Undaunted

Undaunted

Jon Gaunt

TO LISA. MY FIRST, MY LAST,
MY EVERYTHING.

This paperback edition first published in Great Britain in 2008 by
Virgin Books Ltd
Thames Wharf Studios
Rainville Road
London
W6 9HA

First published in hardback in Great Britain in 2007 by Virgin Books Ltd

A catalogue record for this book is available from the British Library.

ISBN 978-0-7535-1367-5

Mixed Sources
Product group from well-managed
forests and other controlled sources
www.fsc.org Cert no. TT-COC-2139
© 1996 Forest Stewardship Council
FSC

The Random House Group Limited supports The Forest Stewardship Council
[FSC], the leading international forest certification organisation. All our titles that are
printed on Greenpeace approved FSC certified paper carry the FSC logo.
Our paper procurement policy can be found at www.rbooks.co.uk/environment

Typeset by TW Typesetting, Plymouth, Devon

Printed in the UK by CPI Bookmarque, Croydon, CR0 4TD

Contents

Acknowledgments

I would like to thank my beautiful wife, Lisa and my daughters Rosie and Bethany for all their love, support, encouragement, but most of all patience while I wrote this book.

Thanks also to my brothers Simon and Jason, who reminded me of some of the good and the bad times that make up my life.

I am also immensely grateful to my agents Michael and Nick for believing in me and finding a publisher, and thanks to Ed at Virgin for his support and guidance. Massive thanks are also due to my editor, Martin Noble, for all his advice and input in the editing of my story.

Most of all, thank you to my colleagues, listeners and readers who have contributed to my rollercoaster of a career. You can write to me at www.gaunty.com.

Prologue: the phone call

Dad was in Hillingdon Hospital.

I knew the way because for the last year I had been belting up and down the M40 into London to appear on *Sky News* at least twice a week.

I used to ring him on the way to tell him to watch the programme. On the way back, as my sugar levels were dropping and night was falling, I'd ring him on the car phone to ask him what he thought.

These chats were often fast and furious and full of obscenities, as we would discuss my opponent on the TV discussion, as mates would talk about a football derby, no quarter given, none taken.

He was dead proud of me and ever since I landed the job on the *Sun* the previous October we had spoken every single day. He would ring every morning and we would argue and moan about what was in the papers. It was almost a one-on-one phone-in and the calls filled a great vacuum in my life because I was bored just being at home and I was missing the daily contact with colleagues at a radio station. He would also slag off other radio presenters that he had been listening to or TV hosts and he was constantly telling me that I could do a better job than them.

'Why don't you get that bloody agent to get his finger out and get you back on the sodding wireless?'

'I am, Dad, but it isn't as easy as that, it takes time.'

'Yeah well, he's taking enough cash off you for that *Sun* job. He should be getting you back on the radio; you're the best wind-up merchant in the country.'

I always thought I was pretty tough when it came to bad news but as I drove like a maniac I surprised myself at how upset I was.

The call had come at five to six on a Tuesday evening.

It was my stepbrother, Jeff. He never rings. We're not close – sorry, we weren't close.

I asked him how he was.

'Not very well, it's Peter, your dad, he's collapsed at Heathrow. My mum has just phoned, she's in a state, she's on her own.'

'Is he dead?'

'No. In a coma.'

So started two and a half weeks of hell.

Four days of hoping he would wake up, then days of waiting for him to die.

Then he was gone and I'm still missing him, aching for him, wanting him.

But why?

Because when I was a kid, my dad was a bastard.

A complete bastard.

1

Sixteen days before Christmas

1973

Christmas was coming. It was obvious. Mum had just bought the satsumas, nuts, dates and those horrible sugar-coated orange and lemon slices that nobody ever eats. She had put all the goodies on the mantelpiece and told us, 'If any of you touch those before Christmas Eve, you're dead.'

It was 9 December 1973, sixteen days before Christmas. I was twelve, Simon was fifteen, Jason was six and Mum and Dad were 41 and 40.

We contented ourselves with underlining what we wanted to watch over Christmas in the *TV Times* and *Radio Times*, the only time Mum and Dad bought those magazines. We agreed on Morecambe and Wise; the rest was open for debate and fighting right up until Christmas Day.

There was a smell of home baking coming from the kitchen and the smell of Players Number 10 fags coming from the shed where Dad was paint-spraying the frame of a secondhand bike which was going to be Jason's Christmas present. Dad had spent weeks working on the bike and it had been a real labour of love, which had occupied him every evening after Jase had been sent to bed. It wasn't a chopper, which every kid in the Seventies wanted, it was a Raleigh 16, with the small wheels. There was only one job left: getting the saddle clean, and that was Mum's job.

Later that night as Tom Jones sang on the telly, Mum sat with the washing-up bowl between her legs and scrubbed the saddle clean.

As Tom sang she scrubbed. There was one pre-Christmas apple left in the fruit bowl and I asked if I could have it.

'Get a knife and we'll share it,' she replied.

Begrudgingly I halved the apple, making sure I got the biggest bit, and headed for the stairs.

'Come here, Jonathan, give me a kiss.'

I walked back to her, kissed her on the forehead, mumbled, 'Goodnight Mum,' and went to bed.

In the morning she was gone. She was dead.

Simon knew something was up. Months later he told me he heard something in the night but he was frozen to his bed.

What he heard was probably Mum complaining to Dad that she felt ill. At first Dad thought it was her period and then, he told me years later, it just happened. She had a massive brain haemorrhage; he rushed next door for his fellow copper and mate Dave Keylock. They got blankets but she died on the living room carpet as we slept in our beds.

He came into our bedroom the next morning and woke us in our bunk beds, he was crying. It was the first time I saw him cry and I only ever saw him cry again on two other occasions. Once, years later, when he had a vasectomy which resulted in him coming home walking like John Wayne and the last time was when he had his piles elastic-banded and he came in with tears in his eyes, walking like an extra in *Brokeback Mountain*.

Simon was silent. I burst into tears, knowing at once that she was gone.

When we went downstairs Pat and Dave, the neighbours, were washing up in the kitchen. There was a fog of smoke; her hushpuppies were still next to the glory hole in the hall, right next to the hole in the cupboard that Simon and I used to shine a torch through looking for spiders. From that moment and for the rest of my childhood, time becomes confused, mixed up; time contracted and expanded, dates became mixed up in my mind; my history felt confused, disjointed.

I know that Mum was buried, or rather cremated, before Christmas and that we all spent a miserable Christmas day at Auntie Olywyn and Uncle Jock's just down the road.

They weren't real relations, Jock had been in the police with Dad but had emigrated to Canada years ago with his family and had returned very reluctantly a year or so ago. Olwyn was lovely, just like my mum – a big woman, a real mother earth figure. Jock was a security guard at the Jaguar factory. He'd been a sergeant in the police before emigrating and I felt that he was now bitter about his demotion in status. They had five girls but two had already left home and they lived in a rambling, ramshackle house on a main road next to the cemetery in which Mum's ashes were buried after Christmas.

I went to the funeral. The church was packed. Mum had been well liked and acted almost like an agony aunt or vicar's wife to the local community. Remember, this was a time when coppers were a real part of their community, not removed by attending diversity courses or speeding past in panda cars. There were four three-bedroom terraced police houses in Bulwer Road. We lived at 74, next to Tom Lilley who had a daughter the same age as Simon and who had shocked the entire area by getting divorced. Alison was the only kid from a broken home that we knew. How times have changed.

Pat and Dave Keylock lived on the other side and they had two boys. Dave was in the CID and Pat was a big noise in the local amateur operatic group. She had a great voice, a great figure and an air of glamour. My old man was once cajoled along with Dave to appear as extras in the chorus in Pat's am-dram production of *The King and I* at the Coventry Theatre. I remember going to watch it. Him and Dave were wearing false tan and little else; they looked like they'd been Tangoed as they stood at the entrance to the king's palace. The old queen who was playing the king, if you catch my drift, refused to have his head shaved and the bald wig hadn't arrived so we're not exactly talking Yul Brynner production standards, but the part allowed Dad plenty of time to indulge his favourite passions of drinking and smoking because he and Dave were only required at the opening of the show and at the finale. In between times they pulled on their coats and nipped over to Smithfield Arms for a few bevvies.

Pat and Dave had two boys; Paul was the same age as Simon, and Richard was a year younger than me. The last police house on the row used to be Jock's and, since they moved out, a succession of other coppers – including the Johnsons, whose eldest son Andy was Coventry's hardest bloke – had lived there.

Because of Dad's job and where we lived, everyone in the neighbouring streets knew us. If ever there was a domestic or a scrap in the chippie over the road, people would run to our house or Dave's to get them to sort out the trouble. There was always trouble in the chip shop because the Polish owner was the only bloke who had a shorter fuse and a worse temper than my old man. I went to school with his son Roman who is now a software whizkid in California and allegedly worth millions.

The chippie was part of a little L-shaped row of shops, which also included a greengrocer, hardware shop, hairdresser and a haberdashery. Of course there was also the ubiquitous VG grocery shop, whose owner had a son who drove a red E-type that I largely blame for starting my obsession with the Jaguaaaaar. It was a tight-knit community, everyone knew everyone, and the police houses and police families were at the heart of this working-class society.

The area has changed completely now. I went back there a couple of years ago after another infrequent and guilt-ridden visit to Mum's grave. It's weird because all through my teenage years I never once went to the Garden of Remembrance and, judging by the state of the headstone, neither did any of the other members of my family. The carved name had faded and some of the letters were covered in moss, which I scraped off with my hands. I walked around the graveyard and wandered over to the church hall where I stage-managed plays for the church am-dram group and behind which Simon and I used to play football when we were in the church youth club.

In a mist of nostalgia I drove up to Bulwer Road and parked my car outside our old house. It wasn't the first time I had been back to the street. Over the years since I had learnt to drive I had often decided to take a diversion and drive past the old place. Each time the area had changed for the worse and when I went back there this time most of the shops were either demolished or boarded up. Roman's dad's chippie was now an Indian takeaway and the police houses although derelict for years were now refurbished and occupied.

I got out of the car and walked up the hill, which used to seem massive when I was a kid but was now just a slight gradient, I nipped down an alleyway and walked down the back entry to the rear of the police houses. The wooden garages were long gone, probably burned down when the police moved out. I remembered Dad going into that garage with his police truncheon in one hand and our hamster in the other. Hammy had developed a growth on his head and Dad said it had to be put out of its misery and he'd therefore taken it into the garage to do the necessary.

Simon and I were inconsolable and as the door closed we suddenly heard frantic and repeated banging. We had visions of Dad chasing the hamster all around the garage, but of course it was just a coincidence because as he went into our garage Dave Keylock in the adjoining one had started to do some DIY. Dad killed Hammy with one blow.

Remembering the incident, I smiled to myself as I stood on my toes and looked over the garden fence. The pond that Simon and I used to keep fish and frogs in had long been filled in but the brick shed was still standing and the garden, although not as neat as when we lived there, was still pretty much in order. I went over to the local newsagents, now also a convenience store selling everything from mouldy veg to porno mags, and remembered how, when I was a lad and the Schofields ran it, they only sold fags, midget gems and newspapers.

Everything was the same but everything was different. I was the stranger in these streets and I didn't see anyone that I knew. The area had changed: there was an air of menace about the place, an atmosphere of mistrust and, although populated by many different communities, there seemed to be no sense of community. My old man said Coventry changed the day the police were merged with the Brummies and became the West Midlands force and when the old police boxes – like the one in Jubilee Crescent in Radford, where we would nip into with him for a cup of tea – were demolished. In my opinion it also changed when coppers were awarded a decent living wage and were able to buy their own houses and as a result no longer lived in the areas they policed.

It was so different to when I was a kid when everyone knew everyone and everyone looked out for each other. We would play football on the common over the road or go for long bike rides with Shipham Fish Spread sandwiches and a bottle of dandelion and burdock, with the only rule being we had to back home with hands washed before tea or when it got dark.

I know this sounds like a bad case of rose-tinted spectacles and nonsense about 'when summers were summers and beef tasted like beef' and all that other nostalgia, but the truth is that my childhood up until the moment Mum died was both unremarkable and special in equal measure. We were loved and encouraged, safe and secure.

Mum always put Dad and us three before her own needs and desires. She loved us to bits. She was a proper mum who had always been there for us, and she didn't have a career. She worked as a cleaner or a school dinner lady for pin money while Dad worked shifts for the police.

Dad made DCI Gene Hunt out of *Life on Mars* look like Sir Ian Blair when it came to equality and political correctness. Twenty-three years later this TV programme was Dad's favourite and I would joke with him that he watched it as if it were a documentary rather than a work of fiction. He would laugh and say, 'Yeah but it was better back then, at least we banged the bad uns up.'

He was right: Dad was a thief-taker not a political correctness and diversity note-taker. He loved telling tales of how the light on the stairs down to the cells would mysteriously go out as a prisoner would start his descent.

'Yeah it was weird 'cos as the lights went off, some of the bad bastards would trip and fall down the concrete stairs, ah diddums.' Then he would laugh like a drain.

There were scenes in *Life on Mars* that could have come straight out of Dad's career.

A year before the Coventry and Birmingham pub bombings our house had been used overnight as a vantage point to stake out a house in Bulwer Road that the police believed was connected with the IRA. When I got home from school one day the house was full of Dad's CID mates dressed in their 'uniform' of flares, black leather jackets and medallions. Every one of them had a fag on the go and my old man was directing operations while Mum was making the tea and cutting up sandwiches.

'Now listen, lads, just pretend there's no one here, just act normal.'

That was quite hard to do as they had set up a camera on a tripod behind the net curtains and another copper was lying spreadeagled, fag in mouth, on the settee with a pair of binoculars trained on the house opposite.

'It's nothing to worry about. Me and the lads need to keep an eye on those peat cutters to make sure the Irish bastards aren't up to no good. Don't tell anyone that we're here and keep quiet; you'll have to go and play in your bedrooms but keep the lights off and keep away from the bloody windows.'

It was quite exciting. It was like being in an episode of *Z Cars* and I was dead proud of Dad. I mean, how many other kids' dads were on the hunt for terrorists? We went to bed later that night with the cream of Coventry's CID either keeping surveillance or playing three-card brag.

When we came downstairs in the morning, it was like entering an opium den. We had to practically cut our way through the cigarette smoke, the fumes of which almost smelt as rancid as the whisky breaths of the bedraggled coppers who were all now playing brag and eating Mum's freshly prepared bacon butties. Of course nothing came of the surveillance, apart from a row between Mum and Dad about how much money he had lost playing cards that night. This row started at teatime and culminated in his throwing his dinner at the wall. The food slid down the wallpaper as Mum stared at him and put him down again.

'That was mature, Pete, wasn't it?'

We kept quiet. We knew the script. After a lengthy silence Mum cleaned up the mess but the stain seemed to remain on the wall for ages as a reminder of his foul temper.

2
Not fit for man nor beast

1973

They say you shouldn't speak evil about the dead but my old man was a right bad-tempered bastard and he wasn't the best or certainly the most faithful husband in the world. However in the last year of Mum's life the two of them seem to have found a way of getting on and the rows usually about money or womanising had decreased massively.

Exactly one year before the day of her death Mum and Dad had also been confirmed. They had got into religion primarily to get me into the Bluecoat C of E School because I had, unlike Simon, failed my Eleven Plus. Some things never change! But I think it had helped them in their relationship, or is that wishful thinking? I even remember walking in on them messing about on their bed when we were staying at a guesthouse in Cornwall.

As for Cornwall, every year we would be packed into my old man's Austin 40 and head off in convoy with Uncle Harry and Auntie Teresa. They weren't relatives either, just friends, and with fag in one hand and the route written on a piece of

pped from a Weetabix box in the other we'd embark
mammoth twelve and a half hour trip to the southwest.
The old man would be puffing away like a laboratory beagle for
the whole journey, with us three crammed in the back with all
the windows shut just waiting for the moment when Jason would
puke. He was the worst traveller in the world and to this day you
only have to show him a copy of *Auto Express* and he feels
queasy.

Mum always made sarnies because Dad never wanted to stop
and if we moaned he had this amazing ability even on a
one-in-ten incline to keep on smoking and driving while
smacking seven barrels of shit out of us in the back without ever
missing the bite point on the clutch. But we had some brilliant
holidays in Cornwall; at first we would stay in caravans and then
graduated to a B&B in a small market town called St Columb
Major. The Glanville family owned this guesthouse and although
not in any way grand it was homely and we had several happy
holidays there. It even had a four-hole putting green in the
garden. On our last-ever family holiday their five-year-old girl
battered Jason over the head with one of the golf clubs.

The holidays always consisted of fish and chips, long cold days
at Harlyn Bay body-boarding on wooden boards and trips on the
Tri-Star or the speedboat *Apollo Nine* down the estuary at
Padstow.

So this fairly typical working-class upbringing all contributed
to the church being packed for Mum's funeral. I remember
standing at the front of the church, staring at the empty trestles
waiting for her coffin to be placed on them.

Afterwards the vicar, who was later to help put me in care,
came up to Simon and me and said that Mum would have been
proud of us if she had been there.

I couldn't resist it and replied, 'Surely if you believe in the
afterlife, she was!'

I didn't go on to the Crem. I couldn't stand the thought of
her being cremated or even seeing her disappear behind the

curtains and years later when we saw my old man off, we decided to leave the chapel before the curtain rolled back and the coffin disappeared. I went back to the house where Jason had been left with Pat Keylock and waited for the others to return.

Mum's relatives arrived back at the house first, in a minibus. She had 13 brothers and sisters and they all lived in Hull. They wanted us three lads to go back and live in Mum and Dad's home town but Dad wasn't having any of it, mainly because of Mum's dying words.

It was typical of her that, as she lay bleeding and dying on the living-room floor, her final words to Dad were: 'Keep the kids together.' The morning after she died he had sat us down in the lounge and told us about her last words and the promise that he had made to her. I smiled and then cried. Although the sentiment was correct it was a curse for Dad. How the hell could a hard-drinking, womanising, sexist, working-class bloke cope with us three? Even at the age of twelve I knew he didn't have a hope in hell of fulfilling his dying wife's wishes and even if he did he was too selfish to put us, and our needs, before his.

The relatives probably realised this too and either way they weren't keen on Dad. They never had been – they knew him, or thought they knew him too well. Fuelled by alcohol, mutual suspicion and grief, the inevitable funeral row broke out, resulting in Mum's relations leaving earlier than planned.

Distance meant that we had never had that much to do with the majority of them, apart from the annual visit to Hull where we stayed at my Auntie Jean's and Uncle Gip's house. These two lived at 33 Leonard Street in Hull, the family home of the Whittys, Mum's maiden name. I have often fantasised about changing my surname to Whitty, or at least combining the two and calling myself Jon Whitty Gaunt!

The house was in a large terrace that still had gaps where bombs had taken out whole families in the war. There was an Anderson shelter in the overgrown garden and there were always feral cats and kittens playing in there. Gip and Jean didn't have any kids and they doted on us. She had one of those massive Seventies knitting machines and every year she would knit three over-big matching jumpers for us boys. After trying them on and the arms being so long that they made us look like extras from *Planet of the Apes*, the usual refrain would go up: 'Don't worry, you'll soon grow into it.' Of course we did by the next visit but by then there would be another jumper to try on.

Gip was my favourite uncle. He wore baggy trousers and a sky blue nylon vest with navy blue piping and his massive arms were full of fading blue tattoos. He smelt of the Brylcreem he pasted all over his black, thinning hair, Old Spice after-shave, roll-ups and real gas that I swear was leaking from his fire in the damp back room next to the kitchen. In between cooking the best fry-ups in the world, he would sit us on his knee and tell us fantastical tales of his adventures at sea, stopping only to let us lick the gum on his roll-up before lighting it and then blowing the smoke all over the two of us. His tales were true, half-true and sometimes completely made up, but they held our attention completely.

'Oh go on, Uncle Gip, tell us the one about the tongue.'

'All right, all right, here lick this then. Now then boys, what's the one thing you must never do on deck in a storm?'

'Talk, Uncle Gip, talk.'

'That's right Simon – and why's that Jonathan?'

'In case the wind changes or a big wave hits the ship?'

'That's right, well this one night we were out fishing in the icy-cold water off Iceland and a right real storm was brewing. It was so fierce I had to tie the wheel with rope to the door of my wheelhouse to keep us on a straight course, and the wind was howling and the rain was belting down. In fact it—'

'It was raining cats and dogs out there,' we both interrupted. 'It wasn't fit for man nor beast out there.'

'That's right, boys, but we hadn't caught enough fish so we just had to keep going and I was convinced that we were right over the little blighters, so I told the lads to start pulling in the nets, as the rain belted it down and the ship tossed and turned. I put on me sowester and went out on the deck and signalled to the young lad to turn the net wheel and then he shouted out, "What, Gip, what did you say?"

'And at that moment we got hit with the biggest wave you ever did see. It was so big I saw whales and dolphins surfing in it.'

'Really, Uncle Gip?'

'Really, would I lie to you boys? And then the boat pitched again and the young lad forgot the golden rule as he tried to shout again but the waves crashed down. He fell over and his teeth clamped together and he bit his own tongue off. It was flipping around like a cod on the deck. I rushed over to it and tried to pick it up but it was more slippery and slimy than a snake and I dropped it again. The young lad was trying to talk but no sound was coming out of his trap and then I made a grab for his tongue once more, just as it was about to be washed overboard, and I managed to get a hold of it and I shoved it in my trouser pocket and rushed down into the fish hold.'

'What happened then?'

'Simple. I whacked it into one of the fish boxes with the fish and covered it in ice, we then changed direction and headed home to Hull. It took seven long days—'

'And seven long nights, Uncle Gip.'

'That's right boys and it was—'

'Raining cats and dogs out there, it wasn't fit for man nor beast out there.'

'Correct lads, but I managed to radio ahead and got our Jeanie down to the fish dock as we weighed the anchor and you never guess what she turned up with?'

'No, what?'

'Her fantastic knitting machine which she does those jumpers on.'

'What these ones?'

'Yeah, would I lie to you boys? Then quick as a flash she's down in the fish store and setting up the machine while I try to find the tongue among all the fish. I found it in the end. It was in the last box. I gave it a shake and told the young lad to bend over and put his gob on your Auntie Jean's machine. He did and you'll never guess what she did next?'

'What? What?'

'She put it on fast speed and stitched his tongue back on there and then.'

'Brilliant and was he okay after that?'

'Well, not really.'

'Why, Uncle Gip?'

'Well, he stood up to speak and say thank you but he actually said, "You thank, Jean Auntie." Auntie Jean had stitched it back on, but it was back to front.'

'What happened then?'

'Oh don't worry it didn't take her long to unpick it and then she put it back on the right way and we all went down the club and had a right good drink, but you remember boys when you go to sea, never ever open your traps on deck when—'

'It's raining cats and dogs out there, it's not fit for man nor beast out there.'

I would later retell and reinvent these stories for my daughters and even without the smell, the fags and the tattoos I could transport them to another world.

Gip was a hard man with the proverbial heart of gold. He had been a salvage man down at the Cape of Good Hope. He and his crew would wait for a storm and the inevitable distress signal to be heard before racing out to try and stake his claim on the cargo. He would often tell us to run into the posh front room, where no one ever went, and get his globe and then, with us sitting on his lap, he would spin it and stop it at all the places he had visited when he was at sea. Simon even reckons that it was Gip, his tales and that globe that made him want to study geography at university.

Years later I learnt that Gip wasn't even his real name. He was actually called Peter, but he had hurt his back at sea and it always gave him gip so the name stuck. After Mum died and especially when I used to lie awake at night in the children's home hearing Andy fart and Gally wank, I used to fantasise that Uncle Gip would come and rescue me, but he never did, he never did.

3

The guilt

After the row, after the funeral, the four of us were left on our own.

The first few weeks I kept expecting her to walk back through the door. I could still smell her, even though all traces of Mum had been removed from the house. Dad and Uncle Bill, my real uncle, had bundled up all Mum's clothes within a day and sent them to the charity shop. The family photos that were in a biscuit tin also went missing. I found them – although Simon disputes this – in the dustbin; I hid them in the shed next to my younger brother's shiny new, secondhand bike. Simon later discovered them and claims to this day that he rescued them and now as the elder brother he seems to have become the unofficial custodian of our history.

That's one of the greatest tragedies of losing a parent so young, it's as if your history is physically and emotionally wrenched from you. Overnight all my certainties, security and points of reference were ripped away from me. From the routine reassurance and love that only a mum can give a child, through to the practical support she provides in simple things like clean clothes and your favourite dinners. As with most mums at the time she only ever worked for pin money so that she was always available for us, was always there to pick us up when we fell and scraped our knees or be at the school gates waiting for us to tell her about our day. She was the nurturer and Dad was the provider so how the hell was he meant to suddenly become both and how the hell were we meant to cope with the completely unexpected loss of our mother?

The first weeks were dreadful. Dad said too much, much too much to us. He kept saying that she didn't deserve to die, that it was his fault and that he was the one that should have been in that coffin. He alluded to the womanising, the rows, the fact that by his own admission he was not a good husband and strangely, most disturbing of all to this twelve year old, he said that had she lived they would have ended up getting divorced. This upset me because, despite the rows and arguments, I actually thought they were getting happier.

But years later when I was living in Hull, Dad's stepdad, whom we called Pop, told me that most of the trips he and my Nana made down to Coventry were the result of fierce rows and threats of Dad leaving or being booted out by Mum. There was I thinking that when we used to pick them up at Digbeth coach station in Birmingham, it was just another happy visit. Pop used to say that Dad was mad but then again he said I was too; perhaps he was right, as he was a psychiatric nurse.

The truth is, though, Mum and Dad were different people and maybe incompatible. They both came from Hull and had met when Dad was an army PT instructor. When he was demobbed he wanted to join the police but he was half an inch too short to qualify for the force in Hull so he had to find one with a less stringent height restriction and that's why, after they had got married, they moved to Coventry. He had vaulting ambition, always wanting to better himself but without the means and perhaps intellect to achieve it. Whereas all Mum wanted was to bring us three up correctly and live in Radford in a police house. There were always rows about buying a house. We even went to see one, but Mum wasn't interested and as she held onto the purse strings there was no way it was ever going to happen. Dad would have to bring home his wage packet and Mum would then divide the money into different pots and then hand him back a few quid for pocket money. This must have been really humiliating for him but she knew and perhaps he did too that he couldn't be trusted with managing the very tight budget they had to live on. There were always arguments about cash or the lack of it, until one day Mum put the whole of his wage packet on top of the coals in the heater in the kitchen.

There was a stand-off as the notes smouldered, us boys shuddered, and then she grabbed the singed notes out of the grate. It was typical of Mum – she managed everything, including Dad, and without her we all began to fall apart very quickly. There was no support network, no real social service input and as with all deaths, once the funeral is out of the way, people have to get on with their lives, so we were largely left to ourselves.

The police were good because they gave Dad a desk job as a collator at a smaller nick which meant he only had to work nine to five. But I felt that from the moment he took this job he was diminished as a man. He wasn't a deskbound kind of guy; he wanted to be out there, nicking bad uns, drinking and womanising and not particularly in that order. He was a good copper too, even though he never passed his sergeant's exams and never progressed from being a constable. He was a brave man who had won a commendation from the Queen for saving a young child from a burning house, which had been lit by her mentally disturbed father. He loved telling this tale of how he had entered the smoke-filled house.

'The bloody place was going up like a goodun when I got there and there were flames coming out of the bedroom windows. One of the neighbours told me that the Jamoc (a

Jamaican) had set fire to the place and that his kids were inside. I kicked down the door and ran up the stairs, I couldn't see a bloody thing – it was full of smoke and it was dark – and then suddenly the black bastard smiled and I saw him, I smacked him right over the bloody head with me truncheon. It should have floored the bastard but he just shook his head and those bloody big lips and then he gobbed in my face and jumped out of the window, stark naked!

'I jumped after him and shouted out and blew my whistle for support. He ran across the road and jumped straight into the canal, I swam after him and rugby tackled him on the other side, gave him another smack on the head and managed to get the handcuffs on him. I left him face down on the bank and gave him another boot for good measure and ran back to the house. The same neighbour was shouting that Dick, my mate, had gone into the house and not come back out. By now there were flames coming out of the roof. I ran into her house, ripped a mattress off the bed and doused it in water and ran back into the nutter's house. The smoke was real bad now and I couldn't see a bloody thing, there was no sign of Dick.

'I kicked in another bedroom door and their was a little bairn, a girl, crying in the corner. I told her not to worry, but she was petrified, so was I, I was bricking it. I picked her up and threw her out of the window into the arms of my mate who had just got back from following me across the canal. Daft bastard had jumped out of the same window as me and the old lady hadn't seen him. We went back to the canal to pick up the fruitcase and took him down the cells.'

'Dad did the lights go off again?'

'Yeah of course they did, son!' He lit up a fag and laughed like a drain.

For all of this he received a medal and a certificate that used to hang proudly in the hallway of our police house. But I think he was more proud of his oak truncheon that had been slightly charred in the rescue but which he refused to replace. Even years later when the police issued a manmade version, Dad still shoved his wooden one down his long truncheon pocket in his uniform. Now he was a deskbound copper and he must have missed the action and the camaraderie of the CID. However he did this boring collating desk job in a vain attempt to keep his promise to Mum and to continue his main role as provider.

However, he was less successful in his new role of nurturer as the only thing he could cook was a superb egg custard tart. But once you've had that for breakfast, dinner and tea it begins to lose its attraction. He could iron as a result of his National Service but he couldn't wash, manage a budget or bring three boys up. I took over most of the shopping because I used to do it with Mum but he was falling apart and that was before he realised that he still needed the shag.

This all happened too soon or at least it did from the perspective of a twelve year old who had just lost his mum. Within a couple of months there was a succession of girlfriends who at first we never met. I had started sleeping in the same double bed as him. I was looking for comfort, reassurance, and love but unfortunately he didn't or perhaps couldn't give it. He would slip into bed beside me in the early hours, reeking of cheap perfume. I hated the fact that he was seeing other women, it seemed that he was betraying Mum – she was barely cold and he was off gallivanting with other women. It felt like he could never have loved her and, with his admission that they would have got divorced if she had lived, I began to hate him. If he really loved her, surely he wouldn't even look at another bird?

However, I too was carrying a guilty secret, a secret that has haunted me for years. I truly believed I was responsible for Mum's death.

I can't even remember what the row was about. She was cleaning the tops of the cupboards with hot water and Ajax. Standing on top of the Formica-covered counter she had just said no to whatever I was demanding and as usual I wasn't taking no for an answer. Simon got involved, I told him to shut up, she screamed at me to be quiet. I answered back again. She swung to throw the cloth at me. She fell backwards and smacked her head on the kitchen stove and her arm on the lino. Her head was bleeding and her arm broken.

The day before she died she scrubbed the church floor with one arm in a cast.

For years I believed that I had killed her. This guilt only increased years later when Simon, just before he left home, shouted in a rage, 'You, you little bastard, you killed our Mum.'

I don't think he meant it, it was just anger, but it confirmed my own guilt.

But the doctors said there was no connection between the fall and the brain haemorrhage. They also say that there is no genetic link with weaknesses in the brain but three more of Mum's sisters went on to die in exactly the same way.

Even to this day I wonder just what would have happened if I hadn't argued with Mum, and if the fall had never occurred. What would have happened to all of us if Mum had lived? Her early death was a defining moment in my life and it contributed greatly to making me the man I became, but I would swap all of that just to have one moment of that love, care and affection that only a mother can give a little boy.

Up to this moment my childhood had been fairly happy, although punctuated with the usual telling off and Mum chasing Simon and me up the stairs with a wooden spoon threatening to tan our backsides.

One day she went to catch Simon's bony arse and missed. The spoon smacked the stair and broke. We sat on the top stair and laughed, the tension was dissolved as she burst out laughing but it still didn't stop her going to a Tupperware party that very same night and buying a replacement plastic one. She was tough and she loved us all unequivocally and without limit, but she knew how to set the boundaries for our behaviour.

That's what I have tried to do with my own children, with massive help from Lisa and without the wooden spoon!

However, thousands of parents have failed or are failing to do this and as a result their kids run riot or at least rings around them.

When Mum died my life was turned upside down: from living by a clear set of rules, in a matter of months all the rules disappeared and I was at sea. However, if I thought that I lacked love, parameters and care in the months after her death, then it was going to become a whole lot worse before it got better.

4

The long wait

I knew that Jeff was in front of us and would probably arrive at the hospital before us but what would he find and would Dad still be alive by the time I got there?

My best hope was that it would be like seven years previously when he had his first minor heart attack. Again I had rushed to see him, fearing the worst but on that occasion as I entered the ward he was sitting up in bed in Nuneaton telling everyone that it wasn't until you needed the NHS that you realised just how brilliant it is and how great the underpaid and overworked staff are. He spent a couple of days under observation, they discovered he had Type 2 diabetes and he was discharged and life carried on as normal.

It was this attack that made him give up the fags after years of pretending he had. Before the heart attack he would nip out to his greenhouse on the pretext of checking on his tomatoes and have a crafty smoke that fooled no one. The doctors remarked that it was good that he had seen the light; it usually takes an amputation for people to finally pack this filthy habit in. Dad had been smoking since the age of fourteen, ever since his own dad died, so giving up the addiction was probably as hard for him as giving up smack with a hell of a lot less help from the NHS than a junkie got in those days.

'Don't worry, darling,' said Lisa, 'Jeff would have phoned if anything had happened.'

'You can't use mobiles in hospital.'

'He would have come out to ring if there was any news. Try not to worry.'

'We should have taken him with us, then none of this would have happened.'

'Don't be daft, you know he's not been well.'

Lisa was right – he had been through a rough year. The diabetes had really started to affect his eyes and although they had been lasered at the local hospital, it was clear from what he said, and what my stepmother Sylvia didn't say when we last saw them, that the doctors thought he was going blind. He was really frightened at this prospect and I had tried to help him by getting a load of his favourite Lee Child thrillers in large print from the library and even some books on tape. He loved his reading, he always had, and the thought of not being able to read depressed him almost as much as the realisation that he would be banned from driving. He loved driving albeit very slowly.

'When you've seen what I've seen, son, and picked up the body parts, you would drive slower too.'

I eased off the gas and smiled as I saw his face in my mind.

Lisa and I looked at each other. It was comforting to know that her parents were with the girls. We had left in such a hurry and I had been so focused on getting to Dad I couldn't even remember if I had said goodbye, let alone kissed them.

As we pulled into the car park I was thinking, *How the hell do I tell them their Grandad's dead?*

For a moment I was back in that bunk bed in Bulwer Road with Dad crying in front of me. I had been through many bad times, even tragic times, but was I ready for this? The automatic doors of the casualty department opened and we walked through.

I saw Jeff. He was dressed in full police uniform, which was to prove a godsend. From the way he looked at me it was obvious that I wasn't too late – Dad was still alive. My stepmum, Sylvia, was in a state of jetlag and shock. They had been travelling for the best part of the day. I embraced her. We cried. Lisa hugged her. I asked Jeff what ward he was on.

He shook his head. 'There's no room mate, all the beds are full. He's in there.'

He pointed to a door and we walked through it.

Dad looked brilliant. He had the best tan ever. He would have been proud of it and he should have been bragging that it was better and cheaper to get than the one I was sporting from Tobago.

As I looked at the tubes coming out of his body I was so glad that I had made the time to see him on the Monday before he flew out on what was to be his last holiday. He was peeling on his shoulders but as usual his hair was immaculate, jet black with only the slightest hint of grey. I used to joke that the only things I had inherited from him was his bad temper and Type 2 diabetes. Why couldn't I have got the hair gene?

He was 72 but he was still a good-looking bastard and seeing him there, unconscious I could understand why he found it easy to charm women and why they found it hard to resist and he even harder to decline their interest.

Only a week or two ago I had phoned him from the pool of the villa I was staying in to tell him that the tan was coming on well to wind him up. His reply was, 'Bugger off, I've only got a few days to go and then I'll be in it too.'

He loved the sun and the Caribbean in particular. Ever since he had retired from the police, he and Sylvia had been on numerous cruises around the West Indies. But this time he was off to Thailand with another old couple and he couldn't wait.

He did look great – relaxed even, and peaceful. But of course he was linked up to masses of machines and his eyes were closed.

How was I meant to react? He looked really healthy but it was obvious he was dying, wasn't it? He wouldn't pull through this, would he? I walked back outside and found the doctor.

'Why's he here? It's one step up from a corridor.'

'I'm sorry, Mr Gaunt, all our IT beds are full. We're ringing round trying to find somewhere to take your father.'

The doctor was about thirty, a woman with lank fair hair and glasses. She was stressed and embarrassed.

'How long will that take?'

She shrugged her shoulders.

And so the long wait began.

5

Abandoned

1974–75

I was alone. Completely alone.

The social worker had gone inside the office to talk to the boss of the children's home. I was in a huge hallway which had a wooden floor and wood panelling on the walls, a large wooden, chipped, staircase descended from the upper floors and in the distance I could hear kids playing and laughing. The place smelt of stale food and sweaty kids. Sunlight poured in from the window on the first-floor landing. I was alone apart from the small case that I had at my feet. I felt like an evacuee, the only things missing were the nametag and the parents missing me back at home.

Dad once told me he had been shipped off to the country during the war, to a place called Stamford. He reckoned that he lived in a windmill and I often wondered whether he thought about his loneliness, his despair as a child when he signed the forms to put me into care.

I doubt it. He was probably too busy shagging the cow he had shacked up with in Mum's house and who had forced us three out of our home.

Through that first year of being a single-parent family Dad had been through a succession of girlfriends, most of whom we never met. However, over the next Christmas we had all had a laugh as he had about three or four on the go at one time. They all sent him Christmas cards and we swapped them over on top of the TV, depending on which one was visiting. There was an Irish nurse who Simon and I really liked — probably because she reminded us of Mum — and we had one lovely Sunday afternoon where we picked her up from the nurses' home and went to a pub for lunch.

Later that night Simon and I told the old man that she was great and that out of all his women he should try and make a go of it with this one. It was weird giving your own dad advice, but we wanted him to be happy, basically because if he was happy then I guess we thought we would be too. However he was more set on the one we, as young teenagers, unfairly christened 'the Slag'.

The 'Slag' was everything Mum wasn't. She wore miniskirts, tight blouses and black bras that I used to wank over when she hung them on the line. She was, as Mum would have said, 'Mutton dressed as lamb', but even as a spotty adolescent I could see what the old man saw in her and I hated her for it.

If it's bad enough as a kid to think of your parents shagging, imagine how much hatred I felt for this pair. I often lay awake at night listening to my old man giving her one, going at it hammer and tongs in Mum's bed, the bed that I had been sharing with him for months night after night. It's like *Hamlet* in reverse. I truly wanted to stab this bint in the arras!

Years later, when I was at university studying *Hamlet*, I realised that it had all been too soon, too sudden for this woman to be trying to replace Mum. Well, that's not true — she never even pretended to want to replace Mum, she wanted to replace Dad's wife and there's a massive difference. A difference I only fully understood as I reached forty and had two beautiful daughters of my own. She wasn't buying the whole package: she just wanted him and unfortunately for us three boys at this point, all he really wanted was her, and I hated her and him for that. Not just then but for years later. I couldn't forgive the selfish bastard for choosing her over us kids, his sons, the ones he promised my dying mum he would look after.

She was going through a messy divorce and lived in the posh end of town. She hadn't had any kids and didn't appear to want them. To me at that time she semed to be a selfish, self-centred cow and as such was a perfect match for Dad. Years later I would tell people that Dad abandoned us because he was going through a breakdown, but the truth was that he chose her over us. The fuck instead of the family. The selfish, selfish bastard.

Now he had done it again. He had lied to me again. He had abandoned me in a children's home.

I'd met him earlier that day at Digbeth Coach Station in Birmingham. I had travelled down from Hull on the coach on my own. I must have been nearly thirteen. Jason and I had spent the last few weeks staying at various relations in Hull including my Uncle Gip's. I didn't realise at the time, but I was on trial. Mum's relatives were trying to work out which one of them would or could take me on. Only a year earlier they wanted all three of us to move to Hull and live with them but now things were different. They all loved Jase, he was the baby, and to be fair he was no trouble. On the other hand I was the spotty adolescent who had already caused a riot and near divorce while living at Olwyn and Jock's.

The 'Slag' had moved in with Dad and us just after Christmas and within a few weeks all three of us brothers had ended up living with these old family friends. I would like to say that us three had tried to make her welcome but we hadn't. It was too early for another woman to be in our home, we were still hurting and we needed Dad's undivided attention, but he needed a woman and at first he tried to make both work. She even tried to buy our affection by giving us a fiver each. Of course we took it and probably spent it on sweets but we knew she was trying to buy us and it wasn't going to work.

The two of them would cosy up together on the settee and I hated the way they kept on displaying their affection for each other. What also hurt was that Dad didn't even bother to put a memorial notice in the local paper on the anniversary of Mum's death. It was as if he had moved on and she was forgotten. Us three watched from the sidelines as their courtship developed. We were excluded. They even started having their meals separate to us and Simon and I began to resent this. Our tactic was to be so objectionable that she would walk out on my old man and we three could get back to normal. There was a fantastic row that Simon and I deliberately caused when they were having a fillet steak dinner. We walked through the back room where they were eating on our knees like Dudley Moore, tugging our forelocks, begging forgiveness for daring to interrupt their meal. The old man went spare and there was a massive argument that culminated in him and the 'Slag' going out for the night and leaving us on our own.

The next day he returned alone. The 'Slag' was nowhere to be seen, and he took us into the front room and told us that we were going to live at Jock and Olwyn's for a bit. There were no tears, no big scene. We just accepted it and if anything I was relieved to be getting out of this atmosphere – surely anything, any place would be better than this?

Jock had got hold of three camp-beds and squeezed them into one bedroom. Simon buckled down to his studies while I, although carrying on going to school, was much more interested in turning a buck by promoting and developing my egg round. Just before Dad had booted us all out I had started this egg delivery service round the local streets, selling a dozen or half dozen door to door for a local farmer.

Now at Jock and Olwyn's I continued the round. I even went back round to Dad's place and sold the 'Slag' a regular half dozen. One week I rang the bell and instead of seeing her come towards me I recognised Dad's familiar shape coming to the door. I asked him if he wanted any and he said, 'No not this week thanks.' I turned and walked back up the path as he turned and shut the door without saying another word. I wanted him to ask me in but I was fucked if I was going to ask or let him know that.

I went round the back of the house and threw eggs at his back window and ran off up the entry.

'Make egg custards with those, you wanker,' I shouted.

That's a lie of course. I never did anything of the sort. I wanted to, but the truth is I wanted to please him more, I wanted him to ask us all to come home and start again, I wanted him to like me, want me, even love or at least tolerate me – so I didn't want to do anything that would make him angry.

I was finding it hard to settle at Jock's. He was a bit of a disciplinarian and I was turning into the typical angry adolescent. The chip shop, over the road, was looking for new staff and there was a furious row when he said I couldn't work there. I didn't think he had the right to stop me but clearly he thought he did. There was an ugly stand-off for weeks until they decided to take us on a fortnight's camping holiday to the New Forest that lasted just two days. We were playing cricket with his girls and I went to throw the ball back and Jock shouted that I threw like a girl and said, 'No son of mine throws like a girl.'

'I'm not your fucking son,' I told him and all hell broke out. I ran off and went back to the tent and pulled out all the tent pegs and laughed as it collapsed as he ran up the path shouting and bawling at me. We went home the next day and within the week Jase and I were on the way to Hull and the trial with Mum's relations.

Jason was left in Hull and I met Dad alone. He chain-smoked as we drove the 22 miles to Coventry. I don't even know where we went to in Coventry; it looked like an old school with temporary classrooms. I asked him where we were, but he wouldn't answer. We pulled into an old playground, he took my case out of the boot, knocked on the classroom door and we walked in.

There was a thirty-something woman who stood up behind a

desk and shook Dad's hand and said, 'Hello Jonathan, I'm Miss Sturdy.' She held out her hand.

I ignored it. 'Who are you?' I said.

'She's your social worker,' Dad replied from behind me.

'What, I haven't got a—'

The door closed behind me. He had left.

I screamed, I shouted, I hit out. I pushed everything off her desk.

Forty minutes later I was listening to the crunch of the gravel under the car tyres as my social worker and I sped up the driveway of the Home.

This was the children's home where I was going to be assessed before being moved on to either foster care or another home, or so they told me. It was opposite a huge park where only about a year ago I had tried and failed to kiss Melanie Evans. She was in my class at school and I fancied her like crazy. I had met her in this park, which was about three miles from where we lived, and we had walked all around it one Saturday morning as I tried to pluck up the courage to kiss her. It was ironic that I was now only yards away from that childish infatuation and courtship but within days I would be miles away from the normal experience of a thirteen year old in terms of morals, sexual experience and abuse.

I knew about the Home because a few weeks after Mum died I had a met a kid dressed in pyjamas and a dressing gown in the back entry behind our house. He was about fourteen and had run away from the home. Dad had talked to him and then taken him back. I remember the kid crying and talking about something called 'pin down'. I didn't know what he was on about but I was soon to find out. Dad calmed him down and then put him in the car and left. Later he told us we should all behave or we could end up in a home and then laughed.

Standing in the hall it was as if the unknown and unnamed kid had been some kind of messenger. However I hadn't done anything wrong, had I? I wasn't bad. All that had happened to me was that my Mum had died.

6

Hurricane

2006

Sylvia began to tell us how it happened. They had been in the immigration hall; the old man was complaining that the queue to get into his own country was longer than the one for the foreigners.

'Sylvia, I feel faint.'

Then he collapsed and banged his head hard on the floor.

'Where were Edna and Ken?' They were the couple they had gone on holiday with.

'Oh Jonathan, it was terrible, they had rushed off the plane and headed for the coach. There was a row on the first and second day, something stupid about a waitress giving your Dad chips instead of rice.'

Trivial details somehow defied the gravity of the situation.

'Did he lose his head?'

'No not really but Ken was acting strange. He didn't seem to want to be with us and hardly spoke to us after that. Your Dad was wound up and he didn't really like the place.'

'Why?'

'Well, they told us it was a little fishing village but it was a three-hour drive from the airport and it was full of sex shops and girlie bars and paedophiles and you know what your dad's like about that.'

I do. He shares the same opinion as me; we'd string the bastards up.

'So you were on your own?'

'Yes.'

Immediately I felt guilty because I had just come back from two weeks in Tobago, staying in a three-bedroom villa. I had thought about taking Dad and Sylvia with us – it would have only cost the price of the flights; I could have easily afforded it. But I didn't. I just wanted to be with the girls and my best mate's family. But if he had come with me, there wouldn't have been the row with Ken, the white-knuckle drive in the minibus with the mad Thai driver to the airport that Sylvia described days later when we went to visit Dad as we waited for him to die.

Then again, as Lisa said, he might have collapsed at Gatwick in front of my girls and the doctors were convinced that this was a massive heart attack just waiting to happen. I guess on reflection it is best that the girls remember him like he was when we went on holiday to Florida the year before.

I thought that I had come up with the perfect solution to the problem of taking elderly relatives away. I booked a house on Sanibel, on the gulf coast of Florida. You can only book these places a month at a time but they are relatively cheap. So the wizard idea was that me, Lisa and the girls would have ten days on our own and then we would fly in Dad and Sylvia, have a week together and then leave them there until the end of the month. Job Sorted.

However Hurricane Charlie had other ideas.

The reason the house was so cheap was that we were gambling on a hurricane not coming in but in this gamble I lost and as the storm approached our Barrier Island we were evacuated from

Sanibel and ran towards Orlando. But for the first time in history the hurricane, after destroying our holiday home, tracked inland and chased us all the way to Disney. On the opening night of the Athens Olympics I sat in a hotel room with the windows and Lisa shaking, trying to reassure the kids that everything would be okay. The hurricane passed right over us. Thank God Mickey Mouse hadn't built the Disney Animal Lodge hotel and we survived the storm.

The next day we queued for hours to get gas and the whole landscape had been torn to bits. I telephoned American airlines to ask them to get Dad off the flight at Miami before it proceeded to Fort Myers where we were meant to meet him. I explained that he was seventy and that he couldn't fly into a hurricane area as he had had a heart attack a few years ago. They were brilliantly efficient and the first thing Dad knew that anything was up was when two burly security guards asked him and Sylvia to please leave the connecting plane. Dad joked later that he thought he was going to get the latex glove treatment and was relieved instead that he was driven to the five-star Fontainebleau hotel on Miami Beach.

This hotel had had previous with Lisa and me, as we had spent one of our first holidays in this place. It's a massive conference hotel right on Miami Beach. When we first stayed there it had certainly seen better times and was in a state of graceful decline but it still had a unique charm and in the massive club Tropicana ballroom you could still feel the presence of those American stars like Sammy Davis Junior who had played the venue back in the Sixties.

When I say play I mean only appear on the stage – I learnt later from a book on the great man that he was never allowed to stay in the hotel because of his colour. He used to have to sleep in a caravan in the parking lot! It's unbelievable to think this kind of racist nonsense was still prevalent in the States only a relatively short time ago.

Times change, thank God, and so had the décor and general state of repair of the hotel when, a day and several nerve-racking electrical storms later, we met up with Dad and Sylvia in the lobby of this famous hotel. We then had possibly the best few days' holiday I've ever had. Dad was relaxed and so was I in his company and he played with the kids like a forty year old or as if he were their Dad not Grandad. He was throwing them about in the pool and getting them to swim underwater and between his legs. He was doing all the things that a normal dad should do and everything that he hadn't done with me since those holidays in Cornwall and Mum's death.

I was jealous but at the same time I realised that he too must now be realising what he missed out on by not being a real father to us three and I even began to feel sorry for him. For years, until the birth of my kids, he had been trapped by the consequences of his selfish actions thirty years previously. Thank God I had released him and myself from this shared history and although nothing was said that day in the pool in Miami, I realised – and I reckon he did too – just how much I loved him, how much I needed him and how stupid I was not to forgive him years earlier than I had.

7
Childhood's end

1975

'So what's your name?'
  'Jon'
  'Bullshit, it's Jonathan.'
  'If you knew, why did you ask?'
  'Just testing.'
  'What?'
  'That you're one of us, another grade one bullshitter. I'm Andy.'
  Andy held his hand out. I shook it. He was about the same age as me with a shock of red hair and freckles. Little did I know when he slid down the banister and broke the silence of the hall that Andy was going to be my guide, my mentor and my best mate in the Home.
  'Where you from?'
  'Radford.'
  'Huh, just down the road then, how come you've ended up in here?'
  'My mum died.'

'What just?'

'No.'

'Where's your old man then?'

'Dunno.'

'Alive?'

'Yeah.'

'What's he do?'

'Works at Massey's.'

Even I was streetwise enough to realise that it probably wouldn't be the wisest of ideas to tell the truth.

'Yours?'

'Don't know and don't care. Your social worker, is she in there with Wilko?'

I nodded.

'Who is it? Sturdy?'

'Yeah.'

'She's a bit of all right, ain't she?'

Before I could answer, the door opened, Andy straightened up and Wilko and Miss Sturdy walked out.

Wilko – Mr Wilkinson – was thin, six foot four and about 55 with a bald head. He was in charge of the Home. He nodded at Andy.

'Andy, take Jonathan up to your room and show him the ropes – where he's sleeping and where to put his clothes.'

Andy picked up my case and started to walk up the stairs, I hesitated.

'Come on, mate, get a move on.'

Miss Sturdy nodded that I should follow Andy and said, 'I'll be back on Monday to see how you've settled in after the weekend. Be good.'

I stared at her and Wilko.

'Come on, it's nearly time for tea, move it.'

I turned and followed Andy up the stairs.

'This is the girls' landing, they all sleep up here and you're not allowed on here after lights out, see that?'

'What?'

He was pointing to the bottom step of the next flight of stairs.

'That knob there – it shines an invisible beam and if you cross it when it's turned on, it sets off an alarm and all hell is let loose. So it's no shagging after dark. You'll have to make do with a wank.'

I laughed but stared at the beam with caution as I passed it and moved up the next flight of stairs.

Andy walked straight into a large bedroom, which had a bow window opposite the door. There were four beds in the room and two were near the window. He walked over to one of the beds and threw the case on it and then immediately turned and pulled the covers off the other. A large fat kid, probably the same age as me, was curled in the foetal position; he had his hands in his underpants.

'Hands off cocks on socks.'

Andy booted the fat lad.

'Out!'

The boy didn't move.

Andy grabbed his hair and yanked him out of the bed. 'I said out, Gally.'

'But this is my bed.'

'Correction. It was your bed but you can sleep over there now, Jon's going in here.'

Gally rolled out of the bed.

'And you can take this sheet with you, you disgusting pig.'

Andy pulled the bottom sheet off and threw it at Gally.

He went over to the fresh bed and took the corresponding sheet off and began to make my bed. I stood and watched.

'Here give us a hand. I ain't your bloody slave.'

I started to tuck the sheet in.

'Not like that, you prat. Don't you know how to do hospital corners? Here, let me show you.'

Andy then gave me a practical lesson on how to make a bed so that the sheet didn't slip.

'You've got to do it right, otherwise you'll only get a bollocking.'

'Ta.'

'Right, come on, bring your case.'

Andy walked out of the room and back onto the landing. There was a huge walk-in cage, made out of wire mesh. The door into the cage was also made out of wire with a great big padlock to secure it. However, the gate was open at the moment. Andy walked in. A large formidable fat woman in her forties was standing in the gloom. All round the edge of the cage there were wooden slatted shelves like we used to have in the airing cupboard at home, which had neat piles of clothes on them.

'You must be Jonathan?'

'Yeah Miss.'

'Open your case.'

I did as I was told. She bent down, picked up the open case and gestured for me to hold out my hands. She placed the case on top of them and took out the clothes. She put them in a pile on the shelves next to a school uniform, which I recognised as mine. Dad must have brought this from Jock's earlier. She took the empty case off me and pushed it under the shelves.

'Take your clothes off.'

I looked at Andy.

He half chuckled, sneered, but indicated to do as I was told.

I took off my skinny rib three-star jumper and my pinstripe Oxford bags and spoons and stood there in my underpants.

'And those.'

I turned away from her and pulled down my pants.

'No need to be embarrassed lad, I've seen worse sights than that in my life.'

Andy sniggered.

I turned again and by now she had a pile of clothes in her hand.

'Now listen, Jonathan, this pile is your play clothes and these are your school set. Keep them clean. You won't get any replacements till next week. Off you go.'

Andy grabbed my hand and we began to leave the cage.

'Hold on, this is for you.'

She held out a small key. 'It's for the drawer in your desk. You can put anything valuable in it to stop it going walkies, can't he, Andy?'

'Yeah.'

'Have you got anything?'

I bent down and rummaged in the case and brought out a Capo di Monte china doll. It was Mum's. I don't think it was a real one but it meant something to me and in fact I've still got it. I nicked it from Dad's house after he threw us out. He wouldn't have noticed because he had just thrown it in the glory hole along with everything else that was connected with Mum before the 'Slag' moved in.

She took it off me and examined it. 'Nice.'

I don't know whether she was being sarcastic or not but I left before I could find out.

Back in the room I got dressed into my play clothes and Andy showed me my drawer. I opened it and put the doll in and locked it.

'What you doing that for?'

'Security.'

'Don't be a prick, they've all got keys for it too, there's nowt such thing as privacy in here or security.'

Andy was right and this is where the abuse of kids in care begins. From the moment they are abandoned, they are effectively institutionalised, damaged. The clothes cage was a symbol that from now on I wasn't someone's special child, I was just another kid in care. There is no longer one special person, a mum, who is going to be there for you, to tuck you up at night, to listen to how you got on at school that day, to turn to when you feel sick or you have that growing pain in the night. From this moment on you are completely and utterly on your own.

In the space of ten or so minutes my childhood ended.

8

Clinging to life

2006

As we waited through the night for a hospital bed to be found for Dad, Sylvia told me more of the story. After he collapsed a man in the queue behind them had tried to give him mouth to mouth until the paramedics arrived. Then an Asian female doctor had arrived and helped. She described this as if it had all happened very quickly and I was relieved thinking, *Well, at least he wasn't without oxygen.* My policeman stepbrother who had been in this situation lots of times before with his job as traffic cop was less convinced. And Jeff was right.

The stranger who helped Dad phoned from his home in Devon and left his number at the hospital. I phoned him back and he told me the bad news – that they had had trouble getting the breathing tube in, it seemed as if there was an obstruction in Dad's throat. He reckoned there could have been at least a gap of ten minutes where his brain didn't get any oxygen. I thanked him for his kindness and promised I would keep him informed. The Asian doctor was contacted and she gave another version of events which contradicted the Devon man's recollection, saying that he was never without oxygen. We obviously clung to her explanation as Dad clung to life. To consider the other version was unthinkable. Dad had always said, 'If you ever have to wipe my arse for me, put a plastic bag over me head.'

I used to laugh at this, but was this now going to become a reality? Every euthanasia phone-in I had ever took part in was now thrown into sharp and tragic relief. It's easy to have a firm view on living wills and euthanasia until you are faced with it and it's your dad or mum lying there. Even though Dad had laughed about the plastic bag and even though he meant it, euthanasia isn't really about the person who is put out of their misery, it's about those left behind, just like in cases of suicide.

Staring at Dad, I recalled the day Lisa and I had taken our first dog to the vets to be put down. She had lost control of her bladder and could hardly walk and I insisted after weeks of this that it would be kinder to her, and a relief to Lisa and me, if we took the final step. I was pretty hard and cold about it because after Mum's death I thought I could handle these situations – but death, any death, has a way of catching you unawares.

As the vet pushed the needle into the neck of Shalagh, our beautiful Labrador, and as she took her last breath I was completely in pieces. It was the deliberate ending of a life and it shook me to the core and that was only a dog. To contemplate taking that decision with a human is easy to talk about in a radio phone-in, but much more difficult and complex to face in real life.

But the point is that first night I wanted my old man to die. If he wasn't going to come back and be the same old miserable lovable bastard he had become in the last ten years I wanted him to have another arrest, cardiac not criminal, and go now. What I didn't want was for him to be left to die slowly or left to die as a dog.

What I didn't know or appreciate at the time was that the decision was not going to be mine or even my brothers' and stepmother's.

9

Nowhere to run to

1975

The first weekend was dreadful. I didn't speak to anyone after Andy showed me the bedroom and the cage. I just withdrew into myself.

I couldn't quite believe what had happened to me, and the fact that I was now in a children's home. Kids like me – police kids – don't end up in places like this. I thought about running away, like that kid had done in his dressing gown a year earlier. But just like him, where would I run? Dad didn't want me and clearly the 'Slag' didn't. I had pissed on my chips at Jock's and all the relatives in Hull thought I was a mental case.

I even began to think that I was mad. Maybe it was all my fault, Mum dying, Jock throwing us out and the relatives hating me. Why couldn't I be more like Simon and keep my bloody thoughts to myself and my big gob shut?

I didn't cry, I couldn't cry. It would not only be dangerous to do so in front of these other 'rough' kids but also it would be a sign of weakness – and any road, what fucking good would it do? No one gave a toss about me. I was on my own.

Andy kept trying to get me to talk as he took me on a guided tour of the Home. It was a large Victorian or Edwardian house in its own grounds with a bungalow set back from the drive where Wilko lived. Some of the other social workers lived actually on our landing in their own rooms to keep an eye on us at night, or as Andy said, to be near the supply of the fresh chickens. There was also a huge communal bathroom with a row of bathtubs with no partition to separate them.

There were about 25 kids in the home ranging from the age of five through to fifteen. As Andy and I were the oldest, apart from Gally who didn't count on account of his being what would now be called special needs but in those days was referred to as a 'mong' or 'spaz', we always got to get in the bath first as we were meant to supervise the other kids. So in reality that meant we got all the clean hot water and dry towels and if they were lucky the younger ones got our dirty water without us pissing in it.

The toilets were in a row and I recall them having no doors on them but my mind might be playing tricks with me. Either way, privacy was at a premium. Downstairs there was a huge kitchen, a dining room and a TV room and a huge wooden-floored playroom with large bow windows that looked out onto the playground and the lawn.

Outside there was a tarmac playground with a shed where we kept an assortment of old bikes that we used to play on every day after school. There was a huge oak tree from which there hung a tractor tyre that we would swing on at every opportunity. Beyond this was a large lawn that sloped off towards a pond at the outer perimeter of the grounds.

On Sunday, after spending all weekend showing me round and trying to get me to talk, Andy was beginning to get fed up with me and I can't blame him. We both had a bath and got dressed into our pyjamas and dressing gowns and went into the TV room to escape each other. Some of the younger kids were already in there, waiting for their turn to have a bath, and Gally was staring

· at the screen, picking his nose. Andy walked straight over to the
TV.

'You two get upstairs and get in the bath.'

'But—'

'Shut it and get up there and don't take too long. What's this
crap you're watching?'

He pushed the knob and switched TV channels.

As the two younger boys left the room for their baths, Gally
exploded.

'I was watching that. Put it back on!'

'So? Fuck off, I wanna watch this, don't we Jon.'

I expected Gally to answer back but instead he flung himself
at Andy and tried to hit him. Gally was a big kid for his age but
it was mostly fat and Andy swerved his fists that were flailing
around like a demented windmill. All the other kids started
shouting, 'Fight, fight, fight!'

Then a couple of social workers emerged out of nowhere and
dragged a snarling, spitting Gally out of the room. They banged
the door shut behind them. Andy, cool as a cucumber, turned
back to the TV, turned the volume up and slumped into a chair
beside me. All the other kids resumed their viewing too.

I could hear Gally screaming, crying and shouting outside as
the workers tried to restrain him.

'Paul, Paul, calm down, calm—'

'*Fuck off, f-f-f-fuck off, the bastard, he always gets his own way, cunt,
leave me alone, get off me, you cunt!*'

'Paul stop swearing—'

'*Fuck off, fucking let me go, let me go, get off me you lezza!*'

'Paul I won't tell you—'

'*Fuck you! fuck off! fuck off!*'

Andy stood up, walked to the TV and turned the volume
down, he turned to me and said, 'Here comes pin down.'

'What?'

It was the first thing that I had said for ages.

'Listen to this?'

Gally was still ranting and raving and fighting in the corridor just beyond the door, I heard other adult footsteps running towards him.

'*No, no, fuck off, fuck—*'

Then I heard a loud thud as Gally hit the floor. Then there was silence, probably as the social workers drew breath.

'They've coshed him.'

'What, you mean they've hit him, Andy?'

'Nah you prick, liquid cosh.'

Andy reckoned that they injected him with something to calm him down. I don't know whether this was true, but it was always the rumour that if you got out of control they would take you out of sight and inject you. One thing's for sure: he didn't sleep in our bedroom for the next few nights and we didn't see him in the daytime either. They had put him in 'pin down'. This is a punishment where they confine you to a single bedroom in your pyjamas for a couple of days. You are not allowed to leave or talk to anyone until you have learnt your lesson and calmed down. This was the 'pin down' that my dressing gown messenger had been talking about in our back entry a year ago.

I was shocked by the brutality of it all, but at the same time it was a relief to have the fat pig out of our room and from that moment on I began to talk again. I wasn't going to be like Gally and rage against the system. It would get you nowhere. I was going to adapt and survive. There was absolutely no point in aggression or silence, I had to become one of these kids and I had to be liked by both them and the people who thought they ran the place.

'Gaunty, what you doing on the bus?'

It was Graham Foster, a mate from school, and he had spotted me at the back of the bus as soon as his head came over the top of the stairwell on the upper deck.

'All right Gray, I've moved.'

'Really, where too then? There aren't any police houses up here.'

'No, no that's right.'

'So where you living then?'

'Er, just up the road.'

'It's true, ain't it? Smithy told me.'

'What?'

'You're in that kids' home.'

'Yeah, yeah it's true.'

'Fuckin' hell, what did you do wrong?'

'Nowt you little prick, we're not all crooks you twat!' Andy's sudden aggression scared me and put the shit right up Graham.

'It's all right, Andy, Gray's okay, he didn't mean to be rude.'

'No soss mate, soss, it's just that, me and Gaunty are mates like and I thought you was living down by the graveyard.'

'I was, I was, but I've just come back from Hull and they don't want me there.'

'Christ, right, right.'

'This is Andy.'

'All right.'

'Yeah and before you ask I ain't done owt either.'

'No, no, of course, of course, it's just a shock like 'cos Gaunty always used to get on the bus down at Heathcote Street. Then when his Mum died, oh soss Jon, I mean like, well like, I was just surprised to see him here like. You a Catholic then?'

'Yeah and you must be a detective.'

'No, no, it's just the badge like, on your blazer, you know.'

There was a few seconds of uneasy silence while Andy and Graham sized each other up. Andy was at the local Catholic Comp whereas I was at the very strict Church of England Comprehensive, Bluecoat. Now that Graham Foster had spotted me on the bus getting on at an earlier stop, I knew the news would be round the school in a flash.

By the end of the day everyone knew that I had been thrown into a children's home and most of them had begun to believe that I was a bad lad and must have committed some heinous crime. At first I was embarrassed but I soon realised that there was no point in getting down about it and that it was easiest just to confront it head on and make out that I was having the time of my life. Actually it made me feel a bit special. I stood out from the crowd and I also wore it like a badge of honour.

'It's brilliant no mum or dad getting on your tits and you can just do what you want when you want and there's loads of great mates and some cracking birds in there.'

I wasn't going to let anyone know how I really felt and after a few days I actually began to believe this mantra too. It was a coping mechanism I guess and I was determined to cope.

However, if I was the top dog in the Home I certainly wasn't at school. Bluecoat was a very strict environment, completely opposite to the Home and was run with a rod of iron and a cane of bamboo by the head teacher Mr Grimes. He was a squat man with short curly black hair whose favourite catch phrase was 'You boy', which he would bellow down the corridor at any slight misdemeanour like wearing the wrong colour socks or walking on the wrong side of the corridor.

I was the kind of kid that would start the trouble and then retreat to the sidelines as the shit hit the fan, but I'll never forget the look of satisfaction on Grimes's face when he eventually caught a mate and me causing mayhem in a history class that was being taught by a crap student teacher. We got all the kids to start clicking their pens in unison to drive her mad and for some reason us two got up on the desks to direct this symphony of Bics when my pal suddenly dropped to his seat.

I looked round and said, 'What's up?'

'The door, the door.'

I turned but it was too late.

'*You boy!*'

Within five minutes we were outside Grimes's office and within seconds we were inside as the fat, sadistic little bastard began to take delight in at last catching us in mid flow. The usual bollocking followed, but then we were saved quite literally by the bell. The school bell rang down the corridor for the next lesson to start, which luckily for us was one that Grimes was teaching. He stopped mid-flow and opened the connecting door into his deputy Mr Fenton's office and called for him to come through. Old Billy Fenton entered through a haze of fag smoke worthy of an entrance on *Stars in their Eyes*, coughing and wheezing. He was a little fat bloke dressed in his usual crumpled cream suit with his grey hair streaked nicotine yellow.

'Mr Fenton, could you please administer the cane to Gaunt and his friend? I have to go and teach.'

Cough, wheeze, sniff and snort. 'Certainly, Mr Grimes.'

Grimes left and Billy stretched and took out the cane.

'Bend over.'

We bent. I think he whacked me first – and Christ did it hurt – and then without stopping for breath, thank God, I heard the cane swish through the air again and make contact with my mate's much bonier arse. He winced, I stifled a tear, but then we heard the Fenton wheeze.

A hundred Embassy a day was taking its toll on this old Maths teacher's health. We winked at each other. Billy brought up some phlegm and gobbed into his hankie and hit me again. But this time there was hardly any strength in the stroke and as the 'punishment' continued the strokes became less and less fierce in direct comparison to the wheezing, coughing and spluttering that were coming from behind us. I even began to feel sorry for the bloke as he puffed out his final command: 'Right, back to your classroom. I'll see you in Maths at two.'

As we left the study we heard the familiar strike of the Swan Vestas on the box and the large inhale as Billy re-entered his smoke-filled lair.

10

Two keepsakes

1975

Katy and I were lying flat on our backs, staring at the sky as we swung on the tractor tyre swing in the grounds of the Home. It was sunny and I could hear Typically Tropical singing that summer's hit 'Barbados' ('Oh I'm Going to Barbados . . .') on the kitchen radio. Katy and I shouted out the words, 'Don't want to be a bus driver all my life.' We giggled; she leaned over and kissed me. I loved her. She was a couple of months younger than me and she had fair hair and a gap in her front teeth which was really sexy. We had been going out for a couple of weeks now, from just after that first weekend when I had spent the whole time not talking to a single soul.

'Why didn't you speak?'

'Dunno, I suppose I was upset.'

'No point. Your dad's just like the rest of them, a wanker. Forget him.'

'Yeah, but he hasn't even been to see me and he only lives down the road.'

'Like I say, he's a wanker, they all are.'

'What about your old man?'

'What about him? I wouldn't want to see him even if he did come. Your best bet is to forget him. There's no point in crying or doing the silent act. You've just got to get on with it and anyhow, we're your family now, fuck the lot of them.'

'Yeah, suppose so. How long have you been in here then?'

'What in the Home? Ages.'

'But they told me that you are only meant to be here six weeks until they can sus out where best to put you.'

The Home was meant to be some kind of short-term assessment centre, but I already knew, because Andy had told me on that first day on his guided tour, that he and his brother Rob had been in there years. Still I clung to the hope that I would move on quickly, even though I was beginning to really enjoy being in the home.

'Here, I've got something for you.'

I sat up and squinted at Katy in the bright sunlight. She had her hand down the front of her trousers; she winced, struggled, tugged and produced a pubic hair. She handed it to me.

'Here I want you to have this.'

I took it. 'Why?'

' 'Cos I think I love you.'

She kissed me and slipped her tongue in. I had hardly ever kissed anyone two weeks ago let alone done French kissing. She rubbed my cock through my trousers.

'You dirty bastard, well I'm not washing them. You'll just have to wear them for the rest of the week. I've a mind to rub your nose in them. Can't you control yourself? Get out.'

I left the cage; Andy and Gally were by the bedroom door laughing. I winked at Andy and smacked Gally around the face and pulled the semen-stained pants back on.

'I used to go out with her.'

'I know, she told me.'

'She's a prick teaser though. You're wasting your time with her. She'll never go the whole way, you've got more chance with Gally.'

'Leave it out, And. I like her.'

I did like her, I felt I could open up to her, tell her about Dad, Mum, my brothers. I still hadn't seen them. Simon told me years later that the first he knew that I was gone from Jock's was when he came home and my camp-bed was missing. However, he never came to visit me once while I was in the Home. Jason didn't even know I had been in care until he was in his twenties and I still don't know how it was that he didn't know, because us two went through far worse together when we were reunited with Dad a few years later. Dad never came to visit either.

The only person who did visit was the local vicar. He was the twat who had come round to Dad's six months earlier and spotted the 'Slag' 's black bra on the line and asked Dad if he was sleeping with her, stating that if he was, then he would be excommunicated or something. I can still remember Dad screaming and balling at him and telling him to fuck off.

I felt like doing the same when he turned up with his Derek Nimmo *All Gas and Gaiters* routine at the home one night. Instead of getting me out of the place, the idiot gave me a prayer book in which he had written, 'With love from all your friends at St Nicholas'. Oh great, thanks a lot, but these are the same bastards who watched Mum scrub the floor with a broken arm and then could only 'tut tut' behind their hymn books as Dad shagged the 'Slag' and abandoned us rather than actually stepping in and helping.

I wish I had told him to fuck off too but I just said thanks for the book and tried to please him in the vain hope that he would rescue me.

Fat chance.

I put the pubic hair in the book for safekeeping and placed both in my little locked drawer underneath Mum's Capo di Monte doll.

11

Bored games

Andy, his brother Rob and me were playing Subbuteo rugby in the playroom. This was the large bow-fronted window room that looked out onto the garden and the tyre swing in the distance. The floor was wooden and other kids were playing with toy cars and chewed up Lego on the floor. It was a summer's evening and it was just getting dark. Everyone was dressed in their pyjamas and woollen dressing gowns and there must have been about ten or twelve of us in the room. Others would have been finishing their baths or in the next room watching TV.

Suddenly the door burst open and Carol and Tina marched in. Tina was about fourteen with fair curly hair, stocky with a bad case of acne that was interspersed with too much facial hair. Carol was the opposite: she was fifteen, tall, voluptuous and scared the shit out of me. She had been making suggestive and crude remarks to me for a day or two, especially at mealtimes ever since the first night when I cocked up my food order.

The system was that one of the kids used to serve each of the tables at teatime and just like the school milk monitor it was always the snottiest, smelliest kid who always pissed his pants that was given this duty. So in our case it fell to Anthony who was so snotty he laid a trail after him or so we joked. Anyway that first night the meal was sausages, mashed potato (Smash not real potatoes) and tinned spaghetti. You had a choice to say either large or small portions because Andy had already explained to me you weren't allowed to leave anything on your plate unless you wanted to get a bollocking and be sent to Wilko's office.

Snotty Anthony, in between sniffs, asked, spaghetti spoon poised and dripping over my plate, if I wanted small or large. I said small because I hated spaghetti. He put the smallest drop on my plate, dropped the spoon and much to the amusement of everyone else on the table then cut me half a sausage and slopped what looked like a teaspoon of mash onto my plate. The basic premise was obviously to stop you being faddy. The kids laughed, the social workers smirked. I sat down.

Then Carol said to Tina and everybody else, 'Ooh I thought he would have a large portion!'

She winked at me, Katy glanced at me, I got a hard on.

Now she was back and from the look in her eye she wanted any portion she could get! The younger kids shuffled on their arses away from me and carried on playing with their cars, Andy winked at Rob. They all seemed to know what was coming.

'You keep guard,' Carol shouted to Tina. Who immediately took up a position at the door.

Carol walked towards me and kicked a dinky toy out of the way, she undid her dressing gown to reveal a baby doll nightie that was see-through and exposed her enormous tits.

Andy said, 'It's your turn, Gaunty.'

'It sure is,' she replied and fondled her breasts.

'No, you slag. I meant the Subbuteo.'

'Shut up, Andy.'

The kids kept on playing. She was upon me, she let the gown slip to the floor and judo threw me onto the wooden floor. In one swift movement she had my cock out and was rubbing it.

She pulled her tits out and rubbed them in my face. The young kids just kept playing cars and Lego and as my face emerged from her cleavage I noticed a Fischer Price Jumbo jet on the floor. She grabbed my face and shoved it into her right tit, saying, 'Suck this, this one's bitter and this one's mild.' She forced my mouth from one nipple to the other. I felt my cock swell and I thought I was going to come off in her hand or piss myself.

Then she hitched up her negligee, shoved my dick into her warm moist fanny and began to ride me. The expression being a piston in someone else's engine best sums up the experience. She was thrusting backwards and forwards; my cock was hurting as my foreskin was being pushed back hard. I remembered how one of the last things Mum had explained to me before she died was how to pull my foreskin back to clean it when I was in the bath. I also remember her saying only to do it in the bath when I wanted to wash it and at no other times. Fat chance. I had been wanking for Britain since I was about eleven but this was something different, completely different.

Suddenly she stopped, I thought she was going to snap my cock off, I was aware that someone was standing over me. It was Tina.

'What the fuck are you doing?' Carol said. 'I thought I told you to keep guard!'

'I wanted to watch. It's not fair.'

'Get back over—'

It was then that I came. I shot my load right up her. She jumped off in disgust.

'You filthy bastard, I wasn't ready.'

Then she looked down at her nightie.

'You bastard, you've spunked all over my nightie.' She picked up her dressing gown and walked out, Tina looked back at my shrivelled, weeping cock.

'*Tina!*'

She turned and ran out slamming the door behind her.

I pulled up my bottoms and wiped my cock on the inside of them, just as Andy turned round.

'Your go, come on,' he said.

12

Intensive care

2006

It was a full twelve hours before, after ringing every hospital in the country, they finally found my dying dad a bed in Woolwich. Bloody Woolwich. That was even further away from his home in Nuneaton than Hillingdon and an absolute nightmare to get to for visiting.

I didn't want special treatment for Dad and he wouldn't have wanted it either, but the least my old man, anyone's old man, deserves is equal treatment. I found out on a radio phone-in weeks later that one of the problems with Hillingdon is that it is the hospital nearest Heathrow so its intensive care beds are often filled with patients, foreigners, who have flown in from abroad, often with two-week-old gun wounds, to avail themselves of our National Health Service. Call me cruel, call me a fascist but I thought that when Dad paid his stamp he was paying for a National Health Service, not a world one?

Hours of waiting went by and I occupied myself by reading anything and everything lying around the room or pinned to the walls. I kept popping back into the room but there was no change, no sign of life. He was just lying there peacefully, even serenely, in a deep, deep coma. It would be days, maybe even weeks before he would come round.

There was nothing we or the doctors could do. We just had to wait and see what happened.

13

Home bitter-sweet home

1975

'What was all that about though?'

'Like I say she's just a slag.'

'Yeah, I know, Andy, but there's got to be more to it than that.'

We were lying in the dark in our beds, the window was open and the night air was still and warm, the only noise was the sound of Gally wanking under his sheets. We were talking about Carol. My knob was still sore and my foreskin still hadn't rolled itself back down again. Andy was his usual sympathetic self.

'Serves you right for being a filthy cavalier and not a roundhead.'

'Does she do that to everyone then?'

'Yeah most of them. Anyway stop talking about it, you're just getting Gally off on it, ain't he Gally?'

'Shut up, Andy, I'm trying to get to sleep.'

'You're meant to count sheep not strokes, you perv.'

Andy threw something at Gally and at the same time said, 'Her dad was fucking her.'

'What?'

'That's why she's in here, her old man was shagging the arse off her.'

'Who told you that?'

'She did, everyone knows don't they, Gally?'

'Yeah, fuckin' slag.'

'You wouldn't say no though, would you, Gally?'

Without waiting for his answer, I asked, 'What, he was fiddling with her?'

'Yeah if you want to call it that, but she probably loved it. She loves it, that's why he started passing her round his mates for a tenner a go.'

'Now you're making it up.'

'You should count yourself lucky, at least she didn't charge you?'

'Don't be nasty, Andy. She must be really fucked up.'

'Don't talk wet, she loves it. She loves the attention. Look at the way she took your cherry in front of everyone, she don't give a fuck as long as she gets the fuck. Did you enjoy it?'

'Yeah, no, I dunno.'

Of course I fucking enjoyed it. What thirteen-year-old kid wouldn't? But at the same time it was brutal, foul. It was abuse.

When you tell people you've been in care they always ask, 'For how long?' But the truth is it doesn't matter whether it's a week or years. The abuse, the damage and the change in values almost happens immediately and is often permanent.

I was only in the Home for a matter of weeks but the experience I suffered and to be truthful enjoyed, damaged me and took the best part of thirty years to put right. After the rules, the amoral code of being in the home, I found it hard to start or maintain relationships with people the same age as myself. I was too sexually advanced or I wanted to sexualise the relationship too quickly. I didn't want to mess about with the social niceties I just wanted to get in their knickers as quickly as possible. I was a slag, a horrible self-centred slag.

★   ★   ★

'Why did you have to do that?'

'Do what?'

'Oh don't come the innocent with me, you fat twat, you know what I mean. Why did you have to shag her, that slag?'

'I didn't, it just happened. I didn't want to, Katy.'

'Bollocks, from what I heard you were loving it.'

'No, well yes, no. Look she just took me, I didn't have much choice, it didn't mean anything. I'm sorry.'

'You're just like all the rest of them. I thought you were different. I thought you were posh like, with your old man being a copper and that, but you're just the same, all you want to do is get your end away.'

'No, no look it wasn't like that. I really like you. I didn't mean to.'

'You didn't mean to? What, don't tell me she forced you to do it, did she? You could have said no, you could have said that you were going out with me, but you didn't, did you? You just gave the fattest slag in Coventry one, didn't you?'

I was really upset. I wanted to be her boyfriend. I wanted to have a relationship with her like any other thirteen year old would. Not just like any other thirteen year old, I wanted to be just thirteen. I loved going out with Katy, but of course I enjoyed what Carol did to me. However, I wanted to be Katy's boyfriend and to have a normal teenage romance, but Carol had stolen that, along with my virginity, on the playroom floor. Andy just laughed and continued to take the piss; he was even more convinced than ever that I now didn't have a prayer with Katy.

The next day I confronted Andy in the playground.

'What did you do that for, Andy?'

'She offered it and I accepted, what's your problem? You're not going out with her.'

'Yes I am.'

'Bollocks, you're shagging Carol.'

'No I'm not, that was just a one off and you know I want to go out with Katy.'

'Well you can. I'm not interested.'

'You've just slept with her?'

'I would hardly call it sleeping. I just gave a knee trembler behind where the bikes are kept.'

'You bastard.'

'Calm down for Christ's sake, it didn't mean anything. Look I'm sorry, does that help?'

'No it does not.'

'Hang on hang on, before you get all high and mighty with me, according to Rob you've been chatting up that black bird Collette. You can't have it both ways.'

I burst out laughing because Andy was right. I had been, in fact I had been doing more than chatting her up. She had given me a blow job without me even asking, in exactly the same place that Andy had shagged my girlfriend, Katy, and this was to set the pattern for the next few weeks as the summer holidays approached.

Sex, everything from mutual masturbation, through fingering and blowjobs to full on shagging was the currency of love and affection – even security and safety – in the home.

Carol was only the beginning of the sex and it was as if the social workers turned a blind eye to it. Surely they must have known that we were all fucking like rabbits? Obviously they knew that we were under age. I guess, just like prison governors turning a blind eye to drug abuse in prisons to keep the lid on a pressure cooker atmosphere; perhaps they allowed the sex to happen to keep us quiet. But they were the adults and we were the kids and we deserved their protection even if it was from ourselves. Effectively Andy and I, being the eldest, ran the place, set the rules, the moral code. It was like a sexual version of *The Lord of the Flies* and it was wrong.

Having sex and such abusive sex at such an early age damaged me and I was one of the lucky ones who managed, almost by accident, to escape the care environment relatively quickly. Others who were in the Home with me didn't have as much luck.

I may not be proud of it now but the stark unpalatable truth is that of course I absolutely loved it as a thirteen-year-old kid. Similarly I loved the way that we developed our own little gang and society in the home with our own rules and systems of protection. The fact that we had been abandoned by the adult world united and strengthened us and we would look out for each other. Crucially we shared a mutual hatred for the bastards who had put us in there. We actually felt special and I was really beginning to enjoy my life in the home – in fact I didn't want to leave. I had even been bought some new clothes and of course as the summer holidays approached I was looking forward to a long hot summer of shagging, shoplifting and general antisocial behaviour.

The nicking was almost as exciting as – no, more exciting than – the sex. It had started with basic shoplifting of sweets and toys but gradually evolved into a shoplifting dare game where both me and Andy had to write a list of items that the other had to nick. I once got stopped coming out of Boots with an opera record, a razor and a pack of sanitary towels. All the store detectives knew we were from the Home and would give us a quick cuff round the ears and tell us to bugger off. No one ever intervened. It was as if the adult world expected us to run wild and we didn't disappoint.

We were also always getting into fights in town on a Saturday or on the bus on the way home from swimming. I don't know whether kids picked on us because we were in care or if we started the trouble. Either way we didn't hang back when it kicked off and I really began to enjoy the violence. We were a gang and woe betide anyone who crossed us.

Care made me the person I am – tough, resilient, aggressive, an achiever – but it also made me cold, negative, judgemental and unforgiving. I find it hard to hug and show outward signs of affection to anyone, including my wife and kids. It's deeply ironic because I end every radio programme by saying, 'If you've got kids, give them a hug, give them a kiss and don't forget to tell them that *you* love them,' but the reality is that from the age of twelve I've found this the most difficult thing to do. I withdraw into myself because experience has damaged me and taught me to believe that I can only really truly trust myself. This self-belief, this coldness, hardness is only beginning to dissipate thirty tears after the damage was done. I am becoming a better person, man, husband and father, only because of the security and non-judgemental and complete love that Lisa has shown me and the fact that I learned how to forgive Dad.

Andy and I were out of breath. We had just had a right go at an old bloke who had looked at us the wrong way as we all got off the bus and the usual had happened. It had started with the usual witty opening – 'What the fuck you looking at?' – and had quickly descended into fists and then boots flying in as we dragged him to the floor and gave him a good kicking before running off over the park. Now we were outside the gates of the home with our swimming trunks and towels in our hands. We looked at each other and shook our heads and laughed and walked up the drive.

Although I was enjoying myself I was clearly on a downward spiral of criminality and amorality and the social workers still hadn't decided what was best for me. I told Andy that their latest idea was to send me to boarding school.

'What, Cleobury Mortimer?'

'Yeah, do you know about it then?'

'Course I do, they try to pack everyone off there.'

Cleobury Mortimer was a residential boarding school out in the country, which they had sold to me as a good enjoyable alternative to the Home.

'What you gonna do in the holidays then?'

'What?'

'The holidays, you sap, you'll be back here, that's what. Don't let them fob you off with that place and anyhow, according to Mark it's full of puffy teachers who want to give you one up the arse.'

'Bollocks!'

'It's true, ask anyone, you're better off here.'

Before I had time to answer back, there was a shout from the house up the drive.

'Jonathan Gaunt, come here please.'

It was Wilko; standing next to him was a woman in her fifties wearing massive specs, a red cardigan, a knee-length dress. Little did I know as I trudged towards the house that this tall, chain-smoking woman was going to prove to be my saviour.

Her name was Rosemary, Auntie Rosemary, and she was my real aunt, but I couldn't remember ever meeting her before. I didn't and still don't remember her being at Mum's funeral. She was married to Mum's eldest brother John and she lived in Hull. We walked into the TV room and sat down. Uncle John was already there, sitting in a wing-backed chair. He was massive, about six foot three with black Brylcreemed hair and a nose bigger than Concorde. He was a man of few words. Rosemary on the other hand was massively intelligent, articulate and well read. She was a matron in a hospital in Hull and a complete stranger to me.

She introduced herself and John to me and told me that she was my auntie and that she couldn't believe that neither of Dad's sisters had taken me. She was also disgusted that none of Mum's family had done anything to help.

'How could they leave you in a place like this?' she kept repeating.

I shrugged my shoulders and kept glancing at John's nose and his short back and sides. He scared the shit out of me.

'Your Auntie Rosemary says that she wants to take you in,' Wilko said as he opened a buff-coloured folder.

'Yes Jonathan but you'll have to live by mine and Uncle John's rules. Is that understood?'

'Yeah, yes I mean of course.'

The door opened and Miss Sturdy, the social worker, walked in.

'This is Miss Sturdy, Jonathan's social worker,' Wilko explained as he stood up and gestured for them to shake hands. 'Well, what do you think, Jon?' Sturdy waited for the answer. I didn't know what I thought and I still don't know what I said. All I do know is that within an hour I was in John's car on the way to live in Hull. Sturdy said that my file would be passed on to the social services in Hull and that they would be in touch. In the eighteen months I spent with Rosemary they never once visited me and neither did Dad or brothers. I was out of the home but supposedly still in care.

14

Rosemary

1975

I put the phone down; the woman who had been tapping on the window of the white phone box threw her fag end into the snow and impatiently opened the door for me to exit.

'About bloody time.'

'Happy New Year to you too love,' I replied as I stepped onto the still glowing ember of her fag and crushed it into the snow. I pulled up the collar on my leather bomber jacket and headed back to Rosemary's.

Later that night the two of us stood in the snow in the back garden and welcomed in the New Year by listening to ships blow their horns on the Humber. It was gently snowing and, for the first and last time while she was looking after me, Auntie Rosemary hugged me and kissed me on the cheek and said, 'Don't worry, Jonathan, this year will be better than last.'

I thought it can't be much worse and to my eternal regret pulled away from her embrace too early and too suddenly. We walked back inside and she poured herself a drink, gave me one of John's beers and switched the TV on. We were alone, Joanne had gone into town to a nightclub and John was down the club.

I was really missing my brothers even though I had just spoken to Simon in a prearranged call from the local phone box. He had told me that Jason was no longer living with him at Jock's but was back with Dad in a new police house in Four Pounds Avenue in Coventry. However, he was spending Christmas with Uncle Harry and Auntie Teresa because Dad had gone to Rhodesia for Christmas with the 'Slag'. I already knew this because I had overheard a row between John and Rosemary where John had screamed, 'If he can afford to go to bloody Rhodesia he can bloody well afford to send us money for his lad.'

Dad had agreed that Rosemary could take me to Hull and the arrangement was that he would pay them for my board and keep; clearly he hadn't kept his side of the bargain. He also hadn't been in touch with me once in the four months that I had been in Hull and he didn't even send me a Christmas card let alone a present that year. The pips went, the money ran out and then there was silence until the woman outside banged the window again with her house keys.

'Is that all you've got to wear?'

'Yeah.'

'We'll go in to town tomorrow and buy you some more, would you like that?'

'Yes, great, thanks.'

Rosemary shook her head and left the room. I was in the back bedroom of her three-bedroom end terrace in the inaptly named Shakespeare Walk. There was nothing poetic about this postwar council house on a large working-class estate in Hull but Rosemary's house was comfortable, clean and cosy.

She had given me Neil's old room as her eldest son was now a nurse and had moved out a few months earlier. There were two single beds in the room, a wardrobe, a chest of drawers, on which I put my mother's china doll, and a window that looked out onto the back garden. I had emptied the few clothes I had onto the bed and now started to put them in the drawer while at the same time looking forward to the trip to town to buy some more.

The journey had been uneventful and I can't really remember us talking much, I also can't really remember saying many goodbyes to the rest of the kids in the Home. As quickly as I had arrived I was gone. I wasn't to see Andy or Katy again for years and years and we never kept in touch. The hard drive had been erased again; I was back at year zero.

To be fair it wasn't a bad place to be. Rosemary's daughter, Joanne, was still living at home and she was studying for her exams. Like her mum and her brother she wanted to go into nursing. Over the year or so that I was in Hull we became quite close and we developed a good relationship which for once I didn't try to turn sexual. We were like brother and sister although of course we were relative strangers. We had no shared history, no common ground.

Rosemary enrolled me in the local comprehensive, which was very different to my school in Coventry. For starters it was about twice as big and was actually on two sites, as two schools – a secondary modern and a comprehensive – had been amalgamated to form one massive comp called Greatfield High. It wasn't only different in size but also in discipline and attitude.

Greatfield, the school in Hull, was a hippy's paradise compared with Bluecoat in Coventry. There was a uniform but it wasn't strictly enforced and there was a much more liberal regime running it. Less able kids seemed to be able to do courses in mechanics and the school had a go kart racing team but the school still had an enviable academic record with quite a few kids going to top universities.

I enjoyed my time there and made some great friends. It was probably the first and maybe only time during my school years that I really had a large group of mates where I felt I belonged. We'd spend nights round each other's houses – never mine though because it didn't feel right to invite them because it wasn't really my home, was it, it was Rosemary's – just doing homework or listening to records or, more often than not, reading the problem pages in *Jackie* magazine.

At last I was mixing with other children of my age – normal children – and once they stopped taking the piss out of my accent (Coventry was considered southern and posh to Hull ears) they really seemed to accept me.

I also had the perfect opportunity to reinvent myself. I was no longer Jonathan Gaunt whose mum had died and who'd been thrown into care, I was now Jon Gaunt From Down South. They knew that Mum had died but I never told them about my time in care, I don't know if I was ashamed or guilty about it but I just drew a veil over the subject. Academically I was doing very well and, aided and abetted by Rosemary and this group of intelligent mates who really wanted to study and escape Hull, I began to see a future for myself.

One night when Rosemary and I were in her living room she said something that changed my life and has become my life philosophy. She was in her nightie and dressing gown, curled up in her chair with her feet underneath her, with the cat in an almost identical position on her lap.

'Well, Jonathan,' she said, 'you've got two choices. You can carry on as you are or you can seize this next opportunity and be whatever you want. Don't just accept where you are, or what you are, or what people think you are. Be yourself and be whatever you want.'

I know it's not exactly Oscar Wilde but it was the single defining moment when I realised I was not going to be a victim. It reminded me of that first weekend when I was in the home and didn't speak to anyone. There was no future in silence. I had to adapt, I had to change, I had to survive, and the same was true now and was to be for the rest of my life. No matter what shit life throws at you, you can recover, you can bounce back. You only become a loser if you accept defeat, if you admit you've failed and then you only consider yourself to be a failure rather than someone who has had a bad experience but who has been made stronger by it.

Rosemary wanted me to go to university and study law. 'You're so bloody good at arguing, you would be a natural, Jonathan!'

Again she was opening up possibilities for me, new horizons; escape routes from my past and background. I got on really well with Rosemary but then again there have been a succession of older women with whom I have been able to communicate and empathise, including in later years Lisa's mum and my large number of female listeners. Maybe I was and am searching for that mother figure who had been ripped away from me at such an early age, but the fact is I've always been able to empathise with women.

There was another aunt, a real one, Auntie Jean Coulson, who I really hit it off with when I lived in Hull. She was married to Mum's second brother, Uncle Harry, who was a dead spit for Ernie Wise. Again these two were unknown to me until after Mum's death and my move to Hull. Jean was a big woman in every sense of the word. She had a massive personality, an unreasonably big ginger hairdo and the dirtiest laugh you have ever heard. She and Harry lived on the eighth floor of a council tower block on the next estate to Rosemary's and I spent every Saturday afternoon and evening with them.

Years later I took Lisa and Rosie, when she was a toddler, to see them. They still lived on the eighth floor but in a cruel twist of fate Harry had developed vertigo. Apart from that they were exactly the same. I haven't seen them since and I don't even know if they are still alive. Typically in Gaunty's life the chapter finishes, the page is turned and I tend to protect myself by looking forward not backwards. It's a familiar pattern; I collude in the process that makes me lose my history, my background, and my family. Is that a weakness or strength? The honest answer is that it's both.

Saturdays were an escape from the mundane normality of evenings at Rosemary's as Jean was the complete opposite of Rosemary, she was vivacious, outgoing, a drinker and bawdy in her humour. She was always teasing me and asking if I had got my leg over any birds that week. I used to get embarrassed which was bizarre when you consider my time in the Home. We watched the wrestling on *World of Sport* and we'd eat a plateload of saveloys with mountains of bread and butter in front of the box. Graham, her only son, still lived at home and he was like a real brother to me, taking me for rides in his souped up Beetle or Cortina. When I went back all those years later he had left home, but luckily was round visiting and he had a daughter the same age as Rosie. I was happy for him.

There is no doubt that the move to Hull was the making or at least the saving of me. If I had stayed in the Home or the residential care system much longer I don't think I would have been one of the survivors. I was too easily led, and Andy and I were already sliding down a path of criminality and general antisocial behaviour that could have only one result.

If Rosemary was my rock, my saviour, my surrogate mother, then John was the opposite and in a way I don't blame him. He had already brought up his own family and now through no fault of his own he had this teenager living in his house. At a time in his life when he should have been looking forward to retirement from a life of heavy manual work as a labourer, he suddenly had to cope with me and perhaps compete for – and fail to win – Rosemary's attention, even love.

However, that first day when we went shopping in Hull he bought everything for me that Rosemary and I selected, including that brown leather bomber jacket I had worn on New Year's Eve and a knee-length green parka on which Rosemary stitched a Union Jack Norton emblem. He never once moaned at having to stump up the cash for clothes and he even paid for me to go on a school trip to Jersey. He lost his head with a relative of Rosemary's who brought some hand-me-down clothes for me to wear, screaming, 'No child of mine is going to wear your cast offs.' But he was an old man, a man of a different generation with different expectations and very few aspirations.

I lived with Rosemary and John in Hull for just over a year and I was doing brilliantly at school – in fact I got the best exam results and report that I ever achieved that year and I was looking forward to going into the fifth year and doing my O levels. That summer I had got a job on a local amusement arcade in the nearby seaside town of Withernsea and I had been having the time of my life. I would walk to the bus stop with John in the morning as it was on the way to the factory where he worked. The bus ride was about fifteen miles and I was in charge of the roundabout and the pinball machines. I was earning good money and there was plenty of opportunity for shagging the holidaymakers on the beach later in the afternoon. Life was pretty good, even though I was now sharing a bedroom with Neil who had moved back in after his latest girlfriend had ditched him.

One night that summer I went to a party with my mates and didn't come home until the next morning. All hell broke out on my return and John tried to cuff me round the ears. I think I hit him back and I certainly told him to fuck off. There was the usual, 'If you want to live here you've got to live by our rules' bollocks and I thought it would all blow over, but it didn't.

A week or so later when I got home from Withernsea, Rosemary was in the lounge smoking and said she wanted to talk to me. She told me that she had had enough of my dirty habits and that Dad wanted me back in Coventry. To this day I don't really know what she meant but certainly when John came back that night from the club I heard another row about the fact that Dad hadn't paid a single penny to them as he had agreed to do for my keep.

So I was going to be booted out – and again abruptly – sent away on my own back to a bloke who didn't want me and hadn't even bothered to contact me, let alone see me, for the past couple of years while I was in the Home or in Hull. I didn't want to go but the decision wasn't mine. I did the only thing any self-respecting fifteen year old would. I went out with my mates, got pissed and shagged some ginger bird in her parents' bathroom.

The next day I got back about nine and was being dropped off at the coach station by Uncle John by twelve, admittedly with two cases now stuffed full of clothes, for the long journey back to Birmingham and an uncertain future.

She stayed in the kitchen crying and washing up as John took me out of the rarely used front door so I didn't have to pass her. Then we got into his car for the trip to the coach station and the long lonely coach drive back to Digbeth to live again with Dad.

I never heard from Rosemary and certainly hadn't seen her until I rang the doorbell twenty years later when I went to Hull with Lisa and Rosie. I sat outside the house for over an hour before I summoned up the courage to walk up the path and knock on the door.

Joanne answered the door and stared at me blankly for a few seconds, before it dawned on her who I was.

'Mum, guess who's here?'

'Who, what?' called out Rosemary from the back kitchen.

'Jonathan!'

She didn't rush to hug me, she didn't even hold out her wet hand that she was drying on a dishcloth as she walked out of the kitchen. The same kitchen in which she had been crying that morning twenty years previously when John took me away.

'Hi Auntie Rosemary, this is my wife, Lisa, and this is Rosie.'

Do I need to draw pictures for you? I certainly didn't for her; she wiped a tear away from her eyes as she looked at Rosie. I had deliberately named my first born after this woman who only looked after me for a relatively short time but who had effectively changed the direction of my life. In twenty years I hadn't bothered getting in touch, and never sent her a birthday or Christmas card let alone visit, but now it was important to show her my young family and to try and say thank you.

She hadn't changed a bit. She looked exactly the same, and she didn't seem to have aged despite now being retired. She led us into the lounge. The TV was in the same place and the collection of brass bells were still on the Cotswold stone mantelpiece where they had been years before. There was no sign of John, was he dead?

'Uncle John's upstairs.'

'He's not well,' Joanna said.

'Would you like a cup of tea, Lisa, and some squash – er Rosie?' She went into the kitchen. Joanna raised her eyebrows. I wasn't sure if I had made the right decision ringing that bell. Everything was the same but everything was different.

Joanne was now married to a sailor and had kids of her own and lived down south.

Later I went upstairs to see John. He was dying and he was wearing an oxygen mask. The gas bottle was next to the chest of drawers where years earlier I had found a copy of *Lady Chatterley's Lover* hidden under his socks or underpants. The book had been well thumbed on certain pages by me for months and then always put carefully back in the drawer. Was this the dirty habit Rosemary was referring to?

She woke him.

'Jonathan's come to see you. You remember Jonathan, don't you?'

I had left Lisa and Rosie downstairs.

He turned and pulled his mask off. He still had that nose. He tried to speak, and he couldn't.

I stood there for what seemed like ages. It was probably only minutes. I walked back downstairs.

'I hear that you're on the radio?'

'Yeah.'

'And don't you write *Emmerdale*?' Joanna asked.

'Yeah, yeah, well I did for a time but not any more.'

How the hell did they know that? Was Rosemary proud? She didn't reveal any emotion and the inevitable silences and small talk followed.

As we got up to leave I actually managed to say it, to say what I had come for.

'Rosemary, I just wanted to say, you know thanks, thank you.'

'What for, don't be daft.'

'No, no it is important I . . .' My voice trailed off, I didn't hug her, I didn't even shake her hand. I turned and left. I heard the door close behind me.

It was to be the last time I ever saw, spoke to or heard from the woman who saved my life.

She died a couple of years ago and I missed the funeral because I only heard about it after the event from Dad.

He had rung me up and we had been chatting about nothing in particular for about twenty minutes when he suddenly paused and said, 'Did you know Rosemary's died?'

'Rosemary who?'

'Auntie Rosemary.'

'Oh right, when?'

'Dunno, Auntie Thel (his sister) saw it in the paper.'

'When's the funeral?'

'Oh I think it's already happened.'

'When did Thelma tell you?'

'A couple of weeks ago.'

'Why didn't you ring me then?'

'I meant to, Jon, but I just forgot.'

I was going to explode but instead said, 'Oh right, right. Well, it's okay, I'll try and get in touch with Joanne and send my condolences.'

'Yeah, yeah.'

'Look, Dad, I've got to go, speak to you later.'

I put the phone down. I was really pissed off. Why hadn't he told me straight away? Did he deliberately wait until after she was buried so that I couldn't go to the funeral? It was over thirty years ago. Why was he still fucking embarrassed about it and what bloody right did he have to stop me paying my last respects? It was all so bloody stupid. I thought that he knew that I had forgiven him, that it was in the past, he didn't now need to deny me my history again.

I was going to have a go at him but just like getting in touch with Joanne or Neil I just let it slide.

Another chapter was closed.

15

Look at the size of you

As I came down the steps of the coach, Dad was waiting for me, smoking a fag. It was the first time I had seen him in two years. In fact I hadn't heard from him since the moment he disappeared from Sturdy's office. He had never been to visit me in the Home and he hadn't phoned or sent birthday or Christmas cards while I was in Hull. But do you know what? I was still looking forward to seeing him. The arrangements had been made for me. I was just told that he would meet me at the coach station in Birmingham.

I got déjà vu but then I realised that I *had* been here before about two years previously when I had been sent back from Hull after the relatives had all rejected me. I walked around the side of the coach and took the case off the driver who was bent double pulling the luggage out of the hold.

'Here, I'll take one of those.'

Dad held out his hand and took the case.

'How was the journey?'

Second sentence and he still hadn't said hello or asked me how I was.

'Fine, fine.'

I would have to get used to him not talking about the Home, Hull or Rosemary. In fact he never once mentioned her name again until he rang me to tell me she had died years and years later. He just drew a veil over the subject and the bastard – just as he did when he threw away our family photos and when he failed to mark Mum's funeral anniversary – was denying me my history again.

'You could do with losing a bit of weight, look at the size of you.'

'Where's the car?'

'Around the back in the usual place.'

We walked round the back of the station and then I could see his black Ford Capri. The windows were steamed up but I could make out two figures in the car.

Surely not the 'Slag', I thought.

It was Jason and Simon. What were they doing here? I knew Jase was living back with Dad but Simon?

'Hi Jon, how are you?'

'Yeah good, Simon, you?'

Simon got out of the car and pulled the seat forward so that I could get in the back. I ruffled Jason's hair.

'Hi Sniffalo.' His nickname, which I had forgotten about these past few years, had suddenly flashed back into my mind.

'Get off, will you,' Jase replied.

Dad pulled out of the car park and we drove to Coventry.

They were living in a police house in Four Pounds Avenue, about three or four miles from our old family home. It was on a busy dual carriageway and one of a pair of police houses set back from the road at the top of a hill. He pulled into the small concrete drive and we all walked into the house. The first thing I noticed was how cold the place was, being at the top of the hill and facing the prevailing wind – and because he was too bloody mean to switch the gas fires on.

It was ironic that it was on Four Pounds Avenue because that was about how much he must have had in his wallet after the 'Slag' cleaned him out.

I learned over the next few days from Simon that one day she had suddenly cleared off back to her mother's with everything in the house — and I mean everything. There was no cooker, fridge, washing machine and the old decorating table from Bulwer Road was now the dining room table. People think I'm making it up when I tell them that we used to sit round this table on empty tea chests with old sheets over them for months, not only for meals but also to do our homework. There was still a TV and a scrappy sofa in the front room but pretty much nothing else.

Jason had been back with Dad and her for about 12 months and had been through pretty rough times but that's his story and not mine. But one thing's for sure: Dad was in a real state. He wasn't as smart as I remembered him and his hair needed cutting and the car needed a wash. These were just little things but for a man as a vain as Dad they were clear signals that all was not well or that he wasn't well.

I was half glad to be back but I was already missing my mates in Hull and the life that I had created there. By the time we reached the outskirts of Coventry and Dad still hadn't spoken to me I was definite that I would have rather still been there. I had escaped all this shit once and it was clear from the way he reacted to me that he didn't particularly want me back. He never once asked me how I was feeling, how I was doing at school or even if I was glad to be back home. Simon must have been having similar thoughts because he had only just recently — and I gather reluctantly — come back to live with Dad as well.

If this was some trashy Hollywood movie or a soap opera there would now be a happy ending where my father, realising his mistake, cuts all ties with his mistress and reunites his boys as per his dying wife's wishes and dedicates himself to bringing them all up all together.

Yeah right!

Actually the truth was that, although the 'Slag' had left him, he still wanted her. I didn't know then and I still don't know now why he wanted us all back together in the same house. There was no concerted parenting effort as far as I could see and certainly no love. Even though she had taken him to the cleaners, the prat was still in touch with her and every Friday and Saturday he made some pathetic excuse that he was going out with his mates when in reality he was off to see her.

How do I know? Because I would follow him on my bike using a short cut through the park and I would see his car arrive outside her mum's house and he would hop out and use his own key to enter. Many nights he didn't even bother coming home and we would be left alone for the whole weekend. This wasn't so bad because at least we could get on with our homework and have the heating on. When he was around he would have the TV on full blast in the front room and there was only a stud partition between that and the back room where Simon and I would sit on hot water bottles trying to concentrate and do our homework.

By this time Simon was in the final year of his A levels. He had started doing sciences but after a year had switched to Geography, History and English, so he spent three years in the sixth form. I was in the fifth year getting ready for my O levels. The only words of encouragement we got from Dad were for us to leave school as soon as possible and get a job. I remember Simon considered the police and there was even a bizarre episode where Dad tried to convince him to get a job as a trainee manager in the local Berni Inn. The same Berni Inn that Lisa and I courted in years later – you can't beat a prawn cocktail, a rare bit of rump, frozen peas, and a schooner of sherry for her and a pint of lager for me all washed down with a bottle of Blue Nun!

Thank God Simon stood firm and kept his head in his books as he eventually managed to escape Dad and get to Durham University but in the meantime he got a Saturday job in Boots photographic department. This was to be a turning point in his life because he met his future wife, Louise, amongst the prints and rolls of film. It proved to be a passport out of this misery because he could begin to spend more time at her house down the road in Kenilworth. Meanwhile I was left at home to look after Jason. I had already taken over the shopping again and when Dad finally did get a secondhand cooker I did most of the meals too.

Over this period Dad's behaviour became more erratic and he became increasingly difficult to manage let alone live with. He would fly off the handle at the slightest provocation or imagined sleight and we began to tread carefully. He never threatened us with any real physical violence but it was best to pussyfoot round him rather than take him on. There was a terrible incident when he was trying to teach Simon how to drive. Simon was in the driving seat and Jason and me were in the back; it was a sunny Sunday afternoon and he had the passenger window open as he smoked and gave directions to Simon. Then he spotted her, about a millisecond after all three of us had seen her on the pavement opposite.

'Pull over.'

'No, don't be stupid.'

'I said, pull over!'

'No, don't be a prat. Hasn't she done enough to hurt us?'

'*I said, fucking pull over!*'

He grabbed the wheel and yanked it hard to the left, Simon tried to pull it back, the wheel hit the kerb and Dad jumped out and ran down the street.

'Dad!' I shouted but he was off. Simon banged the steering wheel with both hands and cried. Eventually he got out of the car and got into the passenger seat. We all sat in silence.

After about ten minutes he returned, walked round to the passenger side and kicked the front wheel to check it was okay; he then got into the driving seat and turned the ignition.

There was a pause and then Simon said, 'You're mad after all she—'

'Don't you talk to me like that!'

By now we were moving. He tried to hit or punch Simon, who retaliated and the old man lost it. He put his foot down and we accelerated at breakneck speed down the road. He started ranting and raving about how he loved her and how we had ruined everything and that he couldn't live without her. We shouted back at him, as he drove all over the road and continued to accelerate. It was terrifying. Jason was screaming and crying uncontrollably.

'Fucking shut up, shut up will you, shut up!'

Dad continued to scream and cry all the way back to the house. He screeched to a halt, we all got out of the car as fast as we could and even before Simon could slam the door shut the fucker had accelerated away. We turned and walked into the house. Thank God he had gone back to find her and left us alone.

This of course on reflection is the time when he was going through some form of mental breakdown. At the time I just thought he was a selfish bastard who only ever thought about the 'Slag' and himself. I think, but I don't know, because I never spoke to him about it, that the betrayal by her made him realise that he was completely on his own. So did he have us back as a security blanket? Well, if he did, it was a one-way street because he didn't offer us any security, any comfort or even love, care or attention.

After the driving lesson Simon began to spend more and more time at Louise's and I was left virtually to bring up Jason on my own. However, the worst part of this time was the uncertainty of when or whether Dad was going to come back.

I remember the first time I found a note. He had gone out on a Friday night, leaving us enough money to get some fish and chips for our tea. I hadn't bothered following as it was obvious from the stench of Brut where he was going and then I found the letter. It was in a sealed envelope that he had left in a kitchen cupboard, propped up against a tin of HP beans that I was meant to heat up with the chips.

It was addressed to the Coroner. I steamed it open over the kettle and read the contents. It was a suicide note saying that he could no longer bear living without the 'Slag' and that he was of a sound mind when he decided to end his life.

I found out years later, because he told me, that he had driven all the way to Flamborough Head on the east Yorkshire coast on several of these occasions after he had left me these notes to kill himself. This was his favourite place from when he was a kid. He and a few mates would cycle the thirty miles from Hull to this desolate and windy outpost and then climb down the cliff and nick the gulls' eggs. In later years he would also tell us that this is where he wanted his ashes scattered.

'Bugger off, Dad. I've had enough of you getting in my hair when you're alive. I don't want to be picking your ashes out of me hair and suit pocket for weeks after we've tried to throw you off that cliff.'

However the old bastard had the last laugh because the final sentence in his will actually stated, 'I want my ashes to be thrown off Flamborough Head' – which we did a few months after his funeral.

He never mentioned the suicide notes directly but he often alluded to them when we were alone. He knew and I knew what he was talking about. He did talk about how she had ruined his life. He tried to move on to the damage it must have done to us three and to try and say sorry but I would cut him off at the pass. By the time he felt ready to apologise I didn't need it, I just needed him.

Of course, he never went through with these suicide attempts. He didn't even take an overdose as a cry for help. Perhaps he expected me to find the note and, as a fifteen year old, actually inform someone about his mental state. But who the hell would I speak to? As a family we had no friends or relatives left to tell: Dad, the 'Slag', or a combination of the two, had alienated everyone who used to care for us. I had probably done my bit too!

Jason and I were more alone here in this grotty, cold police house than even when I was in care. No one gave a shit about us. My year head at school wrote in my school report, 'Jonathan's attitude towards school and his seemingly earnest desire to gain employment have put him in a position which he is finding difficult to cope with.'

Yes, clearly I was finding it difficult, you prat. I had to be mother and brother to Jase while Dad was either pissed, in a rage, or saying that he was going to kill himself. Obviously my schoolwork was suffering but did anyone scratch beneath the surface or try to help? Did they buggery.

We were left alone, completely alone, and then I went and made it even worse for my little brother. As the year progressed I was heading to the age of sixteen and I was getting into punk music and began to want to go and see bands in pubs. When Dad was in during the week I would pretend that I was going to play over the park or going round to a mate's house but unbeknown to him in true teenage style I was throwing my secondhand suits and paint-sprayed shirts out of the bedroom window and changing my clothes in the allotments next to the house.

At the weekend my deception was easier, as I would wait for him to depart on a Friday evening and then just dress, leave Jase a load of crisps and sweets and tell him I would be back on the last bus. I was fifteen, he must have been eight or nine and I left him alone. And not just once but loads of times. But I was always back by half eleven. Then again he wasn't my responsibility: I was his brother not his Dad, why should I feel guilty? However I did and I still do.

Remarkably and with no encouragement I did well in my O levels, gaining nine and only failing Maths which I retook the next year and scraped through. When you consider I moved schools and changed curricula at the end of my fourth year, it wasn't a bad achievement, especially when you factor into the equation that I was pretty lazy when it came to academic work.

Simon is completely different. He's made a success of his life by constantly applying himself and working flat out and it was no surprise when he got great A-level results and went to Durham

University that October. Lucky bastard, with a full grant (do you remember them, Mr Brown?) He was free of Dad and his background. He was the first person in the whole of the extended Gaunt and Whitty family ever to go to university and I am enormously proud of him.

That doesn't mean we didn't fight like cat and dog when he came home just as any siblings would. However, with us two there was another dimension. I resented the fact that he had got out, he had escaped his background while I had been left with a massive responsibility of bringing up Jason and trying to keep my old man on the straight and narrow.

I thought – and if I'm honest I still do – that Simon being the eldest had got the easier ride. He had the longest time with a real mother, he was no problem at Jock's and therefore never ended up in care and then, by virtue of being the eldest, escaped Dad the quicker. I know there's no league table of abuse or neglect but from my perspective he got away lightly and I think this has led to problems between us in later years.

Problems that would only really be sorted out when we stood at Flamborough and literally and metaphorically washed away the ashes and our childhood memories of Dad.

16

A sense of belonging

The first Christmas after Simon went up to Durham, he came home a couple of days early to Four Pounds Avenue and Dad's first words were, 'What you doing back?'

This reaction hurt Simon and soured his relationship with my old man for years. He had come home early, expecting to be welcome but instead he had got the reaction that frankly I had been accustomed to from Dad for months. There was no bed for him and Jase and I were sharing a double bed so Simon had to sleep on the floor among all Jason's Lego bricks. This was the same Christmas where Jason's present, his only present, from Dad was a plastic fort, which Dad handed over in a dustbin bag instead of the more traditional Christmas wrapping.

Unsurprisingly Simon's visits became less frequent and Jason and my misery continued. Again I don't blame Simon for this but he had an escape route, a safe haven at Louise's mum's, and he took it but at the same time that meant Jason and I were left with the old man.

I decided to stay on at school and take A levels in History, English and Geography. I was also increasingly involved in the Belgrade Youth Theatre, pursuing my ambition to be an actor. The Youth Theatre had been started the year I was in Hull and when I returned to Dad's that September several of my old school mates had performed in their first production a couple of weeks earlier. I decided to audition to join and managed to get in at the first attempt with a speech from a play that I had appeared in while I was at Greatfield High.

I had always been in school plays from an early age and it will come as no surprise that I was a bit of a show-off. My earliest acting role was when Mum entered me into a fancy dress competition with a neighbour's son as Bonnie and Clyde – and guess who played Bonnie?

Mum was also working as a door-to-door agent for Grattan's catalogue and there was a suggestion that I could have a go at being a child model for them. Mum was in favour and I was definitely up for it, but my modelling career was cut cruelly short before it even began when Dad announced, 'No son of mine is going to ponce around in his Y fronts, it'll turn him into a puff.'

He had the same reservations when I got into university to study Drama and warned me against the kind of blokes that 'frequent that game'. Unbeknown to him I had already met several of these 'nice boys' as he would describe them, both in the Youth Theatre and by acting as an extra in the annual mystery plays that were performed in the ruins of Coventry Cathedral every summer. I loved acting and the whole theatrical environment. It gave me an escape route from the mundane existence of home and it was stuffed full of other bullshitters who were only too happy to elaborate and hide their backgrounds.

As well as poncing about on the boards I had also managed to get a part-time job at Tesco's as a shelf-stacker. I worked a few hours on Thursday and Friday evenings and all day Saturday and I loved every minute of it. The lads I worked with were the salt of the earth and there was a real gang atmosphere that I had missed since I had been in the Home and in Hull. Roger who was a tattooed 26-year-old butcher and his best mate Tony, the full-time warehouseman, led the gang. We would work hard and then drink and party even harder, frequenting all the 'meathead' bars and clubs in Coventry and concluding every night of excess by eating faggots, peas and chips in the Parson's Nose chip shop or, as it was colloquially known, the 'Parson's Arse'.

These escapades inspired my first professional play *Meat* years later, which launched Tic Toc, my theatre company. We were real lads, drinking, shagging and fighting every weekend and the kind of yobbos I guess whom I would nowadays slag off on my radio show. However, even now I can't help but look back on those times with fondness and a warm glow. We were a gang who looked after each other but who at the same time constantly took the piss out of one another.

It was with these boys that I first went abroad when the supermarket organised a day trip to Bologne. To be frank I don't remember much about the day as we were drunk from when we got onto the coach until the moment we returned twenty-four dishevelled, hungover hours later. These boys gave me a sense of belonging, of being wanted, needed, even loved. Mind you, if I had said this to them they would have called me a right puff and probably given me a dig or two. They were happy, carefree times that allowed me to escape the misery at home.

But of course while I was out boozing, shagging and fighting, poor old Jase was still left at home.

Fortunately things started to get better when Dad decided to buy his own flat. Well, when I say he decided, the real truth is that the 'Slag' persuaded him to get his own place as an investment and to give her credit it was a pretty shrewd move as he picked up a two-bed flat for eight grand and sold it two years later when he married Sylvia for thousands more.

He was still seeing the 'Slag' but pretending that he was going out with other women or his mates. Jason and I were still being left to our own devices most weekends. The flat was part of a block of four and was on the second floor. It was a typical Seventies box flat with two bedrooms and a bathroom with mirrored tiles and black tiles with naked women on them . . . *nice*.

The flat was in an area called Eastern Green in Coventry close to two of the biggest car factories in the city. It was a private estate of quite large houses, well maintained by the car assembly workers who populated the area. Even though the 'Slag' was still in the background, it did feel like a new start.

The best thing for me about this move was the fact that it brought me nearer to Lisa. Correction: if I'm honest, nearer to Rosa, her older sister. Rosa was in the Youth Theatre and, like most of the lads, I fancied her like crazy and tried to weasel my way into her affections.

At about the same time as our move to the flat, I bumped into one of Simon's ex-colleagues at Boots who told me that there was a job going in their record department. Records in Boots – that just goes to show how long ago this was, it was about 1978. I was really into the punk scene by then and this was a dream job that I went after and I got.

Coventry had a pretty lively music scene at the time with loads of local bands that had been inspired by the likes of The Pistols, The Damned and The Buzzcocks who had played venues like Mr George, the Poly or a pub called the General Wolfe in the city. There was still money in the city and more importantly jobs at this time and Coventry was an exciting place to be with a host of bands like The Flys, led by Hazel O'Connor's brother, to the Coventry Automatics who within twelve months would morph into The Specials.

I was never a punk in the sense of wearing safety pins and black leather jackets as me and my mates from the Youth Theatre thought we were a cut above that and favoured wearing second suits, winkle pickers and old macs. My mates in the Youth Theatre were completely different in dress, tastes and outlook from the lads I worked with at Tesco's and as I got more involved with the Youth Theatre I drifted away from the Tesco boys.

I may have dressed with a certain 'style' in the evenings but at Boots I had to be a little more conservative so I bought a brown pinstripe suit and the amount of hard graft I put into the job at Boots can best be assessed by the fact that the painted on pinstripes faded more quickly on the arse of the suit than anywhere else. Still it was a great job and it provided me with the one prop that I was convinced would win over Lisa's sister.

The Bee Gees were massive at the time and every girl's pin-up and their brother, Andy Gibb, was also in the charts. We had a massive display of Andy's records in the shop, including a life-size cutout. I made sure that I had my name on this when it was eventually replaced with a display for Jeff Wayne's *War of the Worlds*, so with pride, a few nerves and a spring in my step I rang the doorbell. Lisa remembers hearing the bell and looking out of an upstairs window and seeing a svelte Andy Gibb standing next to a little fat guy in an ill-fitting, fading brown suit. She laughed at me. Whatever, despite Andy my wooing of Rosa was to prove fruitless and she let me down softly by saying she liked me but . . . as a friend!

I was used to the rejection. I had been going out with another girl Clare for the previous four months and I had spent a fortune on her, including a Farah Fawcett Major poster, a teddy for her nightie and the largest bottle of Charlie perfume you've ever seen, only for her to go on a school field course in Wales and run off with a grebo. I don't know if I was more upset at being chucked or the fact that as a punk she had run off with a biker.

However the knock on the door with Andy wasn't to prove completely fruitless as it introduced me to Rosa's younger sister Lisa. I was already good mates with their elder brother Mikey and quite often would go for an underage drink with him. He was a brilliant pianist, even then, and with my wages from the Saturday job we would always have enough money for the bus fare into and back from town, a bag of chips and the first round. That's all we needed because we would target boozers with a piano and then ask the barman if Mikey could play. He would say yes, we would order a pint, Mike would play and blow them away and before you know it customers were queuing up to buy him a drink and of course they felt obliged to buy me one too. Result!

This is what you call a cheap night out until I went and killed the golden goose and showed Mikey an advert in the local paper for a full-time keyboard player for the Sixties band Chairman of the Board. Before I knew it Mikey had auditioned, left school, and was off to that entertainment capital that is called Leicester and a life of rock 'n' roll excess that would culminate with him topping the charts with King years later. Meanwhile with big brother away, Lisa and I became best mates – that's all, just mates. At the same time I was shown some of the most genuine and unconditional love that I have encountered in my life from her mum and dad.

I had met her mum months before on the bus on the way back from school. It was one of those old Routemasters with a conductor. Rosa and her mum were sitting on the bench seat with their back to the driver's cab looking back down the bus to the open entrance. I got on at a stop after them and Rosa beckoned me to come and sit opposite them. I was in my school uniform but Rosa wasn't and I soon learned that she was having a day off skiving and shopping with her mum, which I thought was a really cool thing for a mum to allow. She was into the punk and theatrical look that we were all developing at that time and her mum had bought her a pair of plastic jelly shoes that were all the rage.

We all got talking and Jo, Rosa's mum, congratulated me on the part I had just played in a recent Belgrade play. She showed a genuine interest and gave me real encouragement. This was something which I hadn't received – apart from that one comment about being a barrister from Rosemary – since Mum had died when I was twelve. I didn't realise then but this was the beginning of a friendship that would develop and grow over the next thirty years.

Jo was married to Mike and they had four children and had fostered two teenage sisters who coincidently had been in care in the Home a few years after me so there was an obvious starting point for conversation and interest. Jo was a good-looking woman in her late thirties and in her own way lively, flirtatious and fun. Mike was grey-haired, played the organ in the local Catholic church, was extremely well read and had been studying to be a priest until he had met Jo and married her years ago. They were both Catholics and family was and still is the core of their lives.

Mike worked permanent nights as an electronic engineer at the GEC to provide for his massive brood. They were an almost impossibly happy family where everyone played an instrument and evenings were spent singing around the piano. They didn't have much cash but whatever they did have was spent on the kids. I was so incredibly jealous of how close they all were and how much each of the children was loved, encouraged and supported. I wasn't alone because over the years a whole assortment of waifs and strays would end up eating and staying at the Roberts home. In fact those of us outside the family would call them the Waltons.

I know it sounds sickly but this was what family life should be about and I can only hope that if Lisa and I have managed to replicate even half of what Jo and Mike achieved then we will have been nearly decent parents. There was always enough food if you turned up unexpectedly and everyone mucked in with doing the veggies and the washing up. They lived in an extended semi just up the road from the flat and I began to spend more and more time at their house in the evening. I particularly got on with Jo and I loved the attention she lavished on me and the fact that she was interested in my background and history.

One of my best mates, Dave Howarth, started to go out with Rosa and a whole gang of us would hang out at the Roberts and frequent their legendary house parties. Dave and I became close as his mum had suffered a brain haemorrhage but survived at the same time as Mum had died. I didn't know Dave at that time but his mum lived for years with a severe mental handicap and I remember when I did get to know him how glad I was Mum hadn't survived the haemorrhage.

Dave's dad, Brian, was a short, bald, fat bloke and a successful businessman until his wife's illness. He dedicated his life to looking after her. I was always struck by what a good cook he was and how he ran a chaotic but warm and welcoming family home. There always seemed to be a new business venture, a home improvement project and a meal on the go at Dave's house and his old man was always at the centre of this whirlwind. I couldn't help but compare Dave's dad with mine and it hurt, it really hurt.

Late at night I would walk home from the Roberts house and wish I was a part of that family and not my own. Well, to be honest, what we had in the flat could hardly be described as a family. Dad was often out in the evening and certainly most weekends we were left home alone. I became the mother figure in the house, doing all the shopping and most of the cooking for Jason and Dad when he was there.

There weren't many rows and he had calmed down quite a lot and almost treated me more like a flatmate than a son. He still offered no encouragement about my schoolwork and all the basic parenting responsibilities were ignored. He never sent us for dental checkups or doctor's appointments, but then again from the day Mum died no one who had 'looked' after me, including Rosemary, had bothered with these elementary parenting tasks. However I was quite happy with this domestic situation because at least it meant I could do whatever I wanted when I wanted and that's a great freedom but immense danger for a sixteen year old.

However these were perhaps the happiest years of my teenage life. I was doing okay at school, loving the Youth Theatre, had great friends and almost a surrogate mother in Jo who was always there for me. At last I had some stability in my life.

17

Don't say a prayer for me now

1979

I had been lucky and fallen into university with grades that nowadays would have been barely good enough to get into a former polytechnic. My only excuse was that my two A level years were difficult to say the least and that I never received one word of encouragement from Dad in my desire to stay on and then audition to get into drama school to become an actor. I did get encouragement from the school in the shape of a grant of a few hundred quid to help to pay for the audition fees for RADA and other drama schools but instead of sending this money off I pissed it all up the wall with my mates seeing various punk bands in and around Coventry.

Through the whole of my upper sixth form I was on a self-destruct mission, drinking too much, staying out too late and hardly bothering with going to school. I was pulled between wanting to leave school and getting a job on the one hand, and staying on and trying to get into drama school on the other. In fact I was doing everything possible to prevent myself reaching my ambition.

I applied to various universities to study Drama, mainly because everyone else was filling out UCCA forms and because I had already spent the drama school audition money on beer and bands. I had an interview at Bristol, which is where I really wanted to go, but they said they would take me only if I took a year out. I told them that with the childhood I had been through I didn't need a year off and if I had one then there was no chance that I would ever come back to education.

But on reflection they were right and I was wrong. I was too young to go to university – just like most kids are at the age of eighteen. I did need some experience of the real world and if I needed it with my background then I'm sure as hell the majority of eighteen year olds need a year off before embarking on further education.

The real reason I was applying to study drama was largely down not to my drama teacher but a truly inspirational English teacher called Delia Dick – stop sniggering at the back. In 1978 she was probably Coventry's only living, breathing *Guardian*-reading liberal. When I had been at the school before I went into care, I hated her and took the piss in every lesson. She couldn't control the English class and we basically ran riot. But after returning to Bluecoat from the more liberal school in Hull she became one of my A-level English teachers and I began to really admire and respect this woman.

She was married to an artist, Colin, a painter. Not a painter and decorator but a real painter! A real-life painter and they shared a real bohemian house, which at the time I would have described as a pigsty in Coventry. Delia introduced me to radical theatre, she used to take a group of us to Stratford and the Arts Centre at the University of Warwick to see revolutionary plays about sexual politics, class and race. This was the woman who showed me that theatre could actually be about the lives of people like me and she truly inspired me to be more than the punky lippy yobbo I was becoming. She gave me a channel to push my anger, my isolation and abuse into something positive, something creative.

Until I started visiting Delia and Colin's house I had never met a real middle-class liberal. Somebody who was interested in art, culture music and could talk about it and get passionate about these subjects just like Roger and Tony from Tesco would about Coventry City. It wasn't just the ideas, it was the whole lifestyle that was both alien and exciting to me. She prepared a salad with couscous and pasta. I didn't know what they were and thought salad was just lettuce, cucumber and tomato. It sounds stupid but remember this was long before Jamie Oliver and his school meal revolution. The salad she made for me that day was more than a meal, it was a symbol of a life outside my experience, a life without borders, a life of possibilities.

I genuinely believe that without meeting and being inspired by this woman, I wouldn't be doing what I do today and I certainly wouldn't have had the rollercoaster life I have both endured and enjoyed. She showed me how to be undaunted by anything or anyone, to embrace the difference, the fear, the strange and mould it to the message that I wanted to shout from the rooftops. Without Delia's influence and without seeing those radical fringe plays at Warwick I would never have formed my own theatre company, never promoted comedy, never gone bankrupt and probably never ended up in radio.

It was Delia who encouraged me to study drama at university rather than drama school and no one was more delighted than her when Birmingham offered me grades of two Bs and a C to get in. Even with all the upheaval at home and the drinking and pogoing, even I could get those grades, couldn't I?

Things were getting better at home as Dad had broken away from the 'Slag'. I don't know how and I don't know why but one day he just told me that he had joined a singles club called Nexus and that she was behind him. He still wasn't encouraging about school, he wanted me to get a job and he was still leaving us at home for weekends, but at least he had stopped leaving the suicide notes and the flat seemed to have given him more self-confidence.

Within months he had met Sylvia and decided that he was going to marry her in the September after my A levels. I was spending more and more time round at the Roberts house and was busy with the Youth Theatre and watching bands.

Although Dad was getting better, we were still not operating as a real family and so it was weird when Dad took Jase and I to meet Sylvia and her kids at their home in Nuneaton. Sylvia was a neat, attractive lady, about the same age as Dad, who had lost her husband, Alf, to cancer at about the same time as Mum had died. She had two girls and a boy. Jeff was the same age as me and was working as a trainee butcher, Deborah was a couple of years younger and Fiona was Jason's age.

The coming together of two families is an odd and unnatural experience. Just because the two adults are attracted to one another, why should the kids get on? On our side we were definitely scarred by the experience with the 'Slag' and so we were particularly wary, and I sensed immediately from Jeff a reserve, even coldness, towards Dad.

Who can blame him? For the past few years he had been the alpha male and now this stranger was vying for his mum's attentions and it was clear right from the outset that Dad was different to Sylvia's first husband. This jostling for position within the new family didn't concern me too much as I knew that I would never live with these strangers as I thought that I would be off to university before Dad married and moved in.

There were several other stilted Sunday afternoons where we all met as Dad and Sylvia's courtship progressed, but its true to say that I never really developed a close relationship with any of my stepbrothers and sisters until Dad lay dying in a coma twenty-five years later. To be blunt, I simply wasn't interested. I thought that I had a passport out of this mess and, just like Simon a few years previously, I was going to grab it with both hands and look forward not backward. As far as I was concerned Jason and Dad could sort themselves out.

The wedding passed me by in a bit of a haze, as I was getting ready to go to Birmingham after being initially rejected for failing to reach the required grades. In fact I had actually only managed to pass two, failing History. I had gone back to school that summer holiday and spoken with Miss Cherry, the formidable but brilliant History teacher that I felt I had let down. She had agreed that I could resit the exam externally next year so I had gone about finding a job, any job, to fill in the year while I retook the exams. I had applied and got a job as a trainee sub-post officer with the post office and I was to start training on the Monday after the wedding. I had already decided that I wasn't going to move to Nuneaton with Dad, about which he was pretty relieved, so as he and Jase made preparations to move, I was left homeless and pretty aimless.

Then, when Jo and Mike said that I could stay at their house until I found a bedsit, my relationship with the Roberts developed and grew stronger. At the same time I got an evening job at a local pub for extra cash and then just like in the movies my life was changed by a phone call.

It was the Drama department at the University of Birmingham offering me a place, despite my results. Evidently the lecturer who interviewed me had liked me and was intrigued, probably in a voyeuristic way, by my time in care, which I had laid on thick as soon as I saw a flicker of interest in his eyes at the interview. It was the survivor instinct kicking in again as soon as I saw a possibility of furthering myself. He had written on my application form to offer me a place with high grades to make me work but to accept me even if I didn't get them. He obviously had sussed out both my academic laziness and the problems I was having at home. Just by chance he had gone into the department that summer's day and realised that they had made a mistake and rejected me and he had reversed the decision.

I was offered the place and was expected to start within two weeks. When I told Dad he said, 'Well done', but wasn't really bothered. However Jo and Mike were absolutely delighted for me. The post office's loss was the theatre's gain or, as Dad might have said, 'Enjoy yourself but don't start licking the other side of the stamp!'

Two weeks later I was sleeping on a camp-bed in the university refectory with about thirty other freshers who hadn't secured a place in a hall of residence and I spent the first two weeks homeless and skint until the grant cheque arrived. Dad had given me a lift over to Birmingham in his car but precious little else and unlike other kids he never once gave me any cash while I was at university. I survived on the full grant cheque and by working on the post, in pubs and at the Belgrade Theatre in the holidays. After a couple of weeks I managed to find some accommodation with a few of the other 'rough sleepers' in a house in Longbridge, miles away from the university.

It wasn't just where I lived that made me feel like an outsider at university, I also felt trapped by my background. Most of the twenty kids on the course were from middle-class backgrounds and it seemed to me that the only way for a working-class kid to survive was to either pretend you were one of them or act as the course clown. Neither of which I was willing to do. So for the first couple of terms I felt pretty isolated and I wasn't particularly happy, which was why I was contemplating leaving and going to Israel to work on a kibbutz with an old friend called Nicolette.

She was a mate from the Youth Theatre, who lived just up the road from Dad's flat and just before I got the phone call to go to Birmingham I had been spending a lot of time with her. We had bought The Specials' first single 'Gangsters' and we played it to death in her mum and dad's front room trying to decipher Terry Hall's mumbled lyrics and like everyone from Coventry at the time bragged to all and sundry that we knew all or at least one of The Specials. All of this is deeply ironic because years later Lisa's boyfriend before me, Marc, was the brother of Roddy

Radiation, their lead guitarist, and Nicolette went on to have a very long-term relationship with The Specials mastermind Jerry Dammers.

When I opened my nightclub, Lynval and Jerry out of The Specials had a very successful dance night there and in truth the name of my theatre and club and the guiding principles of my ambition were modelled exactly on the ethos of Two Tone. That's why I get so angry when people accuse me of being a racist because of my strong views on immigration and integration. I am not and have never been a racist. Coming from Coventry and living through the Two Tone era it is almost impossible to hold these filthy knuckle-dragging views.

Going to university that winter and coming from Coventry was pretty special as Two Tone took off. It felt like Coventry was the centre of the musical universe and when I went to see either The Specials or The Selector it was a huge buzz to realise that most of the kids in the audience were now dressing like us lot had been for years in the Youth Theatre.

I really believed in the whole Two Tone concept of black and white uniting and facing down racism. I also admired the way that Dammers wanted his own label and wanted to take over the means of production and challenge the corrupt record industry. It was similar to punk but with real rhythm and of course it was all coming out of my hometown.

I was so inspired I even had a brief flirtation with forming a band of my own with a couple of guys I met in the students' union. I was the lead singer; we had the rehearsal space, the image, the name – The Precedent – and even the T-shirts. Unfortunately we didn't have the talent, the looks and in my case anywhere near the voice to make it out of the garage. However one of my fellow drama students certainly did have, his name was Simon Le Bon.

The first time I met Simon, I was having a coffee with a couple of mates in the union café when this six foot tall suntanned poser walked over to our table dressed in shorts, trainers and a denim shirt with sunglasses on . . . in October. He was just back from having a year off working on a kibbutz in Israel and as every girl didn't stop saying, he was drop dead gorgeous – and of course he knew it. That said, he became a good mate and he wasn't a bad actor. If he hadn't left at the end of his first year to tour with Duran Duran he would have made a pretty good living on the stage. I'm sure he's kicking himself! He had immense charisma and lit up the room as he entered.

It was Simon who planted the idea of taking a year out and living on a kibbutz in my brain and I shared the idea with Nicolette that Christmas. She was keen too and we started to make preliminary plans so when three months later I ended up back in Hull I was pretty convinced that I was going to pack in college and travel. But my experiences in Hull changed all that.

I went back to Hull because I wanted to see some plays at the National Student Drama Festival that was being held in the drama department at the university. One of my best mates from the Belgrade Youth Theatre, Lawrence Boswell, was directing a play at the festival for Manchester University. It was a play by Ben Jonson and he had set it all to Two Tone and reggae music. It was like nothing I had ever seen and it completely blew my mind.

I had always admired Boswell, he was kind of the ace face in Coventry and most teenagers wanted to be like him. He was the first person in Coventry to wear the secondhand two tone and mohair suits that The Specials were to make their uniform and that every other kid in Britain would be copying later that year. He was a leading actor in the Youth Theatre but to be honest his skills didn't lie in acting, even though he was a good-looking but spotty bastard, whom women couldn't resist. His skills lay in directing. He came in and out of my life for the next ten years and despite going through some pretty ropey passages himself, he is now a massively successful theatre director working at the RSC and directing stars such as Billie Piper and even Madonna in the West End of London. It was seeing Lawrence's production in Hull that made me realise that I too wanted to direct rather than act and it was also both the inspiration for me staying on at university and making my first trip to the Edinburgh Fringe Festival.

I returned to university determined to stop being the outsider and to put my life experience's to good use. For too long I had allowed myself to be intimidated by the middle-class kids who surrounded me. I suddenly realised that my background and my terrible childhood wasn't a disadvantage but a definite advantage. I knew what life was about. I had lost my mum at twelve, I had been in care, I had survived and I would continue to survive. I wasn't equal to these middle-class posers, I was better than them.

After the Easter break I was walking home after watching some arty film at The Triangle arts centre in Birmingham with an older student mate, Nigel, when we saw a poster for a playwriting competition with a prize of fifty quid. Nigel was my best mate at the time and was in his final year of studying Drama and Theatre Arts at the University of Birmingham. I was still in the first year and struggling to fit in and even though Nigel was the proverbial Birmingham middle-class kid we had hit it off. We would later share a grotty flat with another mate called Jed overlooking an old abattoir in Mosley.

Nigel fancied himself as a bit of a writer and had written quite a few avant-garde plays, which had been performed, but not understood, at the university. He said he was going to enter the competition and I said, in an act of complete bravado and arrogance, 'Don't bother because I'm going to win that.' And I did. However I added insult to injury by writing my play on his typewriter.

The play was about my experiences of being in care and I nicked the title, *You're Wondering Now*, from a song by my favourite group, The Specials. It was basically a 45-minute shout of anger about the abuse that I and the other kids both suffered and dished out in the Home.

For years I hadn't been able to talk about being in care. I was ashamed about it and felt as if it were my fault that I ended up in the Home. I carried the burden of shame just as I had done with the blame for Mum's death. In all those late-night teenage conversations or drunken confessional chats with mates or girlfriends at university about how you lost your virginity I would always skirt around the issue, lie or make a joke about what happened to me. Everybody loved the funny way I told the piston in someone else's engine story and I guess it was funny but it was also horrific. I knew that if I wrote about that time in my life it would help me come to terms with it.

I only wish that I knew that back in 1979 when I wrote that play. It might have been even more successful. As it was, it was really just a scream of pain, but I was canny enough to know that the judges, just like the lecturer who interviewed me, would love the subject matter, and I was right – they liked it and it proved to be the passport that not only helped me through my university career but also provided the foundation for my career in theatre, promotion and entertainment.

Part of the prize was to have the play performed by the Belgrade Youth Theatre in Coventry of which I had been a member since I returned to live with Dad when I was about sixteen. A mate of mine directed it and believe it or not the kid who played my character was none other than the movie star Clive Owen. At this juncture I should add he didn't have the movie star looks or even the teeth that make women swoon now and which have earned him fortunes at the box office.

No at this point in his life he was a thin, gangly, acne-scarred teenager who stank. But even at that young age and looking like that, he was, and remains, one of only a few people I have ever met who actually lights up a room when he enters it.

Clive was sixteen at the time and had just dropped out of sixth form; he was sharing a grotty house in Coventry with Lisa's sister and a few other mates. The state of the house was aptly summed up by the name they called it, Smegma View, I kid you not! Clive comes from a much more deprived background than me and he had real empathy with the character and it was his central performance that made the play such a success and convinced me that I wanted not only to be a director but a writer for the theatre.

A year later we took the play to the Edinburgh Fringe Festival and as with most new plays we performed to the proverbial one man and his dog. However the trip and the experience led me into a fifteen-year relationship with the Fringe and to becoming one of the biggest promoters of alternative comedy and fringe theatre in the country while at the same time carving out a career as a TV writer and showbusiness entrepreneur.

I formed a university society via the student union with a couple of mates with the express aim of taking plays to the Edinburgh fringe but in reality of course it was a front to take my own work there. I was aided and abetted by a mate called Tim Hawkins. He was a giant of a man, who came from a very respectable middle-class family in Huddersfield. He owned a blue mini van, had a speech impediment, loved rugby, didn't want to or couldn't act but was brilliant at the technical side of theatre. We hit it off and became good friends and Tim was to prove to be instrumental in Tic Toc, the theatre company, happening a couple of years later. We didn't share a house but we spent loads of time together drinking and plotting and devising the kind of theatre we wanted to create.

I was now living in a grotty house in Selly Oak with four girls. I had a single room because it was the cheapest and I was absolutely infatuated with a girl from Southport, who shared a twin room with a fellow drama student. I used to spend hours trying to charm the pants off this convent-educated schoolgirl who was now studying Spanish but she was having none of it. However, she was a great sounding board and she was genuinely interested in my background and childhood. Those late-night conversations sitting on the edge of her bed as her roommate slept opposite really helped me sort out my mixed up and fucked up emotions and attitudes.

If she was a good listener, her roommate was the complete opposite. She was a sweet little rich girl whose mum and dad had divorced. It had affected her badly. She was studying drama with me and she was a pretty good actress but her life experiences were completely different from mine. She was spoilt rotten and for her twenty-first birthday her divorced dad gave her expensive diamond earrings, sketches by Picasso and a brand new yellow mini car. I must admit I found it hard to sympathise with her weeks later when she couldn't understand why her mini has been vandalised when she left it overnight in Sparkhill in Birmingham. As I said, we were just living different lives. It was also my first real experience of that middle-class well-moneyed society.

But she was a treasure compared to the real monster that shared that house with me, who was a committed but objection-able vegan. This woman is probably the sole reason why I hate vegetarians and support fox hunting. She was an aggressive vegetarian and hunt saboteur. Every Saturday Tim and I would be watching *Grandstand* and she would slam through the front door carrying huge petrol carriers full of a mixture of Jeyes fluid and other noxious ingredients that replicated the smell of a fox that she was going to spread all over the local woods to confuse the hounds.

She was the worst kind of religious, political, anti-fox hunting zealot and she wasn't shy in telling all and sundry of them. However the pious cow couldn't see the central conflict in her pro-animal stance. She smoked like a bloody trooper. I swear there were laboratory beagles at the time with less of a habit than her.

We had regular run-ins but the final straw came when Lisa and Rosa came to visit one weekend. They had decided to cook us all a meal and disappeared into the kitchen at the back of the house to prepare a Roberts favourite, a classic spag bol for my mates and me. I heard 'Millie Tant' trundling down the back alley of the house as she came back from her latest jaunt to save Basil Brush and the next thing I heard were screams of 'Flesh! Flesh!'

I ran into the kitchen to see Millie with steam coming out of her nostrils dressed in camouflage gear, throwing the saucepan of mince into the sink.

'What's up, what's up?' I screamed.

Snot bubbling out of her nose, Millie sobbed, 'Flesh, flesh, they're cooking flesh in my frying pan!'

'What?'

'I'm sorry, er, I didn't realise it was your pan,' Rosa tried to explain.

'We'll wash it up after.' Younger sister Lisa tried to calm the situation.

More snot and nicotine-stained cheeks. 'Wash, wash, you can't wash it! You've defiled my pan. I can't use that now. It's had flesh in it!'

She pushed past the sink and me and went into the toilet at the back of the kitchen and started to sob uncontrollably.

This overreaction is typical of these single-issue cretins who have never had real struggle in their lives and so get some perverse pleasure by trying to empathise with a single cause like the starving millions or a bloody fox. It's the same warped logic that makes young kids wear plastic wristbands and follow overpaid pop stars in demanding that those of us who actually pay tax should drop the debt. Then they march unwashed, unkempt but very definitely kept by Mummy and Daddy on the streets of London demanding troops out. They all make me sick.

After the frying pan incident I couldn't stand living with this woman any longer and so I managed to get a room in a shared flat in Mosley with a couple of my older student mates, Nigel and Ged. This was the flat over the bakery with the picturesque view of the old abattoir in the back yard and it was to be the location to rest my multicoloured head for the final two years of my university life.

I say multicoloured because Le Bon had convinced me to come into Birmingham City centre and get my hair dyed the same as him. He came out looking superb, the quintessential new romantic, I came out looking like Worzel Gummidge on acid, but I guess it made a statement. Yes, I looked a prat and combined with my multicoloured jumper and several ear studs I guess I won't have many grounds to complain when my daughters start to express themselves.

The following weekend I cycled all the way from Birmingham to Coventry to show off my new hairdo to the Roberts' family. It was a distance of over 22 miles but I was pretty fit at the time and even relatively slim because I was cycling to and from college and snorting industrial amounts of amphetamine speed. I've got to admit I loved speed, I loved that head rush and that adrenaline release and I was doing enough drugs at university to last me a lifetime. I only gave it up when I got Tic Toc off the ground about a year later. I haven't touched anything stronger than a Solpadine since and I am now vehemently anti-drugs and favour a zero tolerance policy to both dealers and sellers. Years later when I promoted raves in Scotland I saw the effects that real drug misuse could have when I saw a girl nearly die in front of me as five thousand kids continued to dance.

Everyone took the mickey out of my hair but I had a great night at Jo and Mikes and told them how my play had won the award and that I had now moved away from the Vegan nutter. The next day I planned to cycle to my old man's in Nuneaton for Sunday lunch but had a puncture on the way and so I had to call him to come and pick me up halfway between Coventry and Nuneaton.

'Bloody hell, what have you done to your fucking hair?'

'I've dyed it.'

'I can see that, fucking hell, what's Sylvia going to say about that then?'

'What's it got to do with her?'

'All right, all right, don't bloody start. It's just a bloody shock, that's all. Mind you, you look like you've lost a bit of weight.'

'Yeah.'

'Been exercising?'

'Yeah, you could say that. What's for lunch?'

'Beef, she puts on a good spread, you know.'

We set off for Dad and Sylvia's house. It was the first time I had seen him, Jason, Sylvia and the rest of my new family since I had gone to university six months before. I had phoned Jason once or twice but had only spoken to Dad earlier this week to invite myself round.

They were still living in the house that Sylvia owned with Alf, but it was clear that Dad wasn't happy there and they told me over dinner that they had put down the deposit on a new house that was being built in a field behind them. Dad was uncomfortable living in another man's house and I understood why. After the initial reaction, jokes and laughs about my hair, the day turned into the usual boring stilted event that it would always be as we all tried to make polite conversation.

The problem was we were all completely different people. I didn't really have anything in common with Sylvia's family, apart from the fact that Dad had married their mum and I didn't even have much in common with Jason because of our childhood. A childhood that of course no one ever mentioned. Dad hadn't told Sylvia about me being in care or even living in Hull and it was as if my history was being denied me again.

Worse, I was complicit in the deception and it made me both angry and upset. I was happy that he was away from the 'Slag' but I was no more part of this new family and his and Jason's new life than I was when he was with the 'Slag'. I was still excluded, still on the outside.

While at university I carried on making the occasional Sunday afternoon visit to see Dad and later when I was living with Lisa we would dread trekking over there for lunch, normally as a result of having a horrible hangover from the night before or of being bored to death by the quietness of the house. They were a different family to us: they were quieter and I presume, but don't know, that Alf was a quieter, more sane man than Dad and I never ever truly felt comfortable in the house.

As Dad tied a napkin around the neck of the wine bottle that I had brought to drink I felt as if I was slowly being strangled too, the real Jon Gaunt was being silenced, cowed by the weight of history between Dad and me which could never be spoken about in front of his new wife.

Lisa would ask, 'Why are you so quiet there? Why are you a different person? Why don't you have it out with him and then you could be yourself in front of him. You've done nothing wrong, Jon, you've got nothing to be ashamed of. It was him that abandoned you.'

This line of reasoning would usually have the same result, a massive row between Lisa and me, but she was right – he was to blame for my terrible childhood not me.

However, I do now regret those wasted years and the Sundays that I turned up wasted at Dad and Sylvia's where I wasn't mature enough to form relationships and a shared history not only with Sylvia but also my new brother and sisters and I was largely to blame for keeping my distance. I could have made more of an effort or I could have confronted Dad and got him to talk about what he had done to me and what had happened to me as a result of his actions. I could have done this while he was still a relatively young man rather than waiting another twenty years to confront these demons.

However, newly invigorated, inspired and attired, I set out carving a place for myself within the drama department. Another working-class lad, Tom McGill, had written a play about his experiences of being in a young offenders' institute and he asked me to play one of the parts in the play. Tom was an interesting character who was about three or four years older than the rest of us and who came from Corby where he had been a right yobbo. This resulted in his doing time and meeting a posh, university-educated drug dealer in prison.

Tom had protected this rich lad and in return the dealer lent Tom books and, in a classic bad-boy-turned-good story, helped to turn Tom's life around, got him into education and eventually into Birmingham University. The play was going to be directed by a young female lecturer called Chrissie Poulter.

Chrissie had been a student in the department a few years previously and had also been a contemporary of Victoria Wood.

Chrissie was great at improvisational drama and was truly inspirational as a director but as a businesswoman at that time she would make the deadbeats on *The Apprentice* look like Bill Gates. She had organised the trip to Edinburgh that year, 1980, and financed it. She had rented a slot in an old church hall on the wrong side of town but when we arrived the guy who was meant to be converting it had done a runner with the cash and the equipment. However we all mucked in and converted this old church into a theatre in time to perform in the last week of the festival. It's fair to say that we played to hardly any audience and Chrissie lost a complete packet.

As well as performing in Tom's play I also directed an avant-garde – that's a polite way of saying a crap – play written by another undergraduate starring my mate Phil and Simon Le Bon. Don't ask me what the play was about because I don't even think the bloke who wrote it knew and certainly Simon, Phil and me didn't have a clue. What it did have though was Le Bon dressed as circus ringmaster but with stockings and suspenders on his bottom half. I can't tell you how many times over the years I've searched for the photos of this production. Could you imagine how much they would have been worth, as he was singing 'Save a Prayer'.

The two biggest memories of that trip was the night Simon slept with the whole audience and the career advice I gave to one of the UK's biggest grossing singers. When I say he slept with the audience, you've got to remember most days we played to no one and I don't think we even reached the giddy heights of playing to the proverbial one man and his dog. However, we did once play to an audience of just one, a cracking young Scottish punk girl who stayed around after the performance and who certainly didn't save a prayer or even have a prayer as Simon shagged her through the night in the flat we were all sharing.

Just days later I took Le Bon to one side as he was about to board a train back to Birmingham to meet up with the rest of his new bandmates to go on Duran Duran's first tour supporting

Hazel O'Connor. He was wearing a cream safari suit and a ridiculous panama hat.

'Simon, are you sure you're making the right decision?'

He had decided to leave Birmingham after just one year and risk it with this new band that at the time didn't even have a record deal.

'You're mad. That bunch of Brummie posers hasn't got a chance of making it.'

'Yeah I know, but I can always come back if it fails,' he replied and then, pulling down his hat, his last words to me were, 'See you. This young man's off to make his fortune.'

I was still convinced he was wrong. Two months later I was among three thousand new romantics going crazy as Le Bon entered stage right at Rock City and sang 'Planet Earth'.

Moral of the story: listen to Gaunty and then do the complete opposite, that's the secret of success.

Edinburgh proved to be my salvation too as I began to see the very real possibility of how I could push my own theatrical career while at the same time making money. It's the largest arts festival in the world and what most of the student groups did was rent a hall, convert it into a temporary theatre and then rent out a few slots in the day to other groups to cover the costs of putting on your own show.

Tim Hawkins' old man was a successful northern industrialist and Tim had inherited some of his business genes and that coupled with my gift of the gab meant we were made. We decided that if we were to offer exactly the same service as other student groups but on a more professional level, we could probably both make a grand each. So we set about that winter trundling up and down the motorway to Edinburgh to find suitable venues to convert. Our plan was to convert them by putting in the staging, the lighting rig and the sound equipment and then we would split the day up into nine one-and-a-half-hour slots and hire them out with a full marketing back-up.

By the time I graduated in 1982 we had one venue and my play, *You're Wondering Now* with Clive Owen in it, was performed along with my Lawrence Boswell influenced and, if I'm really honest, rip-off production of *Volpone* on the Fringe. Both got okay reviews and Tim and I made a few quid. The stage was now set to really expand and launch our own professional theatre and promotions company.

18

Into the fringe

I left university and the city of Birmingham as soon as I finished my finals in 1982. My first play about my experiences of being in care, *You're Wondering Now*, was performed that summer in Edinburgh by the Belgrade Youth Theatre and had been directed by an old mate John Vernon. It got okay reviews and John and I had decided to set up a theatre company in our hometown of Coventry. The idea was that John and I would get it going and then Tim would come down and join us to do all the technical side.

I had hardly seen Dad the whole time that I had been in Birmingham but he had helped out with the play by photocopying the scripts at the police station. It didn't occur to me until after he had delivered the copies that he might have read the script and been upset by it. It was after all a savage indictment of what his actions had put me through. Perhaps I even wanted him to read it.

However he didn't comment on it and he didn't come to see the production. He was concerned that I was leaving university without a job and thought I was off my head to try and do something in Coventry. I ignored him and his views pretty much as I had since returning from Hull all those years ago. He wasn't really a part of my life and I wasn't part of his and I was quite happy with this arrangement.

John and I rented a grotty two-bedroom, first-floor flat in Hillfields in Coventry right opposite the main entrance to the Coventry City ground. The flat was a complete hole and we were both on the dole, surviving on pennies and our dream of creating a theatre company.

The first job was to think of a name, I came up with the idea of Theatre in Coventry or Tic and John suddenly said Tic Toc, theatre of Coventry. I wanted to create a unique company that would write and produce plays that were directly rooted in the community of Coventry but that would have a relevance to working-class audiences right across the country. At the same time as being of national importance I also wanted us to produce small-scale plays and events for community centres, schools and day centres in the city. This would keep our feet on the ground and our purpose pure.

The idea wasn't to start up a company so that we would be recognised by larger organisations or to use it as a stepping-stone to a bigger career, Tic Toc was both the journey and the final destination. We were going to be the biggest theatre company in Britain and the best. I had seen too many small-scale companies lose their way after one or two plays and forget the community and audience that they were meant to serve. At the time I really believed that radical small-scale theatre could actually change people's lives and make them question the society they were living in and their part in it.

The name and even the mission statement was the easy part; the rest was much more difficult and not helped by the fact that the flat was falling apart and we were drinking too much to actually get anything together. The final straw for the flat sharing was when I was running a bath and the plug shot into the air as

John flushed the loo and shit came spurting out of the hole into the bath.

The landlord whom we christened Lal Lal the lavatory man, came round and explained it must be a blockage in the downstairs flat that was occupied by an old geezer called Harry. We had never spoken to this bloke but we felt we knew him as each night we would fall asleep to the almost rhythmic coughing, belching and farting of this pensioner and each morning we would be woken by the delightful sound of him expectorating and phlegming up in his sink as a lifetime of bad food and too many rough fags were spat out while he shouted to himself, 'Jesus H Christ!'

Lal, Lal the lavatory man. He tried to unblock the bog with an old broom handle and only succeeded in blocking it further and the stench of excrement stayed with us for weeks and weeks. Apart from the exploding bath with hot and cold running shit I then discovered that he had used Blu Tack to 'seal' the joints on all the gas pipes on the fires in the bedroom and that my single room was actually occupied by thousands as when I lifted the carpet the floorboards were covered with cockroaches.

The only slightly happy memory of this flat is that it is where we ended up celebrating Simon's stag night which culminated with John doing impressions of Rik Mayall doing his Kevin Turvey act, the late Seventies equivalent of bores reciting Monty Python sketches! We were going nowhere and although we talked a good game by Christmas John had had enough and got himself a job with another small theatre company in Coventry and I was left alone in the dingy flat.

I managed to get some work at the Belgrade backstage on the pantomime and I spent a good few weeks smoking dope and operating the trapdoor for the actors to appear through. Another mate from the Youth Theatre moved his stuff in and I wasted another couple of months snorting and drinking until we finally had enough and did a midnight flit, owing Lal the lavatory man a fortune in rent.

An old school friend's sister had an empty house in Eastern Green and she arranged for us to move in there. This was a Sixties three-bedroom semi in the suburbs and it was just up the road from where Dad's old flat was. After a few weeks Tim moved in and at about the same time I bumped into Lisa after not seeing her and the family since I had returned to Coventry in the summer. She told me that I should come and see her mum and dad, especially as I was now only living up the road from them.

She was sixteen and just sitting her O levels and she was going out with Marc, a brilliant guitarist, whose brother Roddy had been in The Specials. She had turned into a beautiful, trendy, talented and highly articulate woman and I began to see her as more than just a friend over the coming months as I re-established contact with the Roberts. Lisa's sister Rosa was on the dole and spent most of her day hanging around the Belgrade with a bunch of other young kids including Clive Owen.

Coventry had changed since I had been away and as The Specials had sung the year previously it had turned from a Boomtown to a ghost town. When I had left the city, three years previously, to go to university my headmaster would boast that every kid from our school managed to get a job when they left but when I returned things were very different. Coventry really was even more of a ghost town than The Specials had sung about, but now it wasn't just the clubs that had closed down: many of the factories had also shut their gates and the city was really suffering.

It was a really depressing place. Even The Specials had broken up and I began to wonder if Dad was right and that instead of trying to do something in Coventry I should have headed off for the bright lights of London like the rest of my Drama Department contemporaries.

Many of the younger kids in the Youth Theatre who had now hit school-leaving age were on the dole and hanging around the Belgrade Theatre and it began to dawn on me that this bunch of talented but directionless kids could be Tic Toc's first actors. I managed to persuade the Belgrade Theatre to let me take these older unemployed youths and create a play with them to be staged in Belgrade's studio at their expense. We were all on the dole but the seven of us created a show, *Only One Escape*.

We spent weeks talking about our experiences of being on the dole and then I created a storyline, which we improvised around, and from this I scripted the final play. The play was pretty angry and quite left wing in a sixth form kind of way. For God's sake we even had a song in it called 'Smash the System'. I wanted the play to appeal to a non-theatregoing audience so I got an old mate Johnny Thompson, who had a band called The City Centre Shakers, to get involved and they punctuated the scenes with songs that commented on the action. For those of you of a theatrical bent, they acted as Brechtian captions or a modern form of a Greek chorus – see I did learn something at university.

The play was fast, frenetic, aggressive and right in the audience's face and set the style for all future Tic Toc productions. These seven kids created the kind of theatre I had only dreamt of before and without their efforts Tic Toc would never have happened. Naturally the star was Clive. He had the main part and most of the attitude. He had dropped out of sixth form and was living in 'Smegma View', a filthy house in the student area of Coventry, Earlsdon. An old school friend of mine, Mick the Miner, was sharing the house along with Rosa, Lisa's sister, and assorted oddballs.

Mick wanted to be a lumberjack when he was at school but as the opportunities for tree felling in Coventry were rather limited, he had gone down the local pit as I went to college. He was as camp as Christmas and nicknamed Lush by his colleagues in the pit but known to everyone on the music scene in Coventry as Mick the Miner.

Clive was on the dole and bumming off Mick most of the time. Clive's usual dress at the time was hardly Armani, in fact it was a pair of dirty drainpipe jeans, a filthy shirt, Doc Martens, an old mac, all topped off with a trilby. He made Pete Doherty look attractive and clean but instead of wasting all his cash on drugs he would get his dole on Thursday lunchtime, head straight into Tesco's, buy five pound of spuds, four meat and potato pies, a few cans of beans and eighty fags. He would then stroll across to the Shakespeare pub to meet the rest of us to play pool but not before he had put all, and I mean all, of the rest of his dole money into the fruit machine.

Johnny wrote a song about this called 'The Loser' and there was a whole scene about it in the play. Once the dole was gone he would spend the rest of the fortnight sponging off Mick and me. Not that I minded because Clive had an easy charm which everyone found hard to resist and also he was a great laugh. He desperately wanted to make it as an actor and it was obvious even at that age that he was destined for great things and I was hoping it was going to be with my new theatre company.

Meanwhile my old friend Nicolette was studying art at the local poly and she agreed to design the poster for me. Jerry Dammers, who was now going out with her, coughed up some money to have the poster printed in more than one colour. We got the play on and we got some good reviews for it but more importantly an old hippy from the local arts council saw it and decided to fund my next project.

This hippy was called David Hart and he was the drama officer for West Midland's Arts. He was about fifty, short and fat with a long beard and looked like a combination of the late John Peel and Bill Oddie. He was a poet and from a completely different class than us bunch of working-class doleites but he admired the energy, passion and politics of the play. David offered me a thousand pounds to write another play. Now remember at this time I was on the dole and carrying some pretty heavy debts from university so a grand was an absolute fortune. Before it disappeared into the abyss of my debts, I opened another bank account and used this lump sum to con the Government and turn it into five times as much.

At this time there were over three million unemployed and so Thatcher had introduced the Enterprise Allowance Scheme. This was a way of getting redundant workers to set up their own businesses and massaging the unemployment figures. The basic principle was that you had to invest at least a grand in your new business and then the government would allow you to pick up a payment of forty quid a week for a year while you got the company off the ground. So armed with this thousand pounds I signed up for the scheme and set up Tic Toc Theatre Company. Tim had been working on *Only One Escape* so I lent him the same thousand pounds, just for a day or two, and he set up a company called Tactic Theatre Company and thus we both picked up the cash. We then re-circulated the grand to other mates so that they could do the same thing and hey presto we were all off the dole and in business, so to speak.

I knew that the next play needed to have a smaller cast because there was no way we could ever support the seven that were in *Only One Escape* and so I decided we would do a three-hander about my experiences of working at Tesco called *Meat*. The idea was that I would write and direct it, Tim would do the technical side and an old school friend of mine, Perry Costello, would join Clive and another bloke, Franny, who had been in *Only One Escape*, in the cast.

I had known Perry since we were both in nursery school together; Mum had been a good friend with his. Perry's dad had died at a similar time to Mum and Perry had also been a star in the Youth Theatre. He had just graduated with a degree in Marine Biology and was now living with his ballet dancer girlfriend Cheryl, another Youth Theatre stalwart, in Glasgow. Perry was a natural comedian and a brilliant performer who should have gone to drama school but his mum wanted him to get a proper degree and was suspicious just like Dad was of a career in theatre. The play had to be ready in time for the inaugural Coventry Festival, which the Belgrade was organising in the summer. The theatre had already offered me a job managing one of the venues, so there was a lot riding on this production.

I decided that the partying and dossing around had to stop. We now had cash behind us. We all had to be committed and professional if we were going to pull this play off and really get off the dole.

A few days later we all met up in a deserted factory in the city centre that the Council had said we could use rent free to start rehearsals for *Meat*. Unfortunately Clive and Franny didn't seem to me to be as dedicated to the project as I was. I told them straight that I wasn't willing to work with them unless they were prepared to put in as much committment as me, they told me to fuck off and that I couldn't do it on my own, to which I replied, 'Can't I? Just you wait and see.'

That night, after the two of them had walked out, I went up to Lisa's house and told her the news that the play would now have to be a one-man show. I was really down and for the first but certainly not the last time in my life Lisa gave me the strength to carry on. We finished that evening designing the first ever Tic Toc logo together and she came up with the idea of replacing Clive with Moz Dee.

Moz had been in the Youth Theatre but was only a bit player when he got talent spotted by some TV director and ended up becoming a bit of a child star. He was in Channel Four's first ever drama *Ptang Yang Kipper Bang*, episodes of *Angels* and even *Adrian Mole* as Pandora's love interest, posh Nigel. He made a fair few bob and unlike most child stars who waste it on fast women and even faster cars like Porsches, Moz's mum and Dad spent his cash on a new *porch* for their terraced house.

Moz was a Roman Catholic and just leaving the fifth form when I rang him and asked him to be in *Meat*. This time I had actually written the play in advance and after reading it he said yes he would love to do it but that he would have to hide the script from his ultra-religious mum because of all the swearing. Months later the idiot left it on the kitchen table, his mum read it and came to the conclusion that it was the work of Satan and that Moz would burn in hell if he spoke my words. But he was sixteen and somehow he talked her round.

Two down one to go and so Tim and I put an advert in *The Stage* newspaper for an actor to play the third part. We auditioned loads of actors but in the end we plumped for a guy called Rob (known as Bobby) who had just graduated from the poly with a degree in Geography rather than all the drama school trained fools who turned up to audition in our deserted factory unit. He hadn't been trained but he had a raw talent, was a good-looking lad and had bags of enthusiasm and dedication but more importantly he was willing to join in our Enterprise Allowance fiddle. We had our final piece of the jigsaw and we started to rehearse.

About six months later I got home and there was a message on the answering machine from Clive. He hadn't rung to ask for his job back but to drunkenly gloat down the phone that he had been accepted at RADA and to inform me that I was 'a fat fucking no mark that was going nowhere'. I was pleased for him and even more so when I heard months later that he had got into the world's greatest drama school by using speeches from my plays. But I don't begrudge him a thing and I am amazed but not surprised by his success.

I finally met Clive again twenty years later. I was taking a piss in the loo at BBC London at the time and he came up from behind me. The next thing I knew I was being lifted up in a great big bear hug. I turned around and it was Clive.

With new teeth.

But of course by now he was a major Hollywood player. He'd come in to do an interview with some pretentious film critic. We ended up talking in the loo for about twenty minutes. He told me that in his last three movies he'd had to shag Julia Roberts, Jennifer Aniston and Angelina Jolie.

My heart bled for him and of course it only goes to show – you can take the boy out of Coventry . . .

All the while we were talking, his people and the critic were fretting over where he'd got to. Clive did eventually do the interview and even said that if it hadn't been for me, he wouldn't be where he was today.

Well, that's fine with me, but fair's fair: the bastard still owes me a trilby hat and about five hundred quid.

At the end of that summer, myself, Tim and the three lads performed *Meat* at the 1983 Coventry Festival and then hit the phones to try and get bookings anywhere and at anytime to perform the play. The play was about three working-class blokes and it was both a celebration and condemnation of their meathead lifestyle, performed in a knockabout cartoon style, which culminated in a food fight in a curry house. So it was perfect for student unions and small arts centres.

As with all my plays, it was fast, furious and frantic, full of swear words, dancing, loud music and theatrical effects. When I was at college I hated all that staid, boring, drawing room theatre and the very reason I wanted to start my own theatre company was that I didn't want to work or compromise in traditional rep theatre. If I could sing I would have wanted to be in a band but as I clearly couldn't hold a tune, creating my kind of rock 'n' roll theatre came a close second and right from the beginning we acted and talked, even lived like a band.

The only problem of course was it was the same middle-class arses that I went to university with who were in charge of booking acts in to arts centres and who controlled the purse strings of the funding bodies like the Arts Council. However, we managed to pick up some gigs, usually one or two a week, and we would pack all the set, props and sound system into a hired transit van and drive off to places like Guildford or Exeter to perform *Meat*. We would usually get drunk afterwards, because just like a band we always insisted on a 'rider' in the dressing room, and then because we had no cash for accommodation we would either crash on student floors or drive back through the night. Once we even did Edinburgh and back in the same day.

These were great times and I guess we really felt that we were part of a band or a gang and I thrive on this kind of gang culture. All through my career I have tended to build a team round my central vision and then we've all worked our balls off to get to our goal.

We also had a rule that what was said in the van or on tour stayed in the van. We called it Van Talk and as a result the five of us became really close. These were fantastic alcohol- and adrenaline-fuelled days where we knew our play was good and we didn't give a fuck if the person who had booked it liked it or us. We graduated to playing trendy arts centres as a buzz about us grew and then we used to be put up in the trendy liberal bastards' houses where we would merge our stage characters with ourselves and I guess scare the living daylights out of the poor sods who had booked us.

Once we were down south for a couple of nights and we walked into the Art Centre's café and asked for some bacon butties. The hippy behind the counter looked at us as if we were something the cat had dragged in and informed us that it was veggie only. He was just chopping up carrots with a massive chopper and Bobby asked him if it wouldn't be quicker to use the food processor that was gathering dust on the shelf.

The prick actually replied, 'No that would seem cruel to the carrot.'

Perry replied, 'If I was a carrot I think I'd prefer the mixer every time.'

The woman who booked us there invited us to stay at her house and on the second night she didn't come home because she was spending a night of vegan passion with the carrot chopper. We got in, raided her fridge and then ransacked her drawers – well, she did say help yourself when you get home.

Bobby found the biggest vibrator you have ever seen in her knickers drawer. He proceeded to chase us with it round the house and the Habitat furniture until he ran out of steam and it ran out of battery power and then we carefully put it back deliberately in a different drawer so that she would know that we had seen it. We were lads off the leash and on the lash and although we were all earning peanuts it was some of the most enjoyable times of all of our lives.

During all this mayhem and debauchery my relationship with Lisa entered a new phase. We eventually started going out with each other but we had to keep it a secret because we didn't know how her mum and dad would react. However, we soon found out.

Lisa and I hitchhiked to Edinburgh after the Coventry Festival and I was amazed that her mum and dad let her but I guess they thought that we were just good friends and that I would act as a big brother figure. The truth is of course I was something different altogether. We went across to Glasgow and stayed for a couple of days with Perry and his girlfriend Cheryl. It was this holiday that really cemented our relationship and on our return Lisa told her mum and dad that she wanted to move in with me. She was sixteen and I was twenty-two.

Her dad went crazy and I must admit I don't blame him. It culminated with him saying, 'If you ever hurt her I'll fucking kill you.' This was all the more frightening because not only did he mean it but he never normally swears, in fact to this day I can probably count on one hand the amount of times he's even raised his voice let alone swore in anger. Still they didn't really stand in our way and Lisa moved in and started her A levels while living with me.

Looking back on this episode I am not very proud of our actions or myself. Jo and Mike were religious at the time, and remember this was 24 years ago, and they must have felt ashamed of what was going on, especially as the parish gossip was living only a few doors away from our love shack.

Now as my daughter Rosie approaches a similar age I wonder – no I don't, I know exactly how I would react if some barely employed camp theatrical bloke with greasy hair and little or no prospects took my daughter away. I would kill the fucking bastard.

Everyone tried to persuade Lisa to go home, including her brother, Mikey, but Lisa was adamant and from that day on we have been inseparable. Of course it hasn't all been roses round the cottage door and a row-free zone but we have now been together for nearly 25 years, seven unmarried and seventeen with the ring and I love her and need her more than ever. She was more mature than me even when she was only sixteen. It has been her cool head, support, strength and of course love that has pushed me on. She's always been there both for the good times and all the bad times that my stupid ambition and dreams have led us into.

Dad didn't really bat an eyelid about Lisa moving in. He knew the Roberts family and he had met Jo and Mike on a couple of occasions but I always got the impression that he was embarrassed in their company because he must have known that I had told them about being in care. Perhaps the presence of Lisa's foster sisters was also a clear reminder. The weird thing is I felt embarrassed, even sorry for his embarrassment. It was as if I was again taking the blame for something, a decision that clearly had nothing to do with me. Why should I feel like this? He was the bastard who put me in care, I was angry but again I didn't say anything, I just bottled it up. If he had complained or passed comment about my relationship with Lisa I would have told him to keep his fucking nose out, after all he had done to me, and I think he knew that and that was the reason for his silence.

I did introduce Lisa to Simon in my local pub and Lisa reckons that it was his approval I sought, his sanction of the relationship rather than Dad's. By this time Simon was married to Louise and living in Reading and had a good proper decent graduate job with Royal Insurance. Simon liked Lisa right from the start and I was pleased.

While studying for her A levels Lisa also became the unofficial designer and stage manager for Tic Toc and more importantly began to share the vision that I had for the company. Because of the success of *Meat*, West Midlands Arts Council offered us

£5,000 towards our next play but Tim and I both knew that this still wasn't enough to sustain the wages of the five of us. We had started to plan a pantomime that we would tour round schools, old people's homes and sheltered accommodation. Over the years the panto became an annual fixture, which was eventually funded by the City Council but at this time there still wasn't enough cash so we revisited our plans for Edinburgh.

At the end of 1983, Tim and I drove up to the Scottish Capital and booked a venue, the Walpole Hall. This was the church hall of the Scottish Episcopal cathedral in the city and although it was slightly off the beaten track we thought that we would be able to sell some spots and make a bit of cash. We were hoping to make about a grand each but we soon realised that there was an awful lot more cash on offer. That first summer we opened the first Tic Toc venue at the festival.

It was a success although we only had student groups renting it and no big names at this point. However within a couple of years we had expanded, so that by 1986 we had three temporary theatres at the festival and a turnover from the promotions of at least fifty grand. Meanwhile we had developed the theatre company and produced three other plays, *BMeX, Holiday 85* and now the soon to be massively successful *Hooligans*. We had also produced a few pantomimes and slowly increased our funding from West Midlands Arts.

We still weren't making real money but we had all got equity cards and we were all off the dole. Perry had long left, fed up of the commuting and gone back to Scotland to set up a very successful production company with his wife. I had taken over his role in *Meat* and loved every minute of it. On the domestic front Lisa and I had bought our first house together, an end terrace for £19,000. One of the future stars of Tic Toc had also joined a year or two ago as well. He was a young lad called Nipper on account of the fact that he was so short. I don't even remember how he joined, he just sort of turned up and started helping out and before we knew it, when Moz suddenly left, he took over his role in *Meat* and he became part of the furniture through the usual Enterprise Allowance route.

An old friend from the drama department, Caroline Butcher, had also joined as a full-time administrator to help with the increasing office demands and bookings. She was married to my old flatmate Nigel, the one whose typewriter I had used to write my first ever play on, so in a sense everything had come full circle. We also recruited a brilliant theatre technician from the Warwick Arts Centre called John Laidlaw who became a vital part of the team and made my mad special effect ideas actually work.

We were now a permanent company of seven and the company was on a much more formal basis. It was now a limited company and had its own offices in a community building in Coventry called Koco. This was a part of the old Renold chain factory which had long since closed down and now the local co-operative development agency had taken it over and converted it into office space for small groups just like us. In fact at this point Tic Toc became a co-operative too not because of any idealised political view that all workers should share the profits of their labour but simply because it was a cheap way of accessing business advice and funding. That said, at the time we did all pay ourselves the same amount but make no mistake about it, there was only one boss and everyone knew it and was happy with it.

I still hold the view that in any business or artistic enterprise you have to have a single vision, a leader. You can't produce plays, or for that matter radio, by committee as evidenced by the turgid output of most of Radio Five Dead. When people tune into me on the radio it isn't to listen to the callers or even to debate the subject but to listen to how I will attack that days headlines. That's why I talk about my family and how issues affect me and mine, there's no point in saying on the one hand there's this view on the other there's this. People want you to be partial, opinionated and they want to either agree or shout you down.

It was the same with my plays. I wasn't interested in reasoned debate, I just wanted to get my world view over and try and convince the audience to think how I think.

'Did you write that play?'

'Yeah, how did you know?'

'I could see your lips mumbling all the words.'

'Oh sorry, hope I didn't spoil it for you.'

'No of course not, I loved it. In fact I would go as far as to say it's one of the best plays I've seen in over thirty years of coming to the Fringe.'

'Thanks, thank you.'

I had been standing on the back staircase of the student union, when this middle-aged stranger had approached me and started talking to me completely uninvited.

'You must be very pleased about the Fringe First – Jon isn't it?'

'Yeah, yeah, it's great.'

'Well, look if there's anything I can ever do to help you in your career, please feel free to give me a ring.'

And at this point the stranger took my hand and put a business card into my palm and closed my fingers over it.

I thought, *Bloody hell, this must be one of these men that my dad warned me about when I said I wanted to go into the theatre!*

As the bloke walked out of the building, I opened my hand slowly; the card had a BBC logo on it and his name, David Hatch. I didn't have a clue who he was.

It was 1986 and just three years after leaving university, me and a couple of mates had managed to get ourselves off the dole and drugs and become one of alternative theatres hottest companies.

My fifth play, *Hooligans*, had just stormed the Edinburgh Fringe and had not only won rave reviews but also picked up a prestigious Fringe First award and a week's transfer to the Donmar Warehouse in London's West End.

Hooligans was about two unemployed lads from Coventry and their mate Mick who had deserted from the army after returning from the Falklands campaign. They embark on a shopping spree fuelled and paid for by stolen chequebooks and credit cards which culminates with them being involved in a football riot similar to what had occurred a few months earlier in Heysel. It hit a real nerve in Edinburgh that year and played to packed houses. The *Scotsman* described it as 'putting a steel toe-capped boot into the complacency of the Fringe' and 'theatrical GBH' and this reaction is probably the reason why David Hatch came to see it. The fact that we also had a very professional set up by this time must have helped too but just like when I won the Sony awards years later, *Hooligans'* overnight success was the result of three years' hard work that stretched right back to that first production of *Only One Escape*. We had created a house style and now we had the experience, talent and personnel to actually realise my dreams.

At the same time as storming the Fringe we were running two theatres in the Heriot Watt University student's union in the centre of the city. Upstairs in the bigger theatre we were promoting acts like Julian Clary, Jeremy Hardy and Harry Enfield, whereas downstairs we had ourselves and acts like Neil Mullarkey and an unknown comic called Mike Myers.

In fact Mullarkey and Myers followed our show and there was only a fifteen-minute turnaround between our show and theirs and as *Hooligans* finished with a riot it was always a close shave as to whether their double act would go up on time. Mullarkey and Myers show was inventive, silly and very, very funny and played to packed houses as well. At the time, the two of them were the warm-up act for Timmy Mallet and his TV show *Wacaday* and it was clear that they had a big future ahead of them.

In fact it was so obvious to me that I even cornered Mike Myers in the bar one night, after hearing that he was splitting up the double act and returning to live in Canada. I told him he was a fool and that he should stay with Mullarkey in England because they were on the verge of making it. Thank God, just like Simon Le Bon years earlier, that he listened but ignored my advice. Six months later he was on *Saturday Live* in the States, swiftly followed by *Wayne's World* and is now a major Hollywood player. I was also grateful because it meant he stopped chatting up Lisa. He was always flirting with her and as I say to the girls now of course she chose the right bloke because they would hate living in LA with Shrek and his millions.

Somehow they never look that convinced.

I later found out that David Hatch (who died in June 2007), the mystery stranger on the stairs, was at that time the controller of radio for the BBC. Not only that, he was one of the men behind the likes of John Cleese, Graham Chapman and Bill Oddie.

We returned to Coventry in early September convinced that Tic Toc was on its way and those dark days after Franny and Clive left seemed like years ago.

19

Hanging on the telephone

1986

'Can I speak to Jon *Guant* please?'

'It's *Gaunt* and you're speaking to him.'

'Hi Jon, I'm Christopher Malcolm and I was wondering if I could produce *Hooligans* in er . . . Australia.'

'Fuck off!'

'Pardon?'

'Yeah very funny, who is this?'

I looked round the office to see which of my mates was trying to wind me up. None of them was on the phone but I was still convinced this was a setup.

'Who are you?'

'I'm Christopher Malcolm. I produce Steven Berkoff, have you heard of him?'

Had I heard of him? He was my hero. I loved his work. Before I had time to reply he spoke again.

'Have you got an agent?'

'Er . . . no.'

'Would you like one?'

'Yeah, of course.'

'Well, look, give this woman a ring but make sure you mention my name. Otherwise she won't take your call.'

He continued to tell me that her name was Phil Kelvin and that she was a very successful agent representing among others Fay Weldon.

I put the phone down and stared at her number on the piece of paper, I was still wary that this might all be a set up by Bobby or Nipper. I picked up the phone without telling any of the other lads about the previous conversation and dialled.

'Goodwin Associates, can I help?'

It was Phil's assistant – a young woman called Flea.

'Er yes . . . it's Jon Gaunt. Can I speak to Phil—'

She interrupted me, 'Sorry she's not here. Can I take a—'

'Oh it's just that Christopher Malcolm—'

'Hold on, Jon, was it? She's just come in.'

Within a week I was sitting in Phil's office, which was in a mews block off Oxford Street.

Phil was a tiny woman in her late thirties. She had short boyish hair, an impish grin and was constantly chewing nicotine gum. She was very successful, with an impressive list of clients and after talking to me for an afternoon said that she would like to represent me.

At last I was a real professional playwright with one of London's most successful agents representing me. Not only that but Phil believed in me and taught me to believe in my own talent. She made me realise that I could have a future as a professional writer, just like Delia Dick all those years before, she showed me an alternative that was easily within my grasp. The only person standing in the way of having this lifestyle was myself.

Within a couple of weeks I was in a posh restaurant in Kenilworth discussing a deal with Yorkshire TV to produce *Hooligans* for the box.

Phil had asked me what I wanted to achieve and had got straight down to work. Yorkshire TV was doing a series of

UNDAUNTED

experimental plays by new writers and she managed to convince the producer, Derek Bennett, that *Hooligans* was ideal for the slot. That's why he and his sidekick, Tim Vaughan, were now sitting opposite Phil and me, studying the menus. Derek said he fancied the asparagus, Tim agreed and Phil nodded. All three looked at me.

'Oh yeah, yeah that would be lovely.'

We then chose the main course and I waited in trepidation for the starter to arrive. I couldn't spell asparagus let alone knew what it was or tasted like. The other three had had a long, involved conversation about how this was the best time of year to eat it when it suddenly arrived. I waited till they started and then proceeded to clear my whole plate, only realising that you're only meant to eat the tips, not the whole bloody thing, when I looked up from my plate. They were all too polite to remark on my ignorance and instead Derek produced a contract that was offering me about five grand for the rights to the play. A couple of weeks later I signed the contract and I was about to officially become a TV writer.

Meanwhile *Hooligans* was touring all over the country and playing to packed houses. Bobby and Nipper played the parts of the two young lads who were on the dole and my old university mate, Tom McGill, played the part of the army deserter. He was perfect for the part as he looked really hard with his short hair and real tattoos and his eyes had a real menace that were obviously the result of his own disturbed teenage years.

Lisa had been stage-managing the play in Edinburgh and one night just before the curtain went up someone had spilt some water on the floor. She had used a towel to mop up the spillage. Big Mistake. It was Tom's towel. He went mental and Lisa is convinced to this day that this was the evening that the Fringe First judges were in and that Tom's performance that evening wasn't acting but absolutely real anger and madness.

Tom had agreed to be in the play until Christmas but of course we now wanted to extend the run and make as much cash as we

136

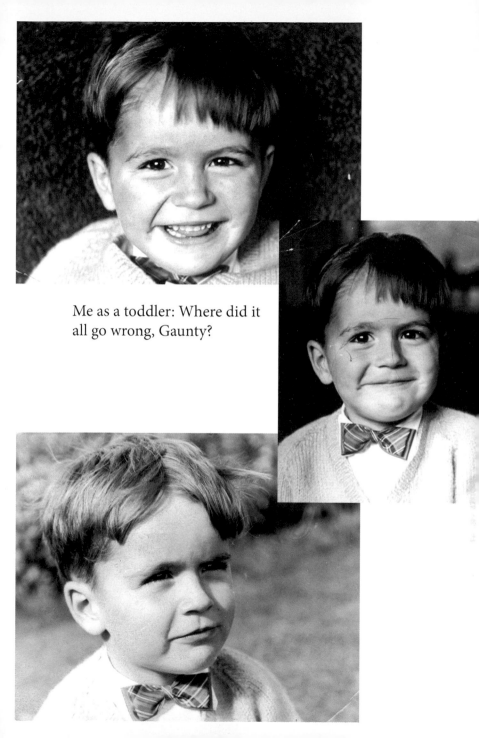

Me as a toddler: Where did it all go wrong, Gaunty?

Left: How come I didn't get my dad's matinee idol looks?

Right: I come from a long line of posers

Above left: Mum, Dad and me, the quietest I've ever been

Above right: Dad and me in Cornwall

My dad's a policeman …

Above: I wanted to be a pop star but didn't have the looks, the talent or the voice.

Right: More Worzel Gummidge than Johnny Rotten

One of my favourite pictures of me and Lisa when we were young and fab … and scruffy

Below: Our first holiday together

CUNARD COUNTESS   Caribbean Cruise 1988

Above: Me and my girls at Sea World
Below: Dad being a real dad to my girls on our last holiday in Miami

Above: Me and Basil, the only fox I don't want to hunt!

Right: What a night! More Sony's than Dixons

Left: Gaunty
relaxes before
battle commences
(© David Sandison/
The Independent)

Right: Another quiet
day at the office
(© David Sandison/The
Independent)

could out of it in the spring. He didn't want to do it and then I made a big, immature mistake. I hadn't told him about the TV offer because he wasn't a member of the company, just a jobbing actor. I let him go at Christmas and recast for the tour. His replacement was good but was no match for Tom. I should have swallowed my pride and asked Tom to at least do the TV version. But I didn't and a few months later we were all at Yorkshire TV filming my adapted version of *Hooligans*.

I had spent a couple of months with Tim Vaughan adapting the script for TV and having long conversations and discussions about the amount of swearing. This felt bizarre because the original script had an inauspicious birth. I was desperately trying to finish writing it and had got stuck so I said, 'Bollocks to this Lisa, let's go and get plastered.'

And I did literally. We had a skinful with the boys and on the way home had started to argue which culminated in me doing the big dramatic one and punching the wall in the house in a rage. Lisa laughed at me and called me 'bloody pathetic' so like the child I am and not having hurt myself enough the first time I smacked the wall again and collapsed in agony. My hand blew up to twice its size and I was convinced I had broken it. Lisa assured me on the way to casualty that 'it had bloody well better be broken or I'll break it for you'.

She needn't have worried because when they showed me the X-ray it resembled the crazy paving that we used to have in the front garden of Bulwer Road. I was in plaster for six weeks and the play was completed by me lying on the sofa dictating the words and directions to Nipper who wrote it in long hand. Now eighteen months later Tim and I were getting to the point where we were trading three 'fucks' for a 'cunt' and changing the liberal use of the word 'fucking' for 'bloody' and even a couple of 'bloomings'. But it didn't matter, what was important was getting it on TV.

I still love doing TV. I love the adrenaline rush, teamwork and excitement of knowing your face, voice or opinions are being beamed into everyone's living rooms. Every Tuesday I get picked up at 4.30 by my driver, an ex-professional boxer from Glasgow called Alan, to take me to Sky News to appear with Eamonn Holmes to review the papers. I don't do it for the money, I do it purely for the craic, being the first to comment on that day's news and to tell a waking breakfast audience what to think of the news and the politicians and stars that are making the headlines.

The excitement, the buzz that I get when I walk into a TV studio is exactly the same now as it was all those years ago when I first started doing extra work and then small bit parts on the TV with Bobby and the rest of the Tic Toc boys.

Shortly after getting our equity cards and at the same time as touring *Hooligans* we got a small-time agent in Birmingham called Val who started finding us TV work. The best part I got was to be Gregor Fisher's (Rab C. Nesbitt) henchman in an episode of *Boon* in Birmingham. This part also gave me the opportunity to drive a Jaguar for the very first time and not just any old Jaguar but a brand new red one that was actually Gabriella Drake's Jag in *Crossroads*. The plotline was that me, Gregor and another Tic Toc actor had tried to give Michael Elphick as Boon a kicking but instead Elphick had slapped Gregor. Then there was a scene where I was in the driving seat and Boon throws Gregor in the back of the car and tells me to take him to the hospital. The technical crew put the car in the right spot, put the wheel on full lock and told me just to put my foot down and pull away as Elphick said his line.

That all sounds pretty simple, doesn't it, and it probably would have been if I had a driving licence or at least knew how to drive but unfortunately I could do neither. When they asked me at the audition I just lied, 'Yeah of course I can drive.'

I wasn't going to miss the chance of working with one of my heroes. I had loved Elphick since I had seen him in *Private Schulz* and my old man was more proud of me working with his hero than any other thing I had done in my life. He was also more chuffed at seeing me turn up in bit parts or even walk-ons in TV programmes than the success I was beginning to have with my plays. Is that a case of the power of TV?

I was beginning to see a bit more of him and I think he was beginning to realise that maybe there was a future in this acting and theatre lark for me. He was also happier and more settled than I had ever seen him. He was no longer a drinker and had settled into a quiet domestic life with Sylvia. He was one lucky bastard because he had at last found a woman who could not only control him but also satisfy him with his ambitions.

Sylvia loved the holidays and wanted to live in a nice place and they were ideally suited but she also had her family and their needs at the centre of her universe. After Dad's death she told me how she would drop her kids off at the school gate and drive to her job in Coventry with tears streaming down her face. She didn't want to leave them but just like Dad there was no real support network when she lost her first husband, Alf, in the seventies.

As she told me this story I felt immense guilt because all those years ago Lisa and I used to take the mick out of her behind her back about the way she bought all her groceries from Marks & Sparks. I had her marked down as a bit of a snob when in fact she only did this because she was having to hold down a full-time job and be a single mum at the same time. On holiday in Miami years later I also saw what had attracted Dad to her. She wasn't just this staid boring housewife that I had characterised her as she actually liked to let her hair down and have a good time but the weight of responsibility of having three kids of her own and then having to take on my brother and of course Dad had taken its toll.

So Elphick throws him in the car and barks, 'You better take him to the hospital.'

'Yeah.'

That was my line, hardly Shakespeare but hey, I was getting the best part of two hundred a day.

I put my foot down, the car missed the transit box van that was parked deliberately in front and sped up the road, stopping about two hundred yards away. Easy. Until I heard the director on the megaphone shout, 'Yeah that was good but can you do it a bit faster next time please?'

Shit! Was I going to have to reverse this forty grand beast as well? No, thank God, a prop man ran up, opened the driver's door for me to get out and put the car back in place, or so I thought. I walked back down the hill to a sweaty Elphick who was taking a huge swig out of his litre bottle of Irn Bru.

'Put your foot down harder, Gaunty, we don't want to miss lunch.'

By which he meant he didn't want to miss having a few drinks in the ATV bar back at the studios. He offered me the Irn Bru.

'No thanks, Michael.'

The last thing I wanted was alcohol if I had to do that scene again. Yes that's right, it wasn't Irn Bru, it was almost neat vodka with just a splash of the stuff made in Scotland from girders. Elphick was drinking heavily at this time; even a bit player like me could see that. However he was still a fine actor and real nice bloke who always insisted on buying the drinks, always doubles, because he was earning more than the rest of us. I've always believed that it was a tragedy that he ended his career, bloated and drunk, playing a pervert in *EastEnders* rather than enjoying the glittering Hollywood career he deserved. As with so many, the drink did get to him in the end.

Right, back to the scene. The cars on its mark, Elphick throws Gregor in the back.

'You better take him to the hospital.'

'Yeah.'

Foot down hard, full lock on, smash. *Shit.*

I had put forty grand's worth of Jag right up the arse of the van in front. Panic, people running towards me, my TV career over before it's even began and then the sound of laughter from Elphick on the street and Fisher on the back seat and then concern from the crew that I was all right. It didn't matter; it was the technicians' fault. They had just put the car back on the wrong mark.

That's the point. TV is a collaborative thing, much more so than theatre and at first I found that really difficult to understand or comprehend. You have to learn to compromise, something that, as you are probably aware, I am not too good at.

The TV version of *Hooligans* proved this to me, I had already made my first mistake by not being humble enough to get the best man for the main part. I now had to learn to work with someone and trust a stranger with my work. Derek had chosen a director called Phillip Casson to direct the play and although he was well known for directing light entertainment programmes he hadn't done much drama. I immediately wrote him off, even before I had met him, and after our first meeting I was even more convinced that he was the wrong man for the job.

We were at the Warwick arts centre performing *Hooligans* when Phil first turned up. He was about 55, short, slightly camp with a mop of grey hair in which he had perched his glasses, which were also on a Larry Grayson style gold chain. Reaction from the cast and me ranged from 'What a wanker' to 'What a fucking puff. What's he know about radical theatre or even football?'

It was the arrogance of youth. We were at the top of our game or so we thought. We were the new boys, tearing up and down the country, kicking ass and we didn't need some silly old twat whose claim to fame was directing the frigging Muppets or Ted Rogers's *321* directing our play. But we were wrong. Casson was a genius. This was the man who, back in the Sixties when he working at Granada, had directed classic pop footage of people like Jerry Lee Lewis. He told us that he was the first director to take the camera off the stand and follow the action or the hands of the pianist. Yes he had directed the Muppets but that was a worldwide hit and who doesn't love the Muppets and above all else he had some great ideas for my play.

When he came to direct the play we had a great week and I learnt so much from watching him direct and also we had a good laugh. Just like Elphick, he wouldn't let you have a single spirit and if you dared ask for a slimline tonic with your gin he would reply, 'No chance, you hairy-arsed beer drinker.'

However the highlight of *Hooligans* getting on the TV was the fact that Brian Glover actually introduced the film and said that if he were forty years younger he would have loved to play Nipper's part of the Skinhead. This was the moment I knew that I had made it and my old man actually rang me up to say well done and 'Was that actually the real Brian Glover?'

The most embarrassing aspect of that week, though, was the day we all bumped into Tom McGill who should have been in the film. We were all drunk, standing outside a curry house in Leeds when Tom just walked by. It was as if it were a dream – why would he be there? But of course Chrissie was from Leeds and he had, purely by coincidence, been visiting. There was an embarrassed silence and it was obvious why we were near the TV studios. I have never had the chance to say sorry to Tom.

At the same time Phil, my agent, was sending me for meeting after meeting in London with the BBC and others to get commissions and within a few months of knowing her I had a major play commission at the Birmingham Rep, a TV play for the Beeb and the offer of writing for *The Bill*.

The promotions side of the company was expanding too and we had decided to have five theatres at the 1987 festival, which would double our turnover. Also at this point I came up with the idea of promoting new comedy in Coventry. We knew all the comedians from promoting them in Edinburgh and we had all the technical equipment and knowledge, so why didn't we convert the seminar rooms downstairs in the Koco building, get a drinks licence and put on cabaret every Friday? So we did and the Tic Toc Club was born.

Dad helped me get a drinks licence because he knew the local licensing copper and this bloke helped me through the procedure. The fact that I was Pete Gaunt's lad also seemed to help to grease the wheels of the licensing committee and if there was any sign of trouble at the fledgling club the coppers seemed to take an active and non-aggressive approach. I began to see a little more of Dad during this period as he had retired from the police after doing thirty years and he was chuffed to get out of it. He said if he had his time again he wouldn't join and that the job had changed too much for his liking.

I actually went to his retirement party with Lisa, which was held in the Police Club where years and years previously me and Simon had gone to the annual police kids Christmas party. He had a good send off and the very healthy pension allowed him to go on his first of many Caribbean cruises with Sylvia and much to my surprise, especially after the Simon and 'Slag' incident, he declared that he was going to set himself up as a self-employed driving instructor!

Once we had taken over the seminar rooms we opened a café in the Koco building and Lisa's mum was employed to manage it. Dad would often pop in for a coffee – 'Black please and just half a cup and top it up with cold water love' – and he would sit and while away a few hours either talking to me and the boys or Jo. It was clear that he was proud of me at this stage and was fond of telling people that Jon Gaunt, the one who is always in the local paper, was his lad. This was weird because it was genuinely the first time he had ever shown his pride and I felt it was all to do with the stardust element of the work.

What was also weird was the way the Tic Toc boys got on with Dad and how they all thought he was a good laugh and loved his jokes and police stories. He made quite a go of the driving school and I began to help him with his books and in return he taught Lisa, she passed first time. She said he was a polite and patient teacher, which differed greatly from Nipper's reaction when he taught him which was, 'Bloody hell, Jon, your dad's a nutter, if you put a foot wrong he gives you a right bollocking.' Still Nipper passed first time too.

I was still keeping my Dad at arm's length at this time and I certainly hadn't forgotten or forgiven him for what he had done to me but I could clearly see that he was a different man and I put that change down to getting out of the police, but mostly to his relationship with Sylvia.

The Cabaret Club was a success and sellout from the word go. We were probably the first comedy club outside London. Our success was helped by the fact that there was a whole new crop of talented comedians desperate for gigs and they would travel to Coventry for as little as forty to seventy quid a night. We had everyone from Julian Clary, when he still had Fanny the Wonder Dog and called himself the Joan Collins Fan Club, to Paul Merton, when he was still called Paul Martin and was a civil servant, through to Harry Enfield, Mike Myers, Jo Brand, Mark Thomas, Lee Evans, Eddie Izzard and of course on a regular basis, Frank Skinner.

In fact I think we were the first people to give Skinner a paid gig. I paid him £20 to appear on the bottom of the bill and that was £19.99 too much. He was dreadful. At the time he was called Chris Collins and I think he was still drinking but I really admired the way he gave up the booze and refused to give in and within a matter of months of hard gigging in the Midlands and London he became a real star of the circuit. We took him to Edinburgh a year or so later and although his own show bombed he also performed at our late-night cabaret club and went down a storm. Now I think he is one of the best stand-ups in the country. Bobby and Nipper formed a comedy duo called the Cheeky Chappies and they acted as comperes for the nights and became as popular with the Coventry crowd, if not more so, than the fledgling TV names we were bringing up.

So my playwriting career was taking off. We were touring constantly and the Edinburgh business was booming. This was the point where I should have jumped ship, left Tic Toc, moved to London, become a full-time writer and lived the literary life.

But did I?

Did I hell!

20

House in the country

Eighty-seven had been a brilliant year for the City of Coventry, Tic Toc and myself. The football club had won the FA cup and Nipper, Bobby and me had travelled down to watch the mighty Sky Blues beat Spurs 3–2. Like thousands of other supporters we had returned to Coventry to be greeted by the sounds of horns blaring and every building being decked out in sky blue. The celebrations had gone on all night and we had been drinking in a great Irish pub called The Blackhorse with the rest of the Tic Toc crowd through the night. The pubs never closed and the next day the city centre was jammed with thousands of city fans to greet their heroes.

If Coventry City's victory had been a triumph for the underdog then so had Tic Toc's success and growth ever since we won that Fringe First. We now had funding from the Arts Council of Great Britain to the tune of £26,000 for a new play, *Stars*.

They had refused to fund *Hooligans*, saying that they thought the script wasn't up to much, so with my typical aggression,

145

when we stormed Edinburgh and won every award going, I sent them a stinking letter enclosing all the reviews and the testimonials from people like David Hatch. I wasn't polite. I didn't play to their rules. I just battered the middle-class liberals into submission. The result was 26 big ones and for the first time in our short history we had enough cash to put on a show properly without cutting corners.

Stars had a cast of five and in a way was a reworking of *Only One Escape*. The plot pre-empted the *X Factor* generation because it concerned five youngsters who were all on the dole but were yearning for stardom. They all just wanted to be famous, famous for anything. They didn't realise that to get anywhere in life you have to work hard. Bobby and Nipper were in it and we auditioned and employed professional actors for the other three parts. At last with the success of the grants and the commercial arm of the business we could all be paid equity minimum and for the first time it seemed that we were making real progress.

We had a packed touring itinerary and we decided to take both *Stars* and *Hooligans* to Edinburgh. Meanwhile my TV- and theatre-writing career was also taking off and I began to consider myself a professional writer and obviously I began to earn more than the others from these outside interests. If I'm truthful this is probably where the rot set in as I began to move away from my gang both financially and timewise. I was being offered opportunities that I couldn't share with them. I desperately wanted the TV success and the money that went with it but I also felt a real loyalty to the Tic Toc gang and also I still had this dream of making Tic Toc the biggest theatre company in the country.

I thought my increasingly high profile could only be a good thing for the company not a negative so I just kept on accepting the commissions and decided to worry about how I would write them or fulfil my commitments later. The lads seemed pleased for me and I didn't detect any resentment from them as my career and bank balance took off and it seemed as if they were happy following in my wake. However, it was clear then and it is clear now that my individual achievements and opportunities were the beginning of the end for Tic Toc.

Yet I still had massive plans for the company. When The Specials were at the height of their fame they had wanted to take over an old cinema in Coventry and turn it into a club for the city but before they could get their plans off the drawing board they had imploded and the dream never turned into a reality. I knew that I could succeed where they had failed and so I started searching with a vengeance for a permanent home for Tic Toc.

At the same time, buoyed up by the cash and success of my writing career, I decided that a real writer didn't live in town but in the countryside so Lisa and I bought a sixteenth-century cottage in the country for ninety grand. Dad loved the fact that I could afford to buy a ninety grand house at the age of 26 but he told me that I was mad to buy a sixteenth-century cottage and that I should have got a modern box, like his on a new build estate.

I told him in no uncertain terms that a Wimpy home did not fit the image I was creating.

He laughed and called me 'a bloody puff' and he was probably right as I was getting a bit up myself to be honest. I couldn't quite believe what was happening to me, and that little boy outside Wilko's office reasserted himself and wanted to show all those fuckers who had written him off that he had arrived and that he was a success.

The house and a new car – a 1.1 red Ford Fiesta – were the physical manifestations of this and on reflection it was a pretty pathetic and predictable and ultimately stupid thing to do. However it didn't stop there because as they say you can take the boy out of Coventry but you can't take the Coventry out of the boy and so I decided to blow all the money from my BBC film commission on a month-long holiday in the Caribbean.

I chose the West Indies because it was hot and exotic but also because it was two fingers up to Dad and a better holiday than he had ever had. However he bored me rigid with advice and travel tips and took delight in telling all and sundry about my trip.

Was he only proud because I had money and a little bit of local fame? I certainly felt so, but I still needed his acknowledgement of my success and that was ultimately pathetic. I also needed to show my brothers that I was more successful than them, which was doubly pathetic and downright childish.

Lisa had never been on a plane before and I had only made short hops to Edinburgh and back on business, so when we settled into our economy seats on the plane on the way to Saint Lucia I really thought I had made it. The lads performed another pantomime around Coventry while we were away over Christmas, cruising the Caribbean with a final fortnight in Barbados. The success didn't stop as even while I was in the pool I got a call from Phil telling me that the BBC wanted to commission me to write a film for them. The champagne cork popped and I pissed another small fortune up the wall.

During this holiday I also proposed to Lisa. It was New Year's Eve and we were on board a cruise ship, pulling out of Caracas in Venezuela as the sun set. She turned me down flat and it was to be another three years before she finally agreed to marry me. She tells me now, twenty years later, that she just bottled out, as I was too big a project! However this rejection didn't stop us both going to the captain's cocktail party later that evening as a storm began to brew.

Before we had left home Dad had told me that there was no need to worry about seasickness because he and Sylvia had cruised the Caribbean many times and that at this time of year it was like a millpond, dead calm. Not this New Year it wasn't. As we took the elevator to the seventh floor, dressed in my hired tuxedo, the ship was pitching left and right. I thought of my Uncle Gip and realised it wasn't fit for man nor beast out there; it was raining cats and dogs out there.

As we entered the cocktail lounge the captain went to shake our hands and tripped over and the cutlery slid off the tables and clattered to the floor. I swear in the corner of my eye I saw that fat bird, Shelley Winters, trying to climb up an inverted

Christmas tree and as she climbed my temperature rose. We sat down and had a drink and a chat with a couple of the entertainers but the storm was getting worse. I should have known this was a bad idea hours earlier when there had been a knock on the cabin door and a little Filipino maid had asked if we wanted seasickness pills and then proceeded to show us the seatbelts under the bunk which we were advised to strap ourselves in with if the storm got worse.

Back in the lounge I was turning a nice colour of green and then the captain announced he was going to the bridge and that he was going to pull in the stabilisers and make a run for the next port. This was all I needed. I told Lisa it was time to leave. She didn't want to, she was getting stuck into the free cocktails, but one look at my face was enough to convince her that it was now or never and so we politely made our exit. Once in the corridor we realised that the lifts were no longer working and so had to walk or rather run down several flights of stairs to our deck.

By this time the ship was really rolling and we were bouncing off the walls. As I ran down our corridor I was pulling off my dickie bow and then jacket and throwing them onto the floor, I was going to puke but I was determined it wasn't going to go all over the DJ. By the time we pushed through the cabin door I was down to my boxers and shoes and spent the rest of the night talking to the big white telephone and calling for Hughie! As a result Lisa missed the New Year's Eve grand buffet and the odds on marriage declined further. Coming from a seafaring family I must have the worst sea legs in the world. I'm also the bloke who was puking, admittedly after a skinful the night before, on the Tristar pleasure cruiser that sails out of Padstow in Cornwall. Lisa just takes it all in her stride while laughing at my misfortune.

We had a fabulous, once in a lifetime holiday but if I'm honest I missed the boys while I was away because for the past four years we had literally lived hand to mouth and in each other's pockets. So while on holiday I plotted and schemed to make my reality of a permanent base for Tic Toc a reality.

In early 1988 Tim decided he wanted to leave and the first cracks in the Tic Toc gang began to appear. To be honest it was so much easier when we were all skint but money and success did begin to change things. We were in the pub one night when Tim said that he could no longer wait for the dream to become a reality and that he wanted to earn more cash now. He had a girlfriend and I think that she was putting pressure on him to move to London and although at the time I resented her and felt let down by him I now understand what was going on.

The moment the lads started to get girlfriends and eventually wives there were obviously, and rightly, conflicting interests. It was no longer a gang with a single shared vision. Lisa and I had been a couple since the beginning, so it was different for us. She was also part of the gang in her own right. The girlfriends of the others would always be outside of that tight circle. They must have also seen the money and lifestyle that I was enjoying and wondered why their partners weren't getting an equal share of it.

Of course the reason why was that, just like in a rock band, it's the writer who makes most of the cash. The lads understood this: they had been on the journey, they remembered that it was me who got them off the dole but the girls didn't have this shared history. I haven't seen Tim from the day he said he wanted to leave and I regret that because we had shared so many good and bad times and of course he wasn't around for the triumph of Tic Toc.

The six of us continued and we took on another new member called Gerard Purfield who was a recent graduate from the University of Birmingham drama department. He was taken on to help with the direction but he had also worked in pubs since he was a lad so he had other skills that fitted our ever-expanding empire. He also reminded me of a younger version of myself and often people thought we were brothers. He still had that devil-may-care attitude that I had possessed when I had first set up Tic Toc but which had inevitably diminished with the pressures and responsibilities that come with running an expanding company.

I was quite jealous of him. He was totally committed to the dream and worked tirelessly to make it a reality and it was great to be bringing on the next generation of talent. I had this idea that as I went off more to work on TV projects outside of Tic Toc, Gerard would take over the day-to-day running of the artistic side of the company.

We had moved out of the Koco building into swish new offices and we were now doing the cabaret club in a snooker hall with a bigger capacity and still selling out. We had a fantastic night with Harry Enfield when he was at the height of his 'Stavros' fame. He had agreed to come and do a one-off gig to try out a new character and we had promised him that we wouldn't sell the night just on the Stavros character. After agreeing the deal I put the phone down and told Lisa to design a poster with the biggest picture of Stavros she could find.

'Yeah but I thought you just said—'

'Don't worry about it, it'll be a sell out by the time Harry gets to Coventry and we'll rip down all the posters before he has a chance to see them.'

The night was a complete sell out but there was nearly a riot because Harry was almost through his act and hadn't done Stavros, which of course everybody had come to see. It was the comedy equivalent of a top band doing a gig, being pretentious and not playing any of their hits. Harry and me would be lucky to get out of here with our lives let alone the profits unless he quickly said, 'Hello Peeps'. Luckily four hundred quid in used tenners and a new character that he introduced just before the end of his set saved the night and our skins.

When he had arrived he had asked if I could lend him four hundred quid in notes for a new character as he had left his prop money on the train. Bobby and I, ever trustful, got him to sign a chitty that he had had the money and he wandered off to his dressing room. That new character that he was trying out was a raging success, not only that night in a snooker hall in Coventry but across the nation as he bounced onto the stage and shouted

'Loadsamoney'. This is a night that has gone down in folklore in Coventry and is almost on a par with all the people who swear that they were at the Sex Pistols gig, and by the way I was at Mr George's nightclub in Coventry just before they went to America and broke up. Years later when I managed to get most of The Specials back together on stage at my club was a similar event but the Loadsamoney night was really special and not just because of the new character but also because we made loads of money!

However the problem remained that it was the landlord of the club that was making the most money on the drink sales rather than us who were taking all the financial risk. The only way to solve this problem was for Tic Toc to become the landlord.

I hit upon the idea of buying a run-down pub in the student area of Coventry called the Pit's Head. This had a large function room upstairs, which I was going to convert into a pub theatre come cabaret room like I had experienced in London. We went to the West Midlands Enterprise Board to see if they would help fund such an idea and they were excited by the proposal and agreed in principle to fund the project. But then – and it could only happen to me – we got gazumped in a bloody recession so the Pit's never got off the drawing board.

I was annoyed but I had sown the seeds of an idea with a potential funder so now all I had to do was find another venue to put the master plan into action. Then it just happened. You know when the sunlight shines through the church window in *The Blues Brothers*? It was magical. I was walking down a street near the city centre when I just spotted this huge white art deco cinema all boarded up. It was the Orchid Ballroom and I must have passed by it millions of times as a kid and Lisa even went to the school opposite it. It was perfect, just a few steps away from the city centre, in a run-down area ripe for regeneration. It was a massive empty shell that no one in his or her right mind would actually want. It was Coventry's answer to an Edinburgh church hall or student union. It was ideal for converting into the Tic Toc Club.

It was in Hillfields, an inner-city area infested by drug dealers, and prostitutes, just the other side of the ring road that encircles Coventry City centre. Back in the Thirties it had originally been a cinema called the Globe, then in the Sixties and Seventies it had been a dance hall known as the Orchid Ballroom. More recently it had been a bingo hall but now it was boarded up and on sale for £215,000. I was doing well but not that well so how the hell were we going to raise the capital let alone the revenue to buy this place?

The first step was to get inside the building. As a result of my writing career, and the success of the theatre company, the comedy club and my high profile in the city, that proved to be relatively easy. I rang up the estate agent, told them who I was, blagged that I had already got the funding from a brewery and a major secret financial institution and they were round the back door with a key within minutes.

Lisa and I went to see the building on our own for the first time; it was musty and smelt of nicotine and neglect. There was one massive ballroom and a smaller room, which was open plan to one side; upstairs there was a balcony, which hadn't been used for years, and the whole place was decorated in reds and oranges. All the bingo tables were still bolted to the maple wood sprung dance floor and the neon-lit bingo board was still hanging over the small stage. There were pens and full ashtrays on the table and trays of dirty teacups on the café counter. It was the Marie Celeste of bingo.

I told the estate agent I would be in touch and continued the blag. I phoned a major brewery that knew what we were doing, both in Edinburgh and at the snooker hall with the Cabaret Club, and invited them down to see the cabaret in action. Two fat brewery reps duly arrived, dressed like CID men, and sat in the audience and tried to look inconspicuous as a brilliant young comedian called Lee Evans treated them to a fantastic performance.

Lee was amazing and very shy, I think we were paying him something like forty quid but he was worth twice as much. He asked if he could use his own mic and we said of course and then he produced a microphone with the longest cable I had ever seen.

It soon became apparent why, as he marched onto the stage and didn't speak for twenty minutes but had the audience in stitches as he got entangled in the wire. He was like Tommy Cooper on speed and the brewery boys lapped it up but I wasn't sure if the next act would be their cup of tea.

Chris Lynham slouched on to the stage dressed in a floral frock with chocolate smeared all over his face and proceeded to rub his breast and crotch during his strange monologue. It was the most surreal and funny act ever with a finale that would never win *Britain's Got Talent*. He stripped naked and put a lit Roman candle firework up his arse as he sang, 'There's No Business Like Show Business'.

'Bloody hell, Gaunty, that's tremendous.'

'What, Chris and Lee?'

'No, the bloody wet sales, they haven't stopped supping.'

If they were impressed by this, wait till they see the Edinburgh operation, I thought.

With the brewery on the hook the next step was the Enterprise Board. They were no strangers to our operation as they had given us a loan of £20,000 and a grant of £5,000 a few years back to buy lighting and staging equipment to help with the expansion of our Edinburgh operation. They were set up to help fund workers' co-operatives which of course we were, weren't we? So one of their lads came down, Lisa and I got the key and I showed them round the bingo hall.

'Look, you remember The Specials?'

'Oh yeah, yeah.'

'Mind your feet on that wire, well they sang that Coventry was a ghost town with all the clubs being closed down. Well, we want to change that by converting this into a cross between a nightclub and an arts centre, but not an arts centre for the middle classes but for everyone, especially the young kids on the dole.'

'Yes I can see that, but how are you going to do that?'

'Well, the basic premise is to take what we do in Edinburgh every year and at the club and provide a flexible space that can put on local bands and small gigs of say a hundred or so up to major acts that will pull in thousands.'

As he picked his way through the detritus I could see he was biting. Time for some more groundbait.

'We reckon we can create at least thirty jobs as well as providing a real cultural asset to the city.'

His eyes lit up.

I told him that I had plans to separate out the two downstairs rooms. One would be the Orchid Suite, capable of holding 300 for local gigs whereas the Majestic Ballroom would hold up to 2,000. At the back of that room I told him that I wanted to build a massive thirty foot glass wall which would have the effect of closing in the balcony, making it a separate room called the Globe Bar which could either act as part of the main room or as a totally separate venue because the glass would be triple glazed.

'And you see that wall there?'

'Yes.'

'Well, that goes out to the front of the art deco façade so I'm going to put a huge round window in there so that the light floods in.'

'Brilliant, and you say you've got a brewery involved?'

'Two.'

Lisa shot me a glance.

'Yeah, we're taking them up to Edinburgh next week to show them the festival set up. Would you like to come?'

As I secured the padlock around the fire doors and walked across the car park he turned to me and said, 'No promises, Jon, but if it was my money I would fund it.'

'When did you decide about the glass wall?' Lisa asked as the bloke drove off.

'Just then, as we walked round.'

'And the other brewery?'

'Don't worry, Gerard's got a name, someone he knows. We'll ring them on Monday and play one off the other.'

21

The end of a dream

1988

The blag was the easy part. We now spent the next few months working on a business plan with a brilliant bloke at the Cooperative Development Agency called John Goodman and, after months of wrangling and rewrites, eventually the Enterprise Board gave us their biggest ever loan of £450,000 to buy and convert the building. We picked up grants from the City Council and a few charities and we were in business. I was now in charge of a building project worth over a million pounds, which would soon have a turnover of a million too, and by God did that feel good and bloody frightening in equal measure. I wasn't yet thirty. I had dreamt the impossible and now it was actually going to happen.

My plans for the building were massive, not small scale. This was going to be a different sort of club and arts centre where the audience would be offered quality live entertainment and not ripped off and treated like cattle. There was going to be no stupid dress code and I wanted to elevate people's expectations of what a good night out was. So that meant decent beer, great acts, friendly security and fair prices. I also wanted the building to be used in the daytime by new theatre groups and local bands so, unlike when we started out, they would get a helping hand.

Okay we had blagged and played fast and loose but the basic business and artistic plan was sound. This was a project that regenerates a run-down building and area while at the same time creating jobs and opportunities for people of all ages to use the facilities. I really wanted it to be a venue which was capable of holding everything from tea dances for the elderly through to bands like The Jesus and Mary Chain and cutting-edge dance clubs run by former members of The Specials. And do you know what? That's what we achieved. It was also to be a kind of Bauhaus where people could rehearse and try out new ideas, music, theatre and comedy. And do you know what? We achieved that too.

This dream of providing more was also part of our downfall though and is best illustrated by the toilet story. When the architect and builder were in the process of converting the building for us they were always asking me to take budget decisions and one of these was the floor covering in the toilet. I could either have tiles, which would last longer but cost three times as much or have lino and replace it every other year. I chose the tiles and that decision was symptomatic of my mistakes. I should have gone for lino and seen how the business grew. I wanted too much too soon. 'Too much too young'!

I told Al Murray, the pub landlord, this tale and he even incorporated it into his act for a time. However, there is a serious point here. I had got myself into a position where I had a million pound building project with absolutely no practical experience. Essentially I was too young and too naïve and I allowed my political principles to dictate the budget rather than the other way round. However, I wasn't interested in creating a club that was appealing to the lowest common denominator where the bogs were filthy, the carpets sticky, the bouncers thugs or the audience got ripped off. Coventry deserved, and I wanted it, to have the best. I could have just opened the club with a lick of paint but Tic Toc was meant to be more than that.

We decided to open the building in stages so we got the builders to get the small room done first and within a few months we were putting on cabaret nights there and then the rest of the building opened a few months later.

Right from the off the place was busy and we were selling more beer than any other of the brewery's outlets so they were incredibly happy. We started to book an eclectic mix of acts: everything from alternative comedians through George Melly to up-and-coming bands like Ocean Colour Scene. My old mate, Dave Howarth, who was now the permanent events manager at the University of Leicester students union, helped me. He had really good contacts in the music industry who could bring in some great bands including De La Soul, Fish out of Marillion and Blur, to name but a few.

Our early success was summed up very eloquently one night by our head of security, Tony Banger Walsh. We were watching a band from the balcony when he turned and gave me a bear hug and shouted over the row the band were making, 'I told you, didn't I Gaunty, I knew you would have it away with this place.'

He dropped me down and I recovered my breath but he was right. We had told people to expect the unexpected and we had delivered. We had really begun to bring some great live and varied entertainment back to the Ghost Town. In May our efforts were recognised when we won a major Arts Council award for the Best Inner City Arts Project in the UK. Lord Palumbo, the Arts Minister, who came to Coventry and was mightily im-pressed, presented us with the award and a plaque which we displayed in the foyer.

A couple of years later Banger would have been squeezing my neck if he could have found me as when we went bust he was left with ten grand's worth of unpaid security bills which he prominently displayed in a photo on the front page of the local paper.

Tony is a big bear of a man and someone who you would much rather have on your side than against you, which is why I'm now glad we're such mates. He's a bit of a legend in Coventry and was a professional wrestler back in the days when wrestling was on the TV every Saturday afternoon, hence his nickname Banger Walsh. I can remember watching him with my Auntie Jean in Hull. When he gave up the ring he set up his own security firm and supplied the bouncers for most of the clubs in Coventry and the surrounding area and in the process became a millionaire. Dad knew him from his police days and recommended him when we bought the club because he knew that being in such a rough area you really needed someone who was respected and perhaps even feared by the local toerags.

'Banger's the man, he won't take no messing and with the toerags and whores round here you need a hard man. Give him a ring and tell him I'm your old man.'

'Ta Dad, I will.'

'Are you sure your doing the right thing with this place son?'

'Yeah course.'

'Yeah, well I know you're confident and that, but the bullshit's the easy part. Now you've got to make it work.'

'Yeah, yeah of course but I've got a good team around me.'

'That's what I'm worried about. That bunch they're all clinging on to your coat tails, you want to watch that.'

'Don't worry about them and at least now your security's been taken off.'

'I wasn't worried about that.'

'Bollocks.'

'Well maybe a little, come on, let's go for a drink.'

That was the first time ever that he had muttered those words and it meant everything to me. We had never been for a pint together before and even this time he only had a fruit juice because he was driving. But he actually wanted to spend some time with me. We talked about the club and what I had achieved and where I wanted it to go.

The security thing was the fact he and the other parents had signed a joint and several bank guarantee with our bank years ago to help us develop the company and now with the massive new investment they were all going to be relieved of this obligation. I had hated asking him to do this for me about three years ago but credit where credit's due – he signed the form without hesitation and it was only now over this pint and his grapefruit juice that I actually realised that he had invested not just money but belief in me. He was trying, albeit at the age of fifty, to be a proper dad.

At the time I had just taken his commitment as a matter of course and I was wrong and immature to do so. Just before we left he had one final word of advice: 'You could do with losing a bit of weight. No wonder Lisa won't marry you!' Some things never change.

We were determined to have no dress code; we were also determined to run a club where women felt safe to come on their own and which was completely drug free – and we succeeded. Banger and his boys helped us to create this atmosphere. Banger's firm was called Mayfair security and he was rightly proud of all the people he had taken care of over the years. Whenever you visited his offices there were hundreds of photos on the walls of Tony with his arm around a celeb.

It became the norm at Tic Toc that if an act sold out, like Martha Reeves or Bob Geldof, we would go into the dressing room and present them with a bottle of champagne. Tony would always follow me in and get one of his lads to take a photo of him and me with the star. Banger would show this to all and sundry saying, 'Here's me with my very good friend, Martha Reeves.' I guess it was good for business but Banger even surpassed his own high levels of self-promotion the night that the ex-lead singer of Marillion, Fish, sold out the venue.

I tapped in the security code of the dressing room and walked in with Banger following in hot pursuit. I asked the tour manager where Fish was, just as the lead singer emerged from the shower room completely stark bollock naked, drying what was left of his hair with a towel. Now Fish is a very tall man and a very, very big man if you catch my drift, but within seconds Banger was next to him, arm over his shoulder and throwing the camera at his lad and shouting, 'Here take a picture of me and my very good friend Fish.'

As the word 'Fish' was spoken and the camera flashed, Banger smiled and put his other hand swiftly over Fish's tackle. Job sorted.

There were many sellout gigs and photos for Banger to add to his collection. But for me the realisation that we had done something remarkable came when Bob Geldof was singing 'I Don't Like Mondays'. He paused in the spotlight after the words, 'And the lesson today is how to die.' The band stopped playing, 2,000 people in the audience stopped singing and dancing, the only light was the follow spot on Geldof and in the dark among the throng I hugged Lisa.

Coventry was no longer a Ghost Town.

That first year at Tic Toc culminated in a spectacular New Year's Eve party where we had the idea of putting on Jools Holland and his Big Band. This was a couple of years before he started his annual Hoot on BBC TV. It was a fantastic night with great entertainment and finished off a great year, which had seen Lisa and me get married at the club, the writing career and the Edinburgh business flourish with the only downside being the retirement of my agent, Phil.

The call had come out of the blue: she had just decided that she had had enough of pushing other people's careers and wanted to do something for herself. She had decided to go to university as a mature student to study film. I was devastated because I really thought we were going places and 1991 promised to be a great year for me. However I respected her decision and wished her well. She helped me find another agent who asked me what I wanted to do. I said I wanted to get into soap operas with the long-term aim of writing my own series. She got the first part of the wish and got me a job on the scriptwriting team for *Emmerdale* but once the regular money started rolling in she forgot the second part which was that *Emmerdale* was only meant to be a stepping-stone to other things.

The problem is of course that soap writing is very lucrative and I kind of got the impression that she saw me as a bit of a cash cow. Although to be fair I wasn't much interested in writing anything else and also the club was taking up more and more of my time.

We had had a good year and the business was profitable, the brewery was even showing us other sites in Birmingham and Leicester where we could repeat the formula. These were heady days where everything seemed possible and my increasing media and TV profile kind of added stardust to any negotiations over mundane but vital discussions about beer volume discounts or loan rates.

However, the building work had gone massively over budget and the initial set up costs were much higher than expected and in all honesty we – no, rather I, because I was the boss – had made some stupid mistakes and decisions on costs and finishes for the club. In my defence I was only 27 when I started the project, which had turned into a business with over a million pound turnover in less than a couple of years but nevertheless I have to take responsibility for my mistakes.

I had seen this potential cash crisis coming and knew something had to be done about it but still hadn't let it get in the way of Lisa and me getting married the previous May.

We had been living together for seven years. Lisa had finally agreed to marry me and it just felt right to go to the next step. We were married in a beautiful Warwickshire village church on 26 May 1990. The weather was perfect and we even had two birds flying in the church as we exchanged vows. It was magical – well, when she eventually arrived it was.

Nipper, Bobby and Gerard had stayed over at the cottage the night before while Lisa had gone back to her Mum's. We arrived dressed in our tailcoats at least an hour early and we had a few stiffeners in the pub before the bride and Lisa's dad were meant to turn up.

Nipper was the best man and did a great job but a word of advice: if you've got brothers, use them. I really wish that I had asked Jason to carry out this function rather than a mate, especially as a few years later I would have to sack both Nipper and Bobby and did not talk to them again for over ten years.

Nipper and I waited on the front row, the stated hour arrived, and then Mikey who was to be the organist took up his position and the vicar went to the door. Nothing happened. Half an hour passed and Lisa's mum was getting edgy and I swear as the clock ticked by towards the hour mark I heard voices in the congregation.

'She's stood the fat bastard up.'

Then the vicar came over, bent down and whispered to Nipper, who turned to the whole church and said, 'Don't worry, the car broke down. She'll be here in a minute.'

Remember this was pre-mobile phone days. Well, in fact they had just come out as my mate Gareth had one, but they were the size of a house brick and you got a double hernia lifting them onto the bar.

This didn't bode well for the wedding as the prat who supplied the car was also the photographer, but eventually she arrived, looking radiant and the ceremony began.

It was a great family affair with Mikey playing the organ, Lisa's sisters Eleanor and Rosa singing and the two lovebirds flying in the sunlight that was flooding in through the stained-glass window.

We had a great reception back at Tic Toc, largely fuelled by unlimited amounts of champagne, courtesy of the Brewery, for all the guests, which they gave as a wedding present. Neil Mullarkey and his new comedy partner Nick Hancock did the cabaret, and local bands supplied the music. My old mate Boswell turned up and true to form shagged someone who shall remain nameless on the darkened stage of the main room. I knew he was in there and I could hear what the dirty bastard was up to because his seventeen bangles were chiming in perfect rhythm in the dark. It was a fantastic day, finished off by me having to bite off Lisa's wedding dress as the ties had got knotted, or at least that's my excuse and the rest is personal.

We flew away on honeymoon to the Seychelles but I knew after two weeks I would return to even more headaches at Tic Toc.

Financially I was still doing okay because I had started writing for *Emmerdale* and the pay was brilliant. I had got commissioned after my very first script meeting, which was unheard of, but I found the actual process of writing quite difficult and extremely stressful, not helped by the fact that I was writing it on a basic Amstrad computer.

Everybody I knew reckoned it must be easy money writing for a soap but that's a bit like when people act the smartarse and say, 'Ooh it must be soo hard to write for the *Sun*, do you have to use pictures?' These idiots have no idea just how difficult it is to adapt to and learn a house style and I would suggest that soap is even harder and more complex than being a columnist in the world's greatest newspaper.

The way it works – or at least worked when I was doing it – was that every month they have an all-day meeting with the twelve members of the scriptwriting team. You are always working three months ahead so when you arrive the producer, who was a guy called Stuart (previously an actor who'd played the part of the baddie in *Poldark*) when I started, would outline the next month's availability of cast members and also tell us where the story had got to. We would then spend the morning and an alcohol-fuelled afternoon knocking round ideas for possible stories and plots.

I knew *Emmerdale* pretty well because I watched it religiously when I got home from school when I was living with my Auntie Rosemary. My experience of running bars and the club also helped to fuel my creative ideas and as a result I got commissioned to write and therefore thousands of pounds at my first ever meeting.

A couple of days after this first script meeting they would choose four writers to script that month's episodes. So they would fax you the storylines for your week's episodes and those of the other three writers. You then had a weekend to flesh out your episode plan and then all four of you would meet up again on the Monday to check that no one's idea clashed. You then had ten days to write 48 minutes of TV.

All of which would have probably been easier if I didn't have the financial worries of Tic Toc hanging over me. Even so the structure is really tight and it's hard to express how down you feel when you go back after they've read your first effort and the big fat bird who was the script editor hands back your script and there are more blue pen marks on it than black as they point out the rewrites that they want.

I found it bloody difficult but at least one of my claims to fame is that I wrote the episode where Amos kissed Mr Wilkes goodbye and left the Woolpack. Not exactly the balcony scene from *Romeo and Juliet* or even *Gone with the Wind* but significant all the same to *Emmerdale* fans.

Writing *Emmerdale* also brought me back into contact with my old teacher Delia Dick as her brother-in-law, a Glaswegian called Jim Campbell, was also writing for *Emmerdale* at the same time. We became great mates and spent many a drunken night in Leeds working on the Farm and one glorious night at Delia and Colin's when he came down to visit.

Colin was still the same and at one point after dinner came into the room with a cock stuffed up his jumper. It wasn't that kind of dinner party, I mean a cockerel which he proceeded to plonk on the table and paint. They were still bohemian and Delia was exactly the same. It was great to see her again, this wonderful woman who had inspired me to go into the theatre, but what she made of *Emmerdale* I'm not too sure.

Mind you, what would the angry young man of twenty-one, called Gaunty, have made of himself as he sold out and wrote soap opera only six years later? But you know what, I didn't see it as a sellout, it was just another way of getting to a mass audience and learning how to communicate with them and although I hated the actual writing I loved the creative atmosphere of the script meetings. It's probably why I enjoy working at Talksport so much these days. I can come in with an idea at nine in the morning thrash it out with my producer, Sean, crack a few dirty jokes around it as we book guests and then by ten we can be discussing it on air with the nation and up to a million listeners.

Jimmy was a much better writer than me and just seemed to get the house style straight away and could knock off the scripts in a couple of days. I think it's fair to say I was the better ideas man but I found the actual work, the craft, really time-consuming and I didn't particularly enjoy it. I think it's similar in business: the entrepreneur who has the idea isn't necessarily the best person to take the company forward and run it on a day-to-day basis and that is certainly the truth with me. I loved the idea of setting up the Tic Toc Club but the mechanics of booking the acts, employing the staff and running the actual business soon began to bore me.

I was also drinking too much again. With a club you always have a drink at the end of the night. If you've had a great night you have a drink to celebrate, if you've lost money on a band you drink to commiserate, it's a vicious circle and it was getting to me. Even the one thing I really enjoyed the most was losing its allure. I used to love counting the sweaty, smelly screwed up notes at the end of the night. I loved it because it meant that the night and the club had been a success. It was the little boy's affirmation that he had made it. It also didn't matter that I had enjoyed that affirmation yesterday, I still needed it again today.

However, even that was getting boring and more significantly and depressingly I was falling out of love with theatre.

We had been touring now for the best part of ten years and I was sick to the back teeth of it. To be fair I hadn't been out on the road with the boys much for the last couple of years but even the thought of booking a tour and organising the publicity, accommodation press and the rest was boring me to death. No matter how hard you toured and how many gigs you played, what real difference were you making to people's lives? In the early days I really did believe that I could change people's opinions, maybe even their lives, by the messages in my plays, but not any longer. Besides, I had fallen out of love with theatre.

The one single TV transmission of *Hooligans* would have been seen by more people than we could ever dream of getting into a theatre if we toured from now to eternity. I had also made a fatal mistake of flogging a dead horse for too long. After the success of *Hooligans* the businessman inside me just couldn't resist the temptation of touring it, along with a new play for just one more time to get a bit more cash out of it but it was self-defeating and was pissing off the rest of the team. However, it was a fact of life that with all my TV commitments and being the front man of the Tic Toc Club, I didn't really have enough time to write more work for Tic Toc.

I did write and direct several more plays for them and I did write, direct and produce a good little play called *Schools Out* in 1990 but in truth it was formulaic and just too easy. The final nail was reading a postcard that Bobby had written to his mum while we were in Edinburgh doing *Hooligans* for the umpteenth time. He was telling her how bored he was with it and couldn't wait to get home and I didn't blame him; however, I was also fed up of the Edinburgh operation and promoting other people's talent as well.

Things came to a head in early January 1991 and I called a meeting. Nick White, who was our financial controller, had told me that we had to seriously look at our costs if we were to have any chance of Tic Toc surviving. The simple hardline truth was that although we were a bunch of seven mates who had achieved almost the impossible by sheer hard graft and a shared vision, the business as it was now could not justify the expense and the cost of all of us.

Tic Toc had changed: we were doing less theatre and more promotion and certainly for the next couple of years if we were going to make the building and the club survive we had to adapt or die, we had to concentrate on promotion. So where did that leave the members who were basically the actors? The dole queue, that's where.

Telling Bobby, Nipper and John Laidlaw that there was no future for them with Tic Toc was one of the hardest things I have ever had to do but it had to be said. I tried to soften the blow by telling them that they could have the rights to the annual pantomimes but that the company couldn't justify paying them a full-time wage at their level when we as a company could get people to do that job for less. I hated myself but I felt I had no choice. Even so, their reaction surprised and depressed me.

Bobby's only suggestions were that I should take a pay cut and that he didn't want to work nights. We were a bloody nightclub! Nipper just stared at me with those puppy dog eyes and Laidlaw was angry, very angry and rightly so. He had been instrumental in our theatre and promotion success and also he had sorted out all the technical aspects of the venue but in simple terms his assistant could now run the place at half the cost.

Things were even more complicated because just like the remaining four of us they had all signed a legal agreement with the bank jointly and severally securing the massive overdraft. Understandably, they wanted to be released from this obligation but the rest of us wouldn't agree. We were acting on behalf of the company, we were trying to save it and if we succeeded, the overdraft would be paid off and they would be free of their obligation. They had taken years of money out of the company and it seemed only fair that they should wait.

Over the years I have agonised over this and beaten myself up over the fact that Nipper and Bobby dedicated themselves to my plays when perhaps they should have gone after the TV version of *Hooligans*. But they didn't, they stayed and now they were stuck in the same rut as me. I wished they had taken the Clive Owen route and called me a fat prick or put up a fight, but they didn't, they just walked away and with them, in essence, went the spirit of Tic Toc.

Later that year the Brewery suggested refinancing the loan and repaying the Enterprise Board their money back and taking on the whole debt themselves. This seemed like an escape route and may well have been a way of releasing the three who had just been sacked from their obligations. However, we were still in a financial crisis and with the help of the Co-Operative Development Agency we went to the Council to ask for more money in the form of a grant or loan to push the project on.

At first they were forthcoming but as the year progressed they took the view that they could no longer support the business and refused to give any more money. The Club limped on for another year as interest rates went through the roof and although the company was intrinsically profitable we just couldn't keep up with the gearing on the loans. In early 1992 the brewery called in the administrators.

I stood in the kitchen of my cottage. I was sweating like a pig even though I was only wearing my dressing gown and I was crying like a baby. It was six in the morning and it was all over. The Brewery had called in the administrators the day before and my dream was in tatters. All I had in front of me was the administrators' meeting later that morning and a very uncertain future. I had lost the lot and I knew it wouldn't be long before I even lost my home.

It may have been January and the beginning of a new year but it was the end of my dream. The Tic Toc Club had gone spectacularly bust with debts way into six figures and I had lost everything apart from my beautiful wife who walked into the kitchen and hugged me. For the first time in nearly ten years I wasn't running Tic Toc.

22

Rave on

'Lisa it's fantastic, it's got three bedrooms, two bathrooms and a sunken lounge.'

I was phoning from Livingston in Scotland. It was just four weeks after the club had gone bust and I was standing in what was to be our new house.

In the last two years of our Edinburgh operation we had been renting a huge leisure and snooker centre in the city called Marco's. Every year we had put in staging, lighting and sound systems to create six theatres. We had promoted some brilliant acts like Roddy Frame, Nigel Kennedy, Tom Robinson and Al Murray and we had become very friendly with the Demarco brothers who owned the centre. I had also become very close to their general manager, Steven Sproule. He was an ex-Scottish squash pro who had a bad back and had gone to seed but who possessed this incredible lust for life and had shared and enjoyed our festival success each year in his venue. Bert Demarco, the older brother, had also been down to Tic Toc when we first found the building and had been impressed by it and my plans and had given me loads of advice and support when we first set it up.

The Demarcos were the biggest leisure operators in Scotland with venues in Glasgow and Fort William as well as Edinburgh. Just as Tic Toc was going bust they were offered the opportunity of running a massive exhibition centre in the new town of Livingston on the outskirts of Edinburgh, called the Livingston Forum. This venue could hold up to 5,000 people for rock concerts as well as playing host to international basketball. The brothers knew everything about snooker, aerobics and fitness but sweet FA about entertainment and rock promotion – though of course they knew a man who did.

When Bert Demarco realised that Tic Toc was going down the pan he had rung me and asked if I would be interested in running the Forum for them. They had been approached by the Livingston Development Corporation to take over the running of this massive venue after the corporation had failed to make a go of it and Bert thought the combination of my skill and experience and their business knowledge would be an unstoppable force.

So that afternoon I had flown up to Edinburgh and Bert and Steven had shown me around the Forum. It was a massive metal structure right in the heart of the new town and had been built by the Glasgow Rangers Chairman, David Murray, to host basketball. Before buying Rangers, Murray had been a massive basketball fan and had built and created this purpose-built stadium with the ambition of creating a basketball team, The Livingston Bulls, that would win the European cup.

There was a large central hall with a maple wood sprung floor that allegedly cost a quarter of a million pounds and there was retractable stadium seating on each side that could hold up to 3,000 basketball fans. It was a magnificent facility and typical of Murray's style: nothing was done by half measures. For a time the team had been incredibly successful but then rumour has it that Murray fell out with the basket ball authorities over his desire to base two teams at the venue so that there was always one playing at home. The basketball authorities wouldn't allow him to do this and as a result David Murray walked away from the game and the Forum, giving the keys to the building free of charge to the corporation as a gift. All they had to do now was run it efficiently to pay the running costs. The corporation had struggled to keep the team going but over the years they had declined and now the forum was largely a white elephant holding the occasional concert, exhibition and rave.

When I looked around it I saw the immediate potential to develop the place both as an exhibition hall and concert venue. It was ideally situated between Glasgow and Edinburgh with a potential audience of five million customers in that central belt of Scotland on its doorstep. Bert suggested a deal where they would pay me a basic fee of a few grand a year plus 20 per cent of any extra income I raised over and above what they already had booked in the diary. It was 20 per cent because there were three brothers and his dad, Bert Senior, who needed a cut, so everything had to go five ways. It seemed a fair deal to me and the icing on the cake was the fact that the Development Corporation owned loads of houses and I could take my pick of them and live their rent free for the first twelve months while we got the venue back on its feet.

Steven's task later that night had been to take me around a few of these houses and now we were in the one I wanted and I was phoning Lisa who was back in Coventry at her Mum's to tell her the good news. It was a three-bedroom brand new bungalow on a small estate in an area called Bankton Wood and it was ideal but very different to what we were used to back in Coventry.

But it was a home and combined with the job it was an escape route from Tic Toc and its aftermath.

The last few weeks since the administrators had been called in had been horrendous and the months preceding it has been an absolute nightmare too. People often ask me if doing three hours of live radio a day is stressful but the truth is I find it a doddle compared to the last few months of Tic Toc. The three hours on air are high in adrenaline and full on, but it's not what I call stress.

Stress is waking up in the morning drenched in sweat, so wet it feels like an animal has been slaughtered in your bed. Stress is knowing that when you get to work there will be thirty phone messages asking for money with the last one being the bouncer threatening to 'break your fucking legs' if you don't pay him by lunchtime. Stress is hiding the post in the drawer because every envelope is brown and every letter is written in red. Being on the radio interviewing top politicians like David Cameron and never knowing who is going to ring and what they are going to say is a walk in the park compared to staring bankruptcy in the face.

We had been fighting a rearguard action for at least six months and although I genuinely thought we could trade and pull through the crisis the absolute bottom line is I should have given up months earlier. However, when it's your baby that is much easier said than done. Everyone on the outside can see that you should accept defeat and with the benefit of hindsight it was an absolute no brainer, but when it's been your dream and your whole life for the best part of ten years you just can't resist giving it one more go.

My old man had sat in the Globe bar with Lisa and I one Sunday afternoon and had been astonished to find out we hadn't been taking any wages for the last six months.

'You've got to let go Jonathan, just let it go.'

'No Dad, you don't understand, we're working on a plan with the CDA. The Council won't let this fail, they will give us another grant or cheap loan.'

'You think so? I wouldn't trust that bunch of Labour shysters as far as I can throw them and you should never have given up *Emmerdale*.'

He was right. I had jacked in *Emmerdale* about seven months earlier. It just all got too much and I took the decision, the wrong

decision again, to leave the TV writing and concentrate on trying
to save the business.

The administrators meeting had started by them saying they
had a preferred buyer.

'Oh yeah, who?' I asked.

'You, Gaunty,' replied the accountant.

'Us? But you've just pulled the plug on us.'

'No Jon, not all of you, not Tic Toc – just you, mate.'

'Oh yeah and who's going to fund that then?'

'We will,' the bloke from the Brewery piped up.

The basic deal was that they wanted me to set up a new
company. The Brewery would then fund my new company to
buy the building from the Administrator and all the other debts
would die with the old limited company and the club and my
vision would continue. But they wanted only me, not the whole
team.

I thought about the offer for at least a second and then turned
it down. I had had enough and not only that it somehow seemed
immoral. I didn't feel that it was right to drop my mates and to
let down – basically cheat – all those local businesses that had
supported me in my dream. I was probably naïve and I later
found out this was a common tactic in the licensed trade, but
even now after all these years I am glad that I turned it down and
moved on.

The club was sold eventually to a couple of unsavoury
characters who tried to emulate what we did and thankfully failed
miserably. Then it was bought for a pittance by a couple of Asian
lads who turned it into quite a successful rock venue, although
to be truthful at the price they got it for they could hardly fail.
It's still open, but renamed and from reports I've heard it's doing
okay, but I haven't been back in the place since the day I left
that meeting.

A few days later Lisa and I went to Rugby to sign on. I was
standing in the queue when I recognised a young lad who I had
thrown out of the club only weeks earlier for trying to deal drugs.

He must have been seventeen or eighteen and can't have worked a day in his miserable life but he signed on and was given his dole whereas I, who had been paying the higher rate of tax and NI, was refused the dole on the grounds that I had been self-employed.

Meanwhile Lisa who had been employed by the company was okay and I had to sign on under her name. It was degrading and demoralising and made all the worse by seeing the lowlife dealer smirking at me as he sucked air through his teeth when he walked past me and out of the office. How could and why should a piece of scum, who hadn't paid a penny in, get money out while I, who had paid loads in was treated like a beggar? I didn't even want more than him but I certainly deserved the same.

This was the least of our worries because it was also becoming increasingly obvious that the house would be repossessed. We hadn't paid the mortgage for months and there was no way we would be able to pay it in the future. We were also carrying heavy personal debts as well as the guarantee on the Tic Toc overdraft. Things looked pretty bleak and that's without the mental anguish of knowing that you had gone down and let down your suppliers, workers and mates who through no fault of their own were now not going to get paid.

I felt a total and utter failure but I wasn't a crook, I hadn't done anything wrong. I had tried to do something positive for Coventry, but I had failed.

There was a creditors' meeting in a hotel on the outskirts of Coventry a few weeks later and the administrators were clear that we as directors had done everything possible to save the company and that there had been no illegal activities or trading and with that we were free of Tic Toc, but not the debt.

Within a week of seeing the house, Lisa and I had loaded up a box van with all our possessions and we started out for our new journey and life in Scotland.

We soon settled in, largely with the help and encouragement of Steven and his wife who were already good mates but we also had excellent neighbours in a couple called Dave and Lorna who instantly became lifelong friends. Dave was on the sick from the tax office but was also a local wedding photographer and Lorna was a big noise in BT. They had two beautiful black Labradors that they doted on who became great pals with our yellow Lab, Shalagh.

Friendships were created and developed by long dog walks and their sense of living life to the full. Steven Sproule also possessed this love for life and I found this energy and glass-always-half-full attitude in many of the Scots I met. They all possessed a can do attitude and it was markedly different to the negativity that Tic Toc fought against in Coventry and I embraced this more optimistic culture completely. Maybe it had something to do with the fact that Livingston was a new town and there was real potential for people to make a new life for themselves. Livingston is like a smaller version of the new town of Milton Keynes and when we moved there years later I found exactly the same kind of attitude among the community. Both might appear to be concrete jungles and lack a soul, but both towns have a young pioneering spirit about them and are brilliant places to bring up a young family.

I started working at the Forum immediately and soon realised there was a hell of a lot of money to be made very quickly. The rave scene was just going legitimate and moving from outdoor venues into the indoors and the Forum had already held a few successful events before Marco's took over. I found out from the books that the lads who were promoting the all-night events were paying seven hundred quid to rent the place. I called in the main promoter with the intention of telling him that there was a new man in charge and the price was not only going up but also going up tenfold.

Davey entered my office. He had ginger hair in a bob and a confident swagger and he ran a rave company called Awesome. He shook my hand and sat down. He knew who I was and he knew that I had promoted before and understood how the business worked.

'Davey, good to meet you.'

'You too, Gaunty, brand new.'

'Brand new,' that was his favourite expression and even to this day Lisa and I use it to each other and have that conspiratorial giggle. I liked him immediatcly, I knew his reputation but he had a charm and warmth about him.

'Now Dave, let's not fuck about mate, you've been having it away with the Council, haven't you? I mean seven hundred fucking quid.'

He laughed.

'Oh aye and what do you propose then, Big Man?'

'Seven grand.'

'A night?'

'Yeah, starting from the one you've got booked in for next week.'

There was a slight pause while Davey stared into mid-distance as his right leg shook up and down, then a smile.

'Okay, no problem, do you want me to sign something?'

We shook hands; he was laughing and kept muttering, 'Seven grand Gaunty, seven grand.' But he knew and I knew that he still had a great deal because he was charging twenty-five quid a ticket and ramming at least five thousand kids in every other week. I think he admired my balls and by putting the price at the right rate he knew that I knew what I was doing. He left the building in his black Merc and I noticed the number plate, of course the Merc was brand new!

Seven grand of course meant that I had already made myself at least twelve hundred quid extra a fortnight and I had only just started in the job. I told Bert the news later that night when I went over to Edinburgh and I saw his eyes light up. His younger brother, Raymond, was equally excited and even did a little jig in the bar.

Bert was cool and very Italian looking with a balding head that he shaved closely to match his designer-stubbled face. Raymond, on the other hand, was short with the biggest comb over since

Bobby Charlton. I started to play five-a-side football with him on a regular basis in the Forum and his hair would keep on dropping down and he would meticulously wind it back up over his head while we pretended we hadn't noticed.

However it was harder to avert your eyes when the black dye he put on what remained of his hair started to drip down his face as he began to sweat. He ended up looking like a cross between Robert Smith of The Cure and Liberty's Shami Chakrabarti with black eyes and what looked like mascara running down his cheeks. That said he wasn't a bad lad.

The other brother, Don, didn't speak much to me or that matter to Bert. He seemed to resent the fact that Bert was the leader and brains of the operation, the brothers were only kept apart and together in business by their dad Bert Demarco senior.

Steven ran the business on a day-to-day basis and although an expert in leisure and bars he hadn't had any experience of the nightclub scene or raves. I told him that we wouldn't be opening the bar except for soft drinks and that we could get away with charging a pound for everything.

'What – even the coke and water?'

'Yeah.'

The profit margin was immense as we were buying in the drinks for 15 pence and the staff requirements were small as everything was served without a glass.

There was only a skeleton staff left at the Forum and I interviewed each in turn and decided who would stay and who would have to go. They were disillusioned and unmotivated but a couple of the younger lads had potential.

I arranged a meeting with the local police and through all the raves we put on we had a great relationship with them. At least 25 of their drug team used to search the kids as they came in and keep on eye on the events. The demand for tickets was phenomenal and we employed Lisa to man the box office and do marketing for other events that we wanted to put on in the Forum.

Although we had the drug squad in attendance there was hardly any need, not because the kids weren't taking drugs, they were, every single one of them, but they dropped the Es before they got into the venue. Undoubtedly there must have been supplies inside but I never saw any real evidence of this, apart from the occasional kid who was dragged out of the toilets by the police and thrown into the back of a waiting van.

The first rave was a real eye-opener and I felt like a real old fart. I was a rock 'n' roll kid and we had prided ourselves when we ran the Tic Toc Club that we never put on raves because we just saw them as glorified discos and of course we were trying to do something different. We were either stupid or principled because judging by the success of Davey and Awesome we could have been raking in the cash for ages. In fact there had been a young lad who had come into the Tic Toc office months earlier asking if he could put on a rave and we had all asked him what the night consisted of, to which he replied in a half-stoned manner, 'Jesus man, where were you in the summer of love?'

'Working and building this place and paying your dole money,' came the reply from Lisa in the corner. The truth, however, was that the rave scene was an alien experience for me.

Davey and his Awesome team had arrived early on Saturday morning and had transformed the basketball court into a rave venue with white drapes hanging from the walls and a stage and dance platforms and the biggest sound system I had ever seen. The doors had opened at eight and the event and the music went on till eight on Sunday morning. I couldn't tell where one song stopped and the other started and looked on in amazement as the kids danced, grinned and gurned in rhythm to the manic beat.

We had security but again there was no need for them as the major difference between this mob and an alcohol-fuelled crowd was there was no aggression or trouble. I bumped into a young lad as I was collecting up empty bottles and I turned and said sorry but I was ready for any trouble, the prat just hugged me and said, 'No bother.' The ecstasy definitely had a positive calming affect on the kids because a similar accident in a nightclub could easily have turned nasty but the Es really chill the kids out.

We had never had any real trouble at Tic Toc either mainly because of Banger's doormen but also because we always had some form of live entertainment on and I feel this too has a calming affect on a drunken crowd. In a pure nightclub that sense of danger is only just under the surface but at a rave it was completely non-existent and that must be down to the ecstasy. But before I could entertain any ideas that these pills were a better alternative to booze an incident happened that confirmed that I was right to knock the drugs on the head all those years previously.

It was the third rave that we had held and it was about two in the morning. The music was pumping and the kids were all dancing like crazy and the tills were almost singing as the cash went in when I was suddenly aware of a commotion in the corner of the bar. Before I knew it a paramedic crash team had burst through the fire doors carrying a wee girl into the sauna that we used as a medical room on rave nights. I had seen other kids suffering from the heat before and I had even seen kids who had obviously dropped one too many pills who then felt suddenly ill but this was something completely different.

As the licensee I was responsible so I rushed into the room to see this girl. She must have been about sixteen and she was almost body popping on the bench as I entered. Her eyes were rolling, she was sweating profusely and she was completely out of it. Her friends stood around pale-faced and shocked and I pulled them out of the room while the medics got down to work. Thank Christ one of the conditions of the rave licence was that Davey had to have an ambulance on standby outside the venue at all times and at his expense.

The girl was still convulsing and scratching at her face as the medics got her onto a stretcher and with the help of a couple of the bouncers secured her to it. They pushed past her shocked mates and hurtled away in the ambulance. The music kept pounding and the majority of the crowd were unaware of what was going on and even if they were, I don't think they would have cared. There and then I saw the truth about this so-called love drug because as soon as this girl started fitting, all her mates didn't want to know. They didn't seem to have the same level of concern as a straight person would have or even a fellow drunk, they seemed to merge into the background, not wanting to be questioned by the police. It was as if they were in denial that this could happen to them, they didn't want to acknowledge just how dangerous their drug taking could be.

The girl pulled through, thank God, but she was in the hospital for several days and of course her story hit the local paper and the regional TV news. To be fair she was only one girl out of 5,000 at that rave to be taken so ill but for her family it's clearly one too many. It became clear that she had taken too many Es and probably had mixed them with vodka while she was waiting in the queue. However it always amazed me that these fit young intelligent kids were and are willing to pop a pill when they clearly have no idea what it could do to them. I know booze can be dangerous too but at least the strength is clearly labelled on the bottle and with the nanny state we now live under you don't need a degree in rocket science to understand that you shouldn't overindulge.

To give him his credit Davey was also concerned and not just because this publicity could have led to the closing down of his raves. He was genuinely worried that one of his customers was so poorly and I found that both strange and kind of comforting.

However, make no mistake about it, he and his crew were hard men and they weren't afraid of dishing out the punishment when they saw fit. I saw or rather heard him doing so a few weeks earlier at about four in the morning. I was in the office carrying out one of my favourite tasks with renewed vigour – counting out the bar takings – when I heard raised voices in the room next door that Davey used for his administration during the event. I heard something hit the wall with a dull thud, and then I heard the same sound again.

'No Davey, I'm sorry, I mean—'

I heard a whisper, then another crack. I came out of the office just as Davey emerged from the adjoining one. He was in a rush.

'Everything all right, Dave?'

'Oh yeah, Gaunty, brand new.'

He smiled and threw some keys in the air and caught them again as he rushed out of the door and into his Merc which then accelerated away from the Forum. A mate of his followed behind in a Luton box van in which they had earlier transported all their gear to the venue. Their office door remained shut.

They returned about an hour later and it was clear from the way that the van swayed as it entered the car park that it was now fully, if not over, loaded, Davey walked back in and went into the main room and stood by the mixing desk. The door of the office opened and a tall thin lad aged about 25 who I had seen around with Davey walked out of the office. Dave's brother was behind him. The lad glanced at Davey in the main room.

'Can I just have a word with Davey?'

'No, best you just went,' replied his brother.

'But—'

'No, it's over. Come on.'

The lad looked at me. It was obvious that he had been crying but he wasn't marked in any way. He was dressed in a white T-shirt, jeans and trainers. It was freezing outside and I remembered him earlier standing outside in the queue wearing one of those sheepskin leather pilot jackets. Davey's brother was now wearing this same jacket. The lad paused, his eyes bore into me but he said nothing, then he turned and walked towards the van. He climbed in and the driver and his mate pulled away, Dave's brother shook his head and walked back in.

'Jesus its cold out there, Gaunty.'

'Nice jacket,' I replied.

'You want it?'

He laughed as I shook my head and he walked over to his younger brother at the mixing desk.

'He was nicking money, Gaunty, and I can't stand thieves.'

Davey was sitting in my office. We were both knackered, it was about seven in the morning and the music was still pumping and the kids were still dancing.

'Yeah but I thought he worked for you?'

'He does – well, he did – but he got greedy. He was selling tickets.'

'I thought that was his job?'

'It is but he's meant to sell them for me.'

Davey had a team of younger lads who acted as promoters selling tickets all over Scotland for the raves. I suddenly realised that they were also working a fiddle on the door. The security staff took the tickets off the kids at the front door in full view of the coppers but they never ripped the tickets. That was because later they would give the tickets back to Davey's boys who would then go outside and resell them, thus getting more people in and more profit. However, white T-shirt boy had been scamming Davey and selling some for himself and pocketing the money. Davey had spotted it and now the lad had to be punished.

'He'll no be back.'

'I don't blame you. I had the same policy at my club. Once they've fiddled you, you can't allow them to keep working because they'll just do it again.'

I had a student working for me at Tic Toc who I found out had been letting people in by the fire exit for a fiver. I caught him red handed and he gave me all the money back and begged to keep his job. I counted the money, looked up and told him to fuck off and paid him off. However I soon heard that Davey had slightly harsher HR policies.

'No Gaunty, I mean he'll no be back in Livi.'

'What I thought he lived here.'

'He did but not any more. He's left tonight.'

'What?'

'That's what the van was for, the cheating bastard. We've emptied his flat and told him to go.'

'What? Where?'

'Who gives a fuck?'

'What, your lads will take him wherever he wants to go?'

'Nah, don't be soft, they're gonna drop him off on the motorway.'

'But what about all his gear.'

'What about it, that's mine, that's his debt.'

It was unbelievable. They had emptied his flat of all his possessions and literally run him out of town dressed in the clothes he stood up in, minus the sheepskin jacket. They had told him quite clearly never to come back. The kid had been in the wrong but surely he didn't deserve this.

Did I do anything about it? No I didn't. I didn't agree with the punishment but then I also didn't agree with the crime. However I realised that I would have to take tighter control of the doors because we couldn't have a position where more people than the fire limit allowed were being let in.

The raves continued and we also started to attract the attention of more traditional rock promoters and the venue also began to be used as a rehearsal space for bands like Deacon Blue, Run Rig and Del Amitri. In fact there was a lovely moment with the leader of Del Amitri, Justin Currie, when the phone rang in the box office and a woman asked to speak to him. Lisa took the call and went into the main arena where the band were set up, he came out and took the call.

'Yeah Ma, hi Ma, yeah I'm sorry, we didn't know until the last minute like.'

There was a pause while he took a telling off.

'Like I say it was a last minute thing and I know it must have been embarrassing, sorry.'

The conversation continued and it was obvious that his mum was telling him off for not telling her that he was going to be on

Wogan the night before, she had only found out about it from her friends when she got to work that evening.

The lead singer put the phone down and rather sheepishly said, 'Mums eh!' and walked back into the room.

The venue was beginning to pick up with live concerts from The Beautiful South, who we played indoor cricket with, through to a sellout gig by Wet Wet Wet who the lads and me played five-a-side with. The best concert though was by Carter The Unstoppable Sex Machine who we had promoted at Tic Toc years ago for about thirty quid but who were now selling thousands of tickets wherever they played.

I had begun to build a small but strong team around me again and I was also part of a bigger team that Steven Sproule had created over in Edinburgh with the rest of Marco's staff. Steven and I were very similar in so much as we liked being the boss and both were control freaks but we also liked to have that gang around us both in business and socially. Lisa and I had some cracking nights out in Edinburgh with them all and it was all welcome relief from the pressures of the last ten years.

The work, when we had it at the Forum, was hard. On a rave weekend I would work from seven on Saturday morning supervising right through the night at the event and not get home until after the clear up at midday on a Sunday. Mind you there was compensation in the form of huge wads of cash that Lisa and I used to count and then stuff under the mattress on a Sunday afternoon.

Although the work was intense and I wanted to make the place a success it wasn't the same kind of pressure as when you own a club outright. It wasn't my ultimate responsibility to pay people and if the toilets got blocked, I just called out a plumber to fix it and sent the invoice to Marco's. This was the nearest to being employed that I have ever been in my career. Even so, I was still responsible for my own tax and NI.

I have never had a proper job or been officially employed in my whole working life and I'm quite pleased with that fact. I believe the best cure for sickness and absenteeism is self-employment, because if you don't work you don't get paid. That said, I was enjoying the lack of total responsibility and it was allowing Lisa and me to recover from the stress and madness of Tic Toc's final years. We were aided and abetted in this by our long dog walks with our neighbours, Dave and Lorna.

Because they came from a totally different background and weren't connected with the arts or entertainment world, they were a refreshing break from the people we had almost exclusively been involved with before. They were also completely non-judgemental and unimpressed by the 'stardust' of my former work, not in a nasty way but they just accepted that's what I did and got on with having a life and a laugh.

It was so refreshing and invigorating not having to perform, justify or play up to a role and I enjoyed being anonymous. They certainly helped me to recover from the depression that I was falling into before we left Coventry. The country itself helped too, I loved the fact that the sky seemed to go on forever and there were real changes in weather from brilliant sunshine to heavy snow in the winter. It was so different to those long miserable dark days you seem to have to endure in the Midlands. This was and is a different country and it was a new start for Lisa and me.

I still love Scotland and if I could get the kind of work I do now up there I would move the family back like a shot. I love the culture and the people and I love the way the Celts as a whole have retained their culture and traditions, how they love their history and are fiercely proud of their Scottish heritage. That's something we have lost or perhaps has been stolen from us English over the years and has obviously been exacerbated by Blair's Labour government over the last ten years.

So Scotland was a fresh start but of course there was still a massive personal debt around our heads and the cottage was still lying empty back in Coventry. The repossession process ground on as our bank accounts were frozen and our credit cards ripped up. When I was at university I was summoned to see the bank manager. He asked me if I had brought my cheque guarantee card in and could he see it? I produced it from my rucksack, he looked at it, pulled open a desk drawer and produced the biggest pair of scissors I had ever seen and promptly cut it in two. It was like being castrated. This time, however, we had castrated ourselves and ripped the cards up, deciding to live on cash and our wits. We could no longer afford to build debt and no one would give us any credit anyway.

Lisa was instrumental in picking me up after the collapse of Tic Toc and that morning when I cried in the kitchen she just hugged me and said everything would be all right and for once in my life I actually let her hold me for ages and ages. In one sense I became the little boy whose mum had suddenly died. The lad who had been betrayed by his dad and put in care, but with that one long hug I was also the strong kid who survived care, separation from his brothers and the death of his mum and the collapse of his business dream but who would now survive this too. Let's face it, when you're in the shit you've got two choices: dig yourself out of it or wallow in it. With Lisa's help I was determined to dig myself out.

The Forum was beginning to make more financial sense, I had cut costs, massively increased income from all sources and begun the slow task of rebuilding confidence in the venue with promoters and customers. It was time for a holiday.

We flew from Glasgow Airport to Miami and spent two weeks in a cheap but fantastic motel in Fort Myers on the Gulf Coast. We had found the Dolphin Inn a few years ago when we had been on a touring holiday in the States and we had become friends with the owners, Donna and Ernie, a couple of Canadians who had made the long trek south to make a few bob before retiring back in Niagara Falls, their home town. Seeing them again made me realise that no matter how bad things had been and were, you can pull back.

Ernie, like most Yanks, had owned businesses that had made him loads of cash. He once earned a real hellhole of a hotel by the Falls and he had also had businesses that went down the pan. He told me the only answer was to come back stronger, tougher and more aggressive and most of all to believe that it is better to try and fail than be one of those losers who snipe from the sidelines and never leave their comfort zone.

His actions backed up his words because within three years Ernie and Donna had sold up, made a fortune and retired back to Canada and out of the godforsaken sunshine and humidity of Florida as Ernie referred to it. He hated the heat but he saw it as a necessary evil to fund his dreams. Lisa and I on the other hand loved the sun and spent most of the days lapping up the rays by the pool and the nights at the dogs with those two or eating in cheap restaurants. It was a fantastic holiday and a real tonic and Ernie inspired me to see Livingston as both an opportunity to regroup but also to relax before moving forward, the dream was in no way over.

We had got back from Florida and Bert had decided that he no longer needed to employ Lisa. He had decided to cut more costs, I was annoyed but in a way relieved. He didn't know but Lisa was pregnant and I was on target to earn enough to keep us all going.

However the sacking of Lisa was a taster of what was to come because by Christmas they wanted me to give up the licence on the building so that they could put a manager in. It was clear what their game was, they were beginning to resent the amount of cash that I was pulling out of the venue. I think Steven, even though he was a mate and had been delighted when we told him that Lisa was pregnant, was also jealous that I was earning more than him and doing less work. But tough titty, that was the deal that they had all agreed to, but as usual deals are fine when you're only talking about them but as soon as the hard cash is on the table, attitudes harden and rules begin to get rewritten.

There was a stand-off. I felt very strongly that I had done every part of my side of the bargain and the venue was heading towards becoming very successful. I refused to give up the licence and there were rows. Steven had split loyalties and disappeared from the scene and therefore never ever saw little Rosie who he was so excited about. I don't blame him; the brothers had put him in a difficult position. It got uglier and ended up in a court case years later which they won and I lost and I ended up having to pay them compensation. The only compensation I have is that the Forum is now demolished and a shopping centre has been built on top of it, as the Forum without me was a total flop.

It was incredibly messy though from December through to the birth of Rosie in March 1993. For a starter without the job we would be homeless. The Development Corporation, after some pressure from myself, agreed to let us stay in the house until the birth at least and again we signed on. Added to this was the pressure of the repossession finally going through on the cottage in Coventry, although to be fair with the geographical distance and the spiritual and emotional miles we had now put between our old home and us it didn't hurt too much. The bank would sell it, in a few months' time, for considerably less than we paid for it. They would then chase us for the shortfall, but at least it was over.

The chapter closed, turn the page and move on.

23

Rosie

Rosie was born on 6 March 1993 just three days after my birthday and three days after the cottage was repossessed.

The timing of the house repossession falling on my birthday was a kick in the balls; it was a constant reminder of bad times. However as the years have progressed I have turned this into a positive, because now I use this landmark date as a time for reflection, a time to consider how far we have come since that dark day and it drives me on to further success. I may not know much of the history of my childhood because it was wiped clean and stolen from me, but I sure as hell know mine and Lisa's history and I'm proud of it and I have learnt from it and it's made me the success I am. It's also meant that our relationship has grown and strengthened as the years have passed and that together we understand our history, know our present and are never afraid of our future.

Having Rosie was a defining moment, even if she made us wait two weeks to emerge into this world. I remember seeing a scan of her in the womb a few days before she was born. She was sucking her thumb as she would for the next nine years. She was beautiful then and as she now develops into a young woman she gets more beautiful by the second. We had bored everybody to death with the initial scan that everyone has. You know the one where the baby looks like a bowling skittle to everybody else except the adoring parents who think they can see every feature.

However, this scan which was taken a few days before Lisa was induced was done to check if Rosie was okay and the image on the screen was completely different to the skittle. This was a baby, no doubt about it, and seeing Rosie in the womb sucking that thumb made me absolutely convinced that abortion is murder. The day of the birth arrived and we entered the maternity ward and the gaze of Sister Black. She took one look at me and said, 'Are you planning on moving in, Mr Gaunt?'

I looked like Sherpa bloody Tensing. I was carrying beanbags, whale music, pain relief machines, tape recorders and even a cuddly toy; the local National Childbirth Trust had convinced us that Lisa had to feel right and comfortable during the labour.

We had been attending the classes for weeks with a load of middle-class first-timers and one other working-class couple from Livi, called Brian and Marie. We had all lain on the floor and discovered our pelvic floor and all the men had been instructed to be both sympathetic and empathetic by joining in the classes. The woman giving the class had said it would feel like passing a grapefruit, which made my eyes water let alone Lisa's.

Then Brian had interjected, 'My only worry is like is it true that afterwards when you're having sex it's a bit like throwing a sausage up a close!'

There was a pause before the middle-class instructor laughed and the rest of us joined in.

But seriously the NCT were a godsend and being so many miles away from our relatives, especially Lisa's mum, they really helped to reassure us.

Back to Sister Black: she was the ward sister and a spinster. She was a living, walking, talking cliché; the spinster sister who is as tough as nails on the husbands and is fiercely protective of her girls, ruling the ward with a rod of iron but who has a real heart of gold. She clearly thought that a dad's role was to provide and his position in the delivery room was *outside*. But these being modern times she had to let men into the inner sanctum.

Lisa, egged on by the NCT, had made her birth plan and decided that under no circumstance did she want an epidural and so the labour began. It was a long, slow and painful experience and that was just for me! No I'm only joking but it did take ages and at one point Lisa was putting the gas and air mask on longer than Jacques Cousteau.

At one point the midwife suggested that she might want an epidural and Lisa was about to say yes when I reminded her of her plan. She shook her head and the labour continued. They then became concerned about the baby so they planted a heart monitor wire to the head and from that point onwards I held onto Lisa's hand and my eyes never left the monitor that showed the wavy beats of our baby's heart.

After what seemed hours the midwife asked if I would like to come and have a look. Now let's face it lads, the honest answer to that question is, 'No fucking way, I'm all right up the top end thanks.' But of course I let go of Lisa's hand and took the few steps to the bottom of the bed and then I saw her. Rosie was emerging. There was this mass of dark thick black hair and then her head turned. Everything was in slow motion.

'One more push, Lisa.'

The shoulders were out and then everything speeded up and before I knew it our beautiful daughter was on Lisa's breast. I was in pieces, crying and searching for the camera. I must have shot at least twenty frames through a tsunami of tears before Lisa calmly and coolly said, 'Jon, take the bloody lens cap off.'

Ten minutes later I was sitting sweating with my newborn child in my arms. The clock on the wall was slowly turning; it felt as if it were actually going backward. They said they would only be five minutes showering Lisa; they had put the emergency cord in my hand in case I needed them but I was afraid to pull it because I thought Rosie was already dead.

Since the midwives had left with Lisa, Rosie had lain absolutely still; I couldn't hear her breathing over the pounding of my own heart.

Do I pinch her? Slap her bum like in the movies, how the fuck do I know if she's still breathing, come on Lisa, come on, what's taking you so bloody long, Jesus hurry up.

Words, thoughts, emotions crashing in, piling up in a motorway accident of a brain, sweating.

Why's it so so bloody hot in here?

And then . . . Lisa was back; being wheeled in a wheelchair. I passed her the bundle.

'All you have to do is blow gently on her eyelids, see.'

The eyes fluttered, Rosie was alive and I had received my first lesson in being a dad.

The lessons are still continuing and I'm still learning. Lisa was a natural from day one.

Rosie was absolutely beautiful and weighed in at nine pounds. Lisa stayed in the hospital for five days and there was only one panic when she was worried that Rosie might be mixed up with another baby when she was taken off for her daily weigh in.

Sister Black had reassured Lisa, 'Mrs Gaunt, don't be so pathetic, there's no mistaking the Gaunt child' – and she was right. All the other babies were puce-coloured with ginger hair whereas Rosie was olive skinned, just like my dad, with a mop of thick, luscious black hair.

She became a bit of an attraction as none of the doctors had ever seen such a dark and hairy Caucasian child; they said it was usual for Asian babies but not whites. When Dad and Sylvia came to visit a few days later the old man said it was a throwback to his great grandad who had married a Red Indian when he was working for the Hudson Bay Company in Canada.

I don't know if he was making it up but one thing was for sure: the birth of Rosie was also the beginning of the rebuilding of my relationship with Dad.

24

Another kind of birth

1993

Lisa and I had returned to Coventry two months after Rosie was born and we were now living in a one-down two-up hovel in a grotty part of Coventry. Lisa's mum, dad and my old man had all tried to find us somewhere better to live before we left the bungalow in Scotland but to no avail. This was the time before the buy-to-let boom and there was hardly any property for rent advertised in the *Coventry Evening Telegraph*. Now there's thousands.

Dad had found a place near where he lived in Nuneaton and I went to look at it and actually it was nicer than the place we eventually moved into but it was in Nuneaton. If you were to ask me, 'What's wrong with Nuneaton?' then you quite clearly haven't been to the place. Still, I appreciated his help and concern.

He had come up to see us after the birth and after holding the newly born Rosie, I had seen a change in him. He didn't seem to want to give her back but eventually she cried for a feed and Lisa took over. As we wet the baby's head he went out to the kitchen and I followed him. He leant against the sink and poured himself a glass of water and he began to cry.

'I'm sorry I'm—'

He said that he was upset not only for mine and Lisa's predicament; thousands in debt, homeless, and jobless but also for my younger brother, Jason, who was going through his own problems at the time.

'It's all my fault, it's all my bloody fault.'

'No it isn't, Dad, look I'll be all right and Jase—'

'No, it's me, it's my fault I shouldn't have—'

Instinctively I put my arm around him, both to comfort and shut him up. I didn't need this. I had enough problems without having to deal with his self-pitying guilt trip about what he had done to us as kids. Or at least that's how I interpreted his words then.

However, looking back, I can see that this was his turning point, this was his road to Damascus moment. Holding Rosie he had begun to confront his own demons, his own history that he had buried for years and he wanted to say sorry, he needed to say sorry and I should have let him. Instead I shut him up and made him bottle it up again for years. How I wish I had the maturity then that I have now because then there would not have been so many wasted years. The reconciliation and forgiveness could have happened earlier and I could have broken free of my past much sooner too. But this was the turning point.

We had moved ourselves back down with the help of Lisa's mum who had come up to Scotland on the train. We hired a similar-size van to the one that we had moved ourselves up in and waved goodbye to Lorna and Dave. We set off to Coventry with a vague idea that I would have to get the writing off the ground again but with the sure knowledge that it would be difficult on two counts: one, that I hadn't written anything for years and two, my literary agent had dropped me nearly as quick as the cheques from *Emmerdale* had stopped falling through her letterbox.

I was thirty-two with a fantastic CV but unfortunately I had only ever worked for myself. What transferable skills did I have? Who would be interested in employing me? I had no cash and I had a credit record that Nick Leeson would be ashamed of and I was returning to my home city from which some people thought I had done a runner after the demise of Tic Toc.

Times were bleak, I was spending a lot of time in bed – in fact *Pebble Mill at One* was my breakfast TV – and little Rosie hardly had any toys to play with. The living room was dominated by cardboard boxes stuffed full with my record and book collections and the only real furniture we had was an oversized leather suite in grey with pink piping.

Stop laughing! Remember this was the early Nineties so cut me a bit of slack in the taste police stakes please. We had dragged this leather suite up to Scotland with us in a hire van when we moved there for work and it had come back down with us when we returned to my home town. When the house was repossessed the bailiff had gone round putting stickers on all our goods but had stopped short of putting a value on the suite on the grounds that even in a distress sale 'nobody would want that'.

But that bit of gross furniture was about to become our lifeline, our saviour. After spending the best part of six months on the dole, Lisa had run out of patience with me, I was spending all my time either drinking cheap lager, sleeping or wallowing in the bath. On reflection I must have been depressed. I had again lost the lot and the plot.

Lisa said we had to get a job, any job, if we had any chance of pulling out of this mess so we decided to wrap up Rosie and head for town. The only problem was we had no cash. Then we spotted the settee. We approached it from either end and we turned it over and shook it like crazy. A few coins fell out of the back of it and we eagerly counted our ill-gotten gains. Not only did we have enough for the bus fare we could also probably afford a coffee and a cream cake – this was pre Type 2 diabetes days – in Coventry's only posh café, Druckers.

We headed into town and several hours of fruitless searching for work later we were on the verge of giving up when we heard a familiar voice shout, 'Oi Gaunty!'

I turned round to see that it was one of my oldest mates, Moz Dee. Nowadays Moz is second in charge of BBC Five Dead but back then he was a DJ on the local BBC radio station.

'How you doing, I thought you two were still in Scotland?'

'No we came back months ago.'

'What's he called?'

'Rosie and he's a she.'

'Sos, sos, so what you up too, I thought you loved it up there?'

'Yeah, yeah we did, but I'm concentrating on my writing again.'

'Bollocks, you're on the dole.'

You know what they say – never try to bullshit a bullshitter and Moz was a prize bullshitter. I laughed and told him the truth and the story of why we were back in Coventry. He was sympathetic and took us into Druckers for a cake and tea.

'I know what you should do Gaunty, you should get a job on the radio like me, you'd be great at it.'

'No, no I couldn't do that.'

There's no way I wanted to be a disc jockey. When I had left Coventry eighteen months earlier Moz was doing one evening show a week. He was second generation Irish and so he had an Irish radio show on the local radio station. You know the sort of thing, plenty of Daniel O'Donnell, The Dubliners and the craic. As the show progressed minute-by-minute Moz became more and more 'Oirish'. It was a cracking little show but it wasn't for me.

'No, no it's not being a DJ, you prat, and I'm on five days a week now, you don't have to play records.'

'What?'

'No all you do is say something outrageous and the old dears phone in and then you either chat them up or put the phone down on them!'

He then proceeded to tell me how much he was earning and that he reckoned that the boss, Andy Wright, would love me and anyway, ' 'Cos of the club and *Emmerdale* and you running off with all the cash to Edinburgh everyone knows you in Cov, you'll be a star.'

I was excited. Lisa and I ran back to the house and Rosie went round most corners on just two wheels in the buggy. Moz had said he would go straight back to the radio station and get Andy to give us a bell. Just like in the movies as we entered the house the phone was ringing, but where was the telephone? We had left in such a hurry we had left all the furniture upside down and the phone was nowhere to be seen. Eventually of course we found it and I tried to get my breath back as Andy Wright asked whether I was free to come and see him.

The next day I was at the studios of Coventry and Warwick-shire Radio (aka CWR), waiting for my big break into radio. When I had left Coventry a year and a half previously, the station had just opened but in the intervening months it had failed to grab an audience and now Andy had been brought in to try and turn the station's fortunes around. He had previously been instrumental in making Radio WM a success in Birmingham and his other claim to fame was that while working in Oxford he had discovered Pam bloody Ayres!

I opened the door and this little weedy bloke with black, thick-framed, National Health glasses held out his hand in greeting. I shook it and he gestured for me to sit down. Andy was a real *Guardian*-reading liberal who rode his bike from Moseley in Birmingham to the station and then caught the train with his bike on it and cycled the short distance to BBC Coventry. But as Moz warned me weeks later, 'Don't let the bicycle clips fool you.' This bloke knew his stuff: he was the archetypal radio anorak.

Andy knew who I was from my club, Tic Toc, and he knew that I had written for theatre and TV and had promoted a whole raft of comedians. He explained that he wanted to shift the focus away from Warwickshire and concentrate on the City of Coventry, as he believed that's where the mass audience was. He said to achieve this he needed Coventry personalities and voices and was I interested?

I was on the dole and about fifty grand in debt. Of course I was bloody interested. He handed over an old reel-to-reel tape recorder called an Uher and showed me how to use it.

'Right Jon, just take this and find a building, any building, and just describe it on tape so that I can hear your voice.'

What could be simpler?

The next day Lisa, Rosie and I went to Coombe Abbey Park on the outskirts of Coventry, near to where our old cottage was. We made the journey in what was now our beaten-up red Fiesta – and let me assure you at this point I really didn't feel like I had made it. I had read in the local paper that the Council had spent a fortune on building a visitors' centre at the park and I went there with the intention of slagging it, and them, off.

As it happened the centre was great and was only the beginning of the Council investing millions in this park as they developed a luxury hotel there too. Coombe Abbey was also special to me because I had worked there as a court jester at the medieval banquets. It was years earlier when I was in the sixth form. I went on to perform with Paul King who went on to find fame but alas no real money as the lead singer of Coventry pop group King who had a string of hits in the Eighties. Paul later became a VJ on MTV and VH1.

Lisa's brother had been the keyboard player in the band but they had split up a few years ago. Paul played the handsome prince and I was the jester or more accurately the village idiot!

'Where have you been?'

'Plucking my pheasants.'

'Good job you haven't got a speech impediment.'

Not exactly Harold Pinter but these were great riotous nights where the large party of office girls used to have loads of medieval food, roughly translated as chicken in the basket, too much cheap red wine and one miniscule glass of mead which would turn them from respectable office clerks into rampant nymphos whose starter for ten was to pinch your arse and if you got lucky they would slip a note in your garter.

It was tacky cheap entertainment but it was a great laugh for both the audience and the performers.

I sat on the damp grass in front of this building with all these memories to inform my piece and pushed the record button.

'I'm standing outside the – no that's no good.'

I pressed the rewind button.

'I'm outside Comb – bollocks.'

'Hi, I'm Jon Gaunt and I'm . . . a twat.'

Rewind, record, and swear, the pattern became predictable. Every time I was convinced it was half good I would play it back and just wince at my voice. As the afternoon wore on I became more and more flustered and more and more angry with myself and all around me.

'Lisa I just can't do it, I can't fucking do it!'

'Of course you can.'

'I can't, I can't, and I sound like a twat.'

'Don't be stupid, try again.'

I was almost crying with frustration. This was my chance to get off the dole and I couldn't do it, I just couldn't do it, I couldn't just talk, just talk into a sodding microphone without either stumbling over my words or putting on a ridiculous posh phone voice. I just couldn't do the simplest thing in the world, be my bloody self.

'Of course you can, have another go.'

'No I can't. Come on, let's go.'

'Don't be so bloody pathetic. You can't give up now.'

'Don't you call me—'

'Well, what else are you? I thought you were meant to be an actor. I thought you were trained for this at Birmingham.'

'Don't you start!'

'Well, you're pathetic!'

'No I'm not. I'll bloody show you!' I pushed the button and in a rage started ranting down the microphone and suddenly the monster was born!

25

Hitting the airwaves

1993

The next morning I took the tape into Andy Wright. He played it in front of me and then smiled and called in his assistant Andy Conroy, who was much younger and was from Blackburn. Years previously, when the club was struggling, Conroy had interviewed me on the radio and tried to stitch me up. I didn't like him.

Smarmy gutless BBC wanker, I thought at the time. *He's never worked in the real world, trying to be funny with me when I'm just trying to do something to stop Coventry being a ghost town and all he can do is ask negative questions.*

I looked him in the eye and I didn't know if he remembered the interview as I did but he held out his hand and said, 'Hi Jon.'

I shook his hand and smiled, through gritted teeth. The tape was played again.

Conroy was more enthusiastic than Andy Wright, 'My God that's brill, that is. Is that your first time Jon, on tape like?'

'Yeah.'

'Bloody hell!'

'Good isn't it?' said Andy Wright.

'Bloody marvellous, when can you start?'

I thought the younger Andy was joking but he wasn't and neither was Andy Wright. Conroy left the office and Wright said that they would like to take me on and that they would spend three months training me up, Conroy would design a training programme and then they would take it from there. Then he said the most remarkable thing: he leaned over his desk, readjusted his glasses, and said, 'In six months' time you'll be the highest paid presenter on the station. You're a natural.'

I was taken aback but still managed to ask him what the starting salary was.

'No, well we don't normally pay when you're training Jon, it's—'

'Well, sorry mate, you can forget it, I'm too old for all that jam tomorrow bit.'

I got up to leave.

'No, no wait a minute, Jon.'

'Look Andy, thanks and all that but I've got a little baby. I can't afford to work for nowt.'

'Okay, okay, I understand. Well how about if we said 300 a week?'

Three hundred quid a week, I was on the dole surviving on about fifty and this man was offering me 300?

'Yeah, yeah that would be great.'

'Of course we'll review it as you go on but if you could start on that?'

'Of course, yeah wow, thanks, when do I start?'

'Monday?'

And that's how I fell into radio. I didn't realise at the time that most kids get into radio by exploiting themselves and by getting exploited to get their first chance. It's just the way the industry works. To be honest, I now believe it's the way it should be and it makes me really angry when some young kid thinks they are above making the tea when they first join my team. In fact it's become a standing joke with all the production teams that I have ever worked with that until you have got Gaunty's tea right then you haven't got a chance of progressing.

But what's wrong with that? That's how it was in the factories years ago and when I first got my Saturday job at Tesco. It was tea first before they let me loose with the knives and rightly so.

However I wasn't a kid. I was a thirty-year-old bloke with house repossession, a bankruptcy and tens of thousands of pounds of debt round my neck and I couldn't afford to work for free.

That said, I worked my balls off in those first few weeks. I constantly listened to the radio and not just BBC Coventry. Wrighty told me to listen to an Australian called Ed Doolan who worked at WM in Birmingham and did a consumer phone-in. I knew the name because, again years earlier, when my play *Hooligans* was a big hit, he had interviewed me when it was on tour in Birmingham, and I thought he had tried to stitch me up.

But now I realised he was just doing his job. I didn't want to be Doolan or even copy him but I respected the way he worked his listeners. Years later he would joke that I was after his job when I stood in for him, I would respond by saying that I was constantly polishing my shoes to dance on his grave. However the sly old fox is still on air and giving the local councils plenty of grief and still holds down a massive audience and I respect him for that.

Andy then started giving me tapes of some American talk jocks and I couldn't believe what I heard, I loved their irreverence, their cheek and their rudeness. It was like nothing I had ever heard on British radio and it made me want to hear more. Meanwhile Andy Conroy was teaching me how to drive the radio desk and how to cue up records and taped inserts. It was a steep learning curve but I loved every minute of it. He was a great teacher and I owe him an enormous amount because without his input I wouldn't have the technical skill to back up my gob! Then after a week or two they let me loose on the

Coventry public and got me to do a live insert into the drive time show from the Coventry fair.

The day after, Andy Conroy and I sat down and reviewed a tape of my insert. Andy started by saying that it was terrible. My heart sank but then he followed up by saying, 'It's just you, Gaunty, you're too bloody big. You just fill the whole radio, it isn't fair on the poor bugger who has to pick up after you, I'm sorry mate, you're not a contributor you're a presenter.'

Within another few weeks they had given me my own show, five nights a week, between six and seven in the evening. The idea was to interview local politicians and talk about Coventry issues and of course open the phone lines to let the people of Coventry speak. Andy Conroy had taught me how to drive the desk and all the technical aspects of presenting but Andy Wright told me the golden rules: 'Just say the first thing that comes into your head, never lie because the audience will always find you out and don't be intimidated. It's your show, your name in the *Radio Times* and you're the star.'

So when that red light went on, I was spectacularly rude to the first councillor that arrived like a lamb to slaughter and Gaunty was in business.

Within six months they had sacked the breakfast presenters, upped my money, and given me the slot but if I'm brutally honest I was still only playing at it. I was only on the radio as a stopgap until I could get back into the theatre or back into TV writing. Even though, in a very short space of time, I had created a stir, got promoted, received more cash and got us out of that hovel and into a better rented house, I still didn't think that this was going to be my career for the next fifteen years.

Then Wrighty told me to go on holiday. Just out of the blue, as we were finishing our lunch – MacDonald's for me and Moz, who was doing the mid-morning show after my breakfast show, and wholemeal bread and half a can of tuna for Wrighty. After lunch, Wrighty asked if he could have a word, we walked to his office and he closed the door.

'Jon, you need a holiday. When was the last time you and Lisa went away?'

'Ages ago.'

'Well, look, take an advance and go and have two weeks in the States. You like Florida don't you?'

He'd obviously been listening to the show.

'Yeah, yeah great.'

'There's only one thing. When you go through the airport buy a transistor radio and listen to all the talk jocks on AM.'

'Yeah sure, Andy.'

We had two weeks at Ernie and Donna's motel in Fort Myers and every day I listened to Rush Limburg, Harold Stern and all the other great talk jocks. Ernie couldn't believe that I had reinvented myself as a talk jock and told me which American jocks were worth listening to.

'I don't know how you bloody get away with it, but it's great.'

The old man was drinking half a mug of black coffee in our cramped living room and had already become a great fan of my new radio show.

'I always knew you had the gift of the bloody gab, but bloody hell making money out of it as well – that's just brilliant. You know what, son, your mum would be proud of you.'

I almost cried but I didn't let him see, it was the first time he had mentioned Mum in years but before I had time to reply he continued, 'But you've got to get yourselves out of this shithole and you've got to take care of Lisa and this little bairn.'

When I got back on the radio the next morning the red light went on and I suddenly knew why Mum had died when I was a kid, why I had been in care, gone bankrupt, written for TV and promoted some of the best comedians and worked with some of the dodgiest Scottish geezers.

It was because I was born to be a talk jock.

26

Talk jock

1994

I loved being the star on my hometown radio station and even though our audience was pitifully small, compared to the big commercial rival, they were incredibly loyal and the numbers began to grow. The meteoric rise I had on the radio reflected on our personal circumstances and meant that over the first couple of years back in Coventry we were able to get out of the 'shithole' and move to nicer and more expensive rented properties. We still couldn't afford to buy anywhere as we had no deposit and with the repossession still around our neck I doubt if anyone would have given us a mortgage.

Once I got the breakfast show slot and had decided that talk radio was what I was born to do, I never had any doubt that one day I would end up on national radio. I was just surprised how bloody long it took. I had rediscovered the arrogance, the attitude, but most importantly the ambition.

Right from this moment I decided that I was not only going to be the best thing on this radio station but on any station and

I set about building a team around me of like-minded individuals. It felt like the beginning of Tic Toc but this time I was using the BBC's money to fund my dream and ambition. I worked with some great people in this station who came to be lifelong friends like Geoff Foster, Kevin Reid and Kev Lee and together we started to create a station sound moulded by the two Andy's that began to build an audience.

I was helped of course because, just as Moz said outside that coffee shop, I knew Coventry and I knew Coventry people and that was a tremendous asset. At the time Victoria Derbyshire was working there too and although she was a good journalist who went on to be on Five Live she never had a chance to be as good or popular as me because she wasn't from the Two Tone city and she didn't understand Coventry people.

Local radio has to be truly local to work, that doesn't mean parochial but it does have to be of its city and about the city. This is what Andy Wright understood and this is why he shifted the focus just to Coventry and of course why he employed me. I'll never forget Victoria's reaction when I was chosen over her to get the breakfast show gig. She had been doing lunchtimes and had been there for much longer than me and obviously saw the gig as rightfully hers. To her I was an untrained upstart. She had a face like a smacked arse when my appointment was announced and she left soon after for a gig in her hometown of Manchester where she could have done as well as me. I'm not sure if she did but she did end up on Five Dead and some people would equate that with success.

A prime example of this local knowledge giving me the edge over a so-called trained journalist was the day not long after I had got the breakfast show when the light suddenly went off in the studio. I hit the pre-fade button that allowed me to talk to my producer on the other side of the glass while the audience couldn't hear.

'What the hell's happening? Has a plane crashed?'

'Don't say that on air because the answer's yes.'

The emergency generator kicked into life and the lights flickered back on. A plane had crashed on the approach to Coventry airport and at first we thought it had come down on a housing estate in Willenhall. For months there had been animal rights protests at the airport as a firm had been exporting live cattle out of the city to the continent for the veal trade.

I had been the first person to interview the bloke behind the project, a man called Christopher Barret Jolly, and I had given him a real rough ride on my Saturday morning show.

He had come off air and said to my producer, 'Blimey he got out of the wrong side of the bed this morning, didn't he?'

The producer replied, 'Same side he gets out every day, that's Gaunty.'

The truth is I couldn't stand the plonker as he was an insufferable snob who had previous for gun running into African states and I took an instant dislike to him.

However the Council were in a difficult position. Remember this was the era before cheap flights, and the airport at Bagington on the outskirts of Coventry was running at a massive loss. Barret Jolly's plan to turn it into the largest port for the live exports of animals was a financial godsend to him and the Council.

Duncan Sutherland, the city's head of economic development, and many of the Labour-controlled Council saw it as a way of finally turning a profit at the airport. However the animal rights protestors saw it differently and had organised a massive demonstration and effective blockade at the airport. I got to know the protestors well as they used to ring the station every day with their views and not only on the protest. I didn't agree with them. I love veal and it's only a cow after all, but I admired their tenacity and passion.

I also knew one of the protestors, Jill Phipps; or rather I should say I knew her old man, Bob.

Years previously I had worked on the post at Christmas and Bob had been the main permanent postman on my student round. His daughter Jill was a beautiful punk at the time and everyone in the Rose & Crown and The Bear which were Coventry's top city centre punk pubs fancied her like crazy. She had got into the animal rights movement in later years and I often spotted her in the City Centre precinct manning a stall collecting petitions on various animal rights issues. This local knowledge and shared history gave me an 'in' to the protestors and although they knew I wasn't on their side they also could see clearly that I didn't think much of Barret Jolly.

The plane crash and its connection to the animal rights protestors and Barret Jolly was a massive story for BBC Coventry and helped us to build the audience because there were so many twists and turns, but nobody could have predicted the final two tragic events that ended the story.

On 21 December 1994 a Boeing 737, which was returning from the Continent after dropping off its cargo of veal calves, crashed in thick fog on the outskirts of Coventry. It narrowly missed hundreds of houses, crashing in the woods only twenty yards from the nearest house. The aircrew of three were killed along with two stockmen who were on the plane.

The next day we broadcast our breakfast show from the living room of one of the houses the plane had clipped on its fateful descent and we listened to the tales of the residents and told the story from every angle to our ever-increasing audience. It's a sad fact of life that bad news sells and it's as true in radio as it is in papers.

Those next few days we were basically a rolling news service for the people of Coventry and it was the lessons learned and the experience I gained during this tragic news event that was to provide the foundation for my award-winning coverage of the Vauxhall car plant closure years later in Luton. Andy Wright always used to say you can have natural talent but it's hours on the clock that count, the more time you put in on air, the better, and of course more experienced you get.

There is also nothing like the thrill of reporting and especially holding together a programme, a live broadcast as a story unfolds, it was the same with the Vauxhall closure and near riot, the events of 9/11 and of course when I was on air in London as the bombers of the Tube started their horrendous massacre on the Seventh of July.

Unfortunately there was a final twist to the veal story when Jill Phipps was tragically crushed to death under the wheels of a 50 tonne cattle truck as she tried to prevent it entering the airport on 1 February 1995. The whole city was in shock and I found the interviews with Jill's friends and especially her mum Nancy some of the hardest I have ever had to conduct. I didn't and still don't support Nancy or even Jill's views on animal rights but you would have to possess a heart of stone not to have been affected by this family's tragedy.

As for Barret Jolly – well, his company, Phoenix Aviation, never flew from Baginton again and it went out of business later that year. In December 2002 he finally got his comeuppance when he was convicted of trying to smuggle in £22 million worth of cocaine in his plane and sentenced to twenty years at her Majesty's pleasure.

However it wasn't all doom and gloom at Coventry. Moz and I had plenty of laughs while we were both working at the station and we were always playing practical jokes on each other. The biggest stitch-up was the day Moz was interviewing Uri Geller in the studio. Uri had been bending spoons over the airwaves and people had been ringing in saying that clocks and watches that hadn't worked for ages were now miraculously ticking. Suddenly Moz glanced up at the clock on his studio wall to go to a newsbreak and it too had stopped.

'Uri, that is unbelievable, absolutely unbel, blooming, believable! You've just stopped the clock!'

'Yes, Maurice, I know. It has happened before in radio and TV studios across the world.'

'No but Uri you don't understand. That clock is directly connected to the atomic clock at Rugby. It cannot stop!'

Uri smiled, and Moz was still amazed as he finished his show and barged into the newsroom.

'Did you lot hear that? He stopped the bloody clock, have we rung the *Telegraph* to give them the story?'

He was full of it and obviously had visions of himself, Uri and the clock being on the front page of the local paper. Then the radio station's chief engineer called him over.

'No, no, hang on a minute mate I just want to ring the paper.'

'No Moz, I've got something to show you.'

He had to virtually manhandle Moz out of the newsroom and down to the operations room.

'What we doing here?'

'See that, Moz?'

'What?'

'That, it's the controls for the clock.'

'Yeah, so?'

'Well, if we pull this lead . . .'

Moz turned to see us all at the door. We were all laughing.

'*You bastards!*'

27

Bethany

I loved working in Coventry. Professionally things were going great and personally things only got better when Lisa fell pregnant with Bethany. Now if Rosie's birth was long and drawn out, Bethany's was much quicker. In fact Bethany tells a story of how she was born in the back of a pizza delivery van! She swears that this is a story I once told her when I was putting her to bed. I personally think that she has just inherited her dad's talent for storytelling and exaggeration. Still her birth story is not too far from the truth because we did only just make it to the hospital.

Four days before the birth we had moved into a large semi in the trendy area of Coventry – yes there is one – called Earlsdon. These were the kind of houses that when Lisa and I first got together and were running Tic Toc we coveted as they were the height of making it in the arty and teaching crowds. We were only renting it, but it was costing us 800 a month so you can see there had been a distinct change in our financial fortunes since I had started on the radio.

Anyhow we moved in and four days later on 8 August 1995 Lisa started having contractions and said she needed to go to the hospital '*right now.*'

I suddenly contracted stomach cramps of my own and ran for the loo leaving Lisa doubled over in agony at the bottom of the stairs. By the time we got into the little red Fiesta, Lisa couldn't sit down so I had to collapse the back seats and she crawled into the back through the hatchback, and kneeled on all fours among the dog hairs and general rubbish as I put my foot down. We rushed into reception and they ushered us straight into an examination room. I took up my usual position at the top end and held Lisa's hand and she was still muttering about me going to the loo when the midwife asked me to come and have a look. 'What already?'

And there she was. There was no time to go to the delivery suite as three pushes and Bethany was out. I swear it was so quick I even caught sight of the England wicket keeper Jack Russell in the room!

Lisa was back home by lunchtime the next day and our family was complete. Now all I needed to do was turn this large rented house into a home.

28

Ullo Jon, gotta new motor?

1995

'Oi Gaunt, you fat prick, if you can afford to run a Jag and come up here you can afford to give me my ten grand.'

I looked round. It was Banger, my ex-bouncer, shouting from the posh seats. I told Alex to keep on walking and ignore him. As we made a swift exit I could still hear him gobbing off, 'Bloody crook Gaunty.'

Since getting back to Coventry and working on the radio, I had made a habit of taking Alex, Lisa's little sister, up to Highfield Road every other week. An old friend and Coventry City Director, Joe Elliot, supplied me with the freebies. The Jag that Tony 'Banger' Walsh was referring to was the XJS I had won in a raffle a few weeks previously.

I had been invited by the head of the City Council's economic development unit to attend a business lunch to promote Coventry. His name was Duncan Sutherland and he had great plans for the city and was a regular guest on my radio show where he used to push his ideas for the regeneration of the city forward to my listeners.

At this particular lunch he bought ten raffle tickets for each of his guests and the top prize was the use of a brand new Jag for a year, all the proceeds going to the NSPCC. I put the tickets in my suit pocket and forgot about them. I was sitting on a table with the 'Great and Good of Coventry'.

Duncan was introducing everybody around the table but my mind was wandering thinking about those bad dark days when the club folded.

'Gaunty, this is—'

'I know who he is, he's the bastard who repossessed my house!'

There was an embarrassed silence and then everyone burst out laughing, including the wanker, sorry, banker.

Over the years Tic Toc had had a succession of brilliant bank managers who understood and supported what we were doing. In the early days they would come and see the plays and many of their junior staff became firm friends and regular customers of our cabaret club. These managers still did their job properly and had made sure that at first our parents secured our overdraft and then took joint and several charges over our houses as security for the expanding company's overdraft. That's okay, that's what bankers do, but the man sitting opposite me was a different kind of animal.

The recession was looming and interest rates were rocketing skywards and he was brought in as the axe man, the company lackey, to close accounts. He had tried to be the hard man with us right from the beginning but had obviously realised how much public support we had. He knew what kind of publicity the bank would get if he pulled the plug there and then, but in several acrimonious and aggressive meetings he clearly set out his stall and thought he had sussed me out as a chancer who needed to be pulled down a peg or two. So when the opportunity arrived he wasted no time in making my life a misery.

Six months after this meal and the purchase of the raffle tickets, Alex and my brother Jason were waiting for me in the control room behind the glass screen at BBC Coventry as I interviewed the bloke from the NSPCC about the draw that was going to be held later that day at Highfield Road for the Jag.

'Oh man alive, would I love to win that, it's every kid's dream to drive a Jaguar.'

The Sky Blues had lost again and we were trudging back to the city centre when Andy Conroy from the radio station bumped into me and said, 'Well done, Jon.'

'Don't be funny, Conroy, they hammered us.'

'Yeah I know, but I mean about the car.'

'What car?'

'Don't you know?'

'Know what?'

Then it dawned on me. At half time as we emerged out of the bar attempting to digest the last of the pie I thought I heard the crowd singing my name and chanting 'You Fat Bastard'.

Jason said, 'Yeah right, you're such a big bloody star, they're really singing your name.'

Jason's sarcasm was misplaced as Conroy continued, 'You won the car, the bloody car! Joe Elliot was just asking me if I had seen you, he's waiting for you in the director's box.'

And he was, along with city hero Dion Dublin. Dion told me later that the first name he had pulled out was fellow player and ex-Villa captain Kevin Richardson, but he knew that he couldn't give it to him as there would have been a riot, so he pulled again and my name came out.

My luck was definitely changing and before you ask – no, I didn't say put it back and draw again, I deserved a change of fortune. I tightened my grip on the keys even harder and smiled. I had half the dream of every Cov kid. I had a Jag.

The other half of the dream is to own a house on Coventry's most exclusive area, the Kenilworth Road. All the houses are set back from the highway, behind a copse, and even though I now joke on the radio that I can afford not to live there, the truth is one day I would like to pull out of a drive on that road knowing that the house in my rearview mirror is all mine.

It's a Coventry thing.

29

From paradise to Luton

1995

Everything was going well. We had two beautiful daughters, a comfortable house and rising audience figures at work. I was convinced we were on our way back up when suddenly we got a visit from the new head of all BBC local radio, a smarmy git called Nigel Chapman.

I'll never forget that first visit as we were all invited into Andy Wright's office to meet this new boss. He sat on the edge of Andy's desk, delicately eating a sausage roll like a cross between Hannibal Lector and Dale Winton. There was an air of menace, mixed with a slight campness, as he told us how he too had started out in local radio.

Upon examination, this boring half anecdote translated into the fact that after Cambridge or Oxford he too had worked at a local station for a week or two before progressing onto the lower reaches of the greasy BBC management pole. He was now on a tour of his local radio empire and he soon buggered off again. I hoped that would be the last we saw of him, but how wrong I was.

When he left Andy muttered to Moz and me, 'He doesn't believe in local radio, he's just doing this job so he can get to London.'

I remember Moz and I laughing at this and calling Andy a twat behind his back because that's exactly what we wanted to do and for Moz it happened soon after. At this point neither of us had any real commitment to Coventry; we had been there, done that and got the T-shirt. That was all in the past. Now, just like Chapman, we wanted to use Coventry and local radio as a stepping-stone to greater things. Ironically a week or so later both of us received a letter from some talent scouts for a new national radio station that was being set up called Talk Radio and we were asked to send off demo tapes.

When I had been promoted to the breakfast show I often wondered if Moz had felt the same resentment towards me as Victoria, but if he had he never showed it. However he didn't need to because a few weeks later he was offered the position of host on the new Talk Radio breakfast show and off he went to London and a mega salary. Andy Wright was brilliant about all this and didn't stand in his way, releasing Moz from his contract without hesitation. Again my respect for Andy went up.

Of course I was jealous of Moz because he had got the break that I wanted and felt I deserved but I had to bite my lip, pat him on the back, and buckle down to making the breakfast show the best I could. The audience figures were going up and the station sound was getting better and better, and in all probability I would have stayed in Coventry for years if Chapman and his henchman hadn't returned a couple of months later and closed the station down.

The news had been leaked to the *Guardian* that the BBC was going to close down CWR and a couple of other local radio stations and Chapman came up in his chauffeur-driven car to deliver or rather confirm the news. He again took up his position on the front of Andy's desk but this time chose not to eat, which was probably a good idea the mood we were all in. He told us that the audience figures didn't justify the costs and that they were going to merge us with BBC WM in Birmingham. It later emerged that he had got this powerful job in the first place by saying he knew how to solve the problem of underperforming stations. He had the genius idea of just closing them down. Problem sorted.

He seemed to take the view – a typical London-centric BBC view – that as Coventry and Birmingham are only 22 miles apart the people must be the same with similar interests and views. But the two cities are millions of mile apart in attitude, allegiances and customs, as any Brummie or Cov kid could have told the BBC if they had bothered to ask. He told us that most jobs would be saved and that people could transfer to Birmingham and that we would maintain our own breakfast show and sports department, but that all the other programmes would come from Birmingham.

It wasn't Wrighty or Conroy's fault that the station was still struggling. The berk who set it up in the first place was to blame from the moment he decided to call it Coventry and Warwickshire and thought you could serve both places equally. This was so incredibly misguided and ill informed and Andy Wright, with the appointment of me and Moz, was in the process of recovering this lost ground. We were now getting it right, the audience was growing alongside the reputation and now Chapman was pulling the rug from under our own and the people of Coventry's feet.

However, Chapman had picked on the wrong station and the wrong city and none of us was willing to take this betrayal by the BBC without a fight. The local Labour MP, Dave Nellist, got a campaign going and a blind man, David Kelly, and his wife took the BBC to high court to try and get them to reverse the decision.

Meanwhile I had Chapman on the breakfast show to explain his decision to our growing army of listeners. He was meant to be on for ten minutes but I kept him squirming in his seat for over an hour while everyone from the directors of Coventry City

Football Club to the Bishop and even Stuart Linnell, who was managing director of the local commercial radio station Mercia Sound, lambasted him. His PR people, back in Birmingham, were phoning and shouting down the line to tell Gaunty to get him off but my magnificent production team and I ignored them. My job was safe – he wanted to keep my breakfast show – but to be quite honest I didn't want or see a future in being just a satellite of poxy Birmingham.

Dad was really concerned about the closure of the radio station and was worried that I would be back to square one. I told him over a Sunday lunch at his place and a couple of bottles of wine that there was nothing to worry about as my job was safe and that anyhow I was so good on the radio someone else would come in for me.

'Oh yeah, yeah I know that son, but those bastards, those puffs at the BBC, you can't trust them. Just watch your bloody back, that's all I'm saying. Remember you've got to think of Lisa and the two kids now too.'

I appreciated his concern and the two bottles of wine were significant because I had started to feel more relaxed at his place and had decided that I wasn't going to suffer in silence at his house. If I could share my life and be myself on the radio with thousands of listeners I sure as hell wasn't going to play someone else at his dinner table. He seemed to accept this and as a result I actually began to look forward to visiting him.

Meanwhile there were demonstrations, petitions, questions in the House and eventually the judicial review but unfortunately it was all in vain and Chapman and the BBC got their way.

Years later I was at an awards ceremony, called the Gillard's, whose aim was to celebrate local BBC radio, and Chapman was there as a guest. He was no longer running local radio and there were new people in charge, Andy Griffee and Pat Loughery, both of whom I would have arguments and fall outs with later in my career but both of whom passionately believe in local radio as I do.

I was getting into a lift after the do and after picking up another award and Chapman jumped in. He recognised me and said, 'Hi Jon.'

'Hi Nigel, I'm surprised to see you here.'

'Oh why?'

'Well mate, this is a celebration of all that's brilliant in local radio and you, you cunt, you single-handedly tried to wreck it.'

He didn't know what to say, everybody else was silent in the lift, suppressing giggles until he got out at his floor and slunk off to his bedroom. Then the lift erupted with laughter and congratulations.

Although I now work on a national commercial radio station I still passionately believe in the need for BBC local radio. The BBC is big and bloated but local radio does something that no commercial company would ever be able to afford to sanction. It gives a voice to the masses, the great number of people who pay their licence fee, who can now have their say about the issues that affect them.

Local radio *should* be the front door of the BBC, the place where people can access the other activities. So when I attack the bloated broadcasting corporation, it is not local radio that is in my sights.

However, BBC Coventry was dead. Most of the staff moved to Birmingham, including Andy Conroy who became second in charge over there, and I started to do the breakfast show on the opt-out station. Following me now at ten from Birmingham was consumer champion Ed Doolan, the man whom Andy Wright had sent me to study about a year ago. Doolan was wary of me and wary of the Coventry audience. I was very popular and he knew that it was better to have me in his tent, pissing out, rather than outside pissing in. So the wily old fox invited Lisa and me over for dinner.

We arrived at his house and were ushered in past all the pictures of him with famous people; it was the broadcast equivalent of Banger Walsh's office. He even had a picture of himself with Nelson Mandela, but fair play to him, he was massively popular and a household name to the Brummies – Doolan not Mandela!

We sat down and the fat Aussie introduced us to his young attractive wife, Chrissie, who offered us drinks before we went out to the restaurant. Then Lisa made the fatal mistake of asking Ed how he first got the job on WM. Twenty-eight minutes later with no supplementary questions, pauses for breath or interruptions, he finished his answer. We were surely in the presence of a radio genius! I decided there and then one day I would take his job and wipe the floor with his audience figures.

Andy Conroy booked me in for a couple of weeks stand-in shifts for the Birmingham show and I thought, here we go, move over Doolan. Then completely out of the blue David Robey phoned me up and asked me to come to Luton.

I knew Robey because he used to be second in charge at WM. He had recently been moved to Luton to have one last go at turning it round and getting it an audience before it faced the Chapman chop. I'll give him his due, Robey came up with a radical plan. He decided to turn it into an all talk station and not play any records at all. He had nothing to lose, I could open my bedroom window, shout and more people would be listening to me than that radio station's audience at the time. He wanted me to do three stand-in shifts on the drivetime show and I said yes because that meant double bubble for the week. I had just won the Jaguar in the raffle so I belted down the M1 in the motor and did the gig.

The first night as I went into the studio the producer told me, 'Don't expect any calls, people in Luton don't like to phone.'

The red light went on, I attacked a councillor, said the number fifteen times and the phone lines lit up like a Christmas tree. The 'producer' sat on the other side of the glass, reading a film magazine and didn't put any calls through. I got to the first travel break and went through to him.

'What's going on?'

'Travel and then it's the film review with me.'

'What about the callers?'

'What about them?'

'Well, mate, where I come from all those lights on that switchboard represent callers who want to talk, how about putting a few of them through.'

'No, we do the phone-in during the last hour.'

'You might, you lazy bastard, but I don't, so get your finger out and let the callers talk.'

Rather grudgingly, lardy arse put down his mag and put the callers through.

The show finished at seven and by five past Robey said, 'Let's not beat around the bush, would you like a job?'

He offered me half a breakfast show. I was to start at eight and finish at ten, five days a week. We argued about the money for a few days and then I decided to take the gig; it was more money and more security as he offered a two-year contract. I kept it quiet from Conroy until I had signed the contract and I regret that because he said, 'Well done, but I always thought that you would go to a bigger station next.'

I don't know if he meant he was lining me up for the breakfast slot in Birmingham but the die was already cast. I was going to be wafted from paradise to Luton.

30

Forgiveness

1995

I might have been leaving Coventry radio but I had no intention of leaving the city. I decided that, because I had the Jag for another nine months or so, I would commute and see how it went before moving my young family.

I pulled into the car park of BBC Three Counties in Luton in my Jaguar looking like Billy Big Boots after already alienating most of Robey's management team during the three-day stand-in. I parked the car and an hour later got the traditional Luton welcome when some yobbo smashed the driver's window and nicked my radio.

The welcome from the staff inside was almost as friendly. My reputation had obviously preceded me and they were frosty, to say the least. The breakfast duo was especially wary as they had lost a couple of hours to me and the consumer champion, an Irish version of Doolan, was also on his toes. The only person who was genuinely welcoming that first week was an old cockney guy called John Pilgrim who was the early morning presenter.

John was to become my closest friend, supporter, mentor and fan and is still the best sounding board I have for my radio ideas and ambitions. I nicknamed him 'The Old Man Not a Boy' because he was about 55 when we met and unlike most people in radio he had actually had a life outside the media world. He had run a borstal and so empathised, sympathised and criticised my tales of woe about being in care and he never has and never will tolerate any of my tantrums. He had the guts to tell me when I was wrong or had gone over the top with a caller or one of my team and he acted as a bit of a father figure to me.

More importantly he was as knowledgeable about the three counties of Beds, Bucks and Herts as I was about Coventry and in the early days he was a great help by whispering how to pronounce the names of local places into my headphones while I was on-air. He then started hanging about and giving me funny one-liners to react to the callers and he was so generous because he never wanted to be credited for them on air. He just seemed to get his satisfaction from me getting the laugh off the punter. He also didn't mind if I ignored his suggestions, he was only bothered about the sound on air. In simple terms Pilgrim was a great supporter, he spent hours talking to me about the show and just like Andy Wright he believed in me.

In between eating greasy spoon breakfasts in the local café and chain-smoking, he would bull me up and encourage me to go further, push the envelope that little bit more on air. The same thing that happened in Coventry happened in Luton and within months Robey bowed to the inevitable and gave me the whole breakfast show. I now started at seven and finished at eleven. This meant I followed on directly from John Pilgrim's early-riser show so he became an integral part of my team as well and the audience got to know him as The Old Man Not a Boy.

At this point Lee 'Rat Boy' Agnew was producing the show. Lee got his nickname because he was a little runt of a man who looked like the archetypal football hooligan. The sort of kid you see on the front of the *Sun* described as a 'feral youth' – you know, the kids who end up getting rewarded with a safari holiday by some left-wing liberal lesbian of a social worker. But underneath those looks and the blue Harrington jacket was a great producer with a fast brain and quick wit. Lee had only just graduated but he had a natural ability to produce. He was a quick learner and totally dedicated to the show and to me.

The other member of the team, and one of the most vital, was the phone operator, the Japanese sniper, Luton girl Lorraine Maguire. She was short and could barely see over the glass partition hence the nickname. She had graduated with some poncy creative media degree from the University of Birmingham and had returned to her hometown to get some real work experience.

We hit it off straight away and eventually she graduated to being a co-producer with Lee. 'Little Orphan Amy' took Lorraine's place on the phones, so called because on air I depicted her as a young girl with no family and definitely no boyfriend. The team was complete and over the months we all played up to the characters. We were still doing a news show but with loads of interaction and lots of what Conroy would call 'light and shade'. So we could do the heavy stuff and then have a laugh.

The audience lapped it up. There were a few ground rules: you couldn't break the conventions, for instance Amy couldn't suddenly contradict the picture that the audience had of her or Lorraine couldn't say I was lying when I made up that her boyfriend was a gay boy called Quentin Gervase Dechatterly-Decasulay Smith. It was a form of zoo radio, a bit of a circus but with only one ringmaster.

We were aided and abetted in this creation by the fact that Robey only stayed for a few months after I took over the breakfast show; he went off to be the manager of WM in Birmingham. Everyone expected me to follow him but he never offered me a show, probably because of the run-ins we had had in the few months he was in charge. The bottom line is he didn't really get my show and I never showed him any real respect or gratitude for the break he gave me. In essence we developed a 'hate–hate' relationship. This is all the more bizarre because we have worked together on and off for over ten years during our careers and I would say that I have saved him his job on at least two occasions and he would say he made me a star!

With him safely out of the way we had a succession of managers who largely let me get on with it, mostly because the audience figures were rocketing. When I arrived at the station they were in single figures. I bet the regional manager, David Holdsworth (nicknamed Reg), by the time I left they would have hit 20 per cent. I was right but I'm still waiting for him to pay up. The rest of the station, apart from the already successful consumer show, seemed to be influenced by my style and the whole station began to sound like a unit. Robey, in his short tenure, had also managed to get rid of most of the dead wood while he was around so we had a fairly young team that grew up together.

I spent five years at Luton and they were probably the happiest and most fulfilling parts of my career so far. I was earning good money, had great mates and it's no exaggeration to say that the audience adored me. The local paper, the *Luton News*, offered me a job as a columnist, after I suggested the idea to them, and I received the princely sun of 25 quid a week to rant and rave about local councillors and national issues. I learnt a great deal from this experience and it stood me in good stead when I finally pushed through the doors of the *Sun*, years later.

The Jag had been returned after the first nine months in Luton so I was now making the trip in my beaten-up red Fiesta, which by now had gone round the clock. Every morning I would start it up and the fan belt would slip, squeal and whine, a bit like my listeners – only joking! I would hurtle down the M1, usually with a raging hangover, arriving at the studio five minutes before I was due to go on.

I've always liked to arrive just before the start of a show otherwise I find you have all the arguments and discussions with your production team and then your brain turns to cotton wool when you get on air. I prefer to have the rows and work out the arguments live on air with the listeners; it's more exciting and immediate that way. Likewise I'm much more interested in what the listeners want to say than the experts or the suits. Of course you need guests but the listeners are the most important element of the show.

I also tell new presenters never stay with a boring call or go to a crap caller or a regular just because you haven't got another caller on the board, because one thing is for sure: one boring caller will only get you another fruit loop. You have to trust yourself to pull the right trigger points to get them to call and if they don't call it's not because people in Luton or wherever don't like to phone, it's because you are a shit radio presenter.

I was also massively helped in Luton by the fact that the town was very similar to Coventry and the people were alike. It had the same ethnic mix, the same sort of industry, and the same attitudes. I knew these people. I was from these people and I knew exactly how to entertain, inform, educate and goad them into reaction. Man alive, it was exciting but the commuting was killing me. It was time to move and time to get back into the property market.

I liked Luton but not enough to live there so Lisa and I found a new build house on the outskirts of Milton Keynes. Over the months we watched it being built I shared the excitement and frustration with my listeners. Even sharing the initial house search with them too, they were fully involved. This is a massively important part of phone-in. If you are going to ask people to tell you about their lives, their innermost feelings, then you have to be able and willing to share yours.

So my life and that of my family became public property. As the girls grew up they learnt this and they understood that the little old lady who stopped us in the supermarket and wanted to talk to us, because she felt she knew us, was important and not a pain. She was a friend and should be treated as one. The same with autographs: I love people recognising me and wanting to talk to me and get a photo and a signature. Who wouldn't? It's a validation that they love you, care for you and most importantly of all will be loyal to you and listen to you.

There is no place for false modesty in a talk radio broadcaster. I know I am good at my job but I also know that I need good callers to make the show and to attract those callers you have to work and work at your act. As Andy Wright said, you have to build up the hours on the clock, you must always be prepared to expect the unexpected and be ready to go with the flow and chuck out the running order if a caller comes on and starts a debate or tells a story that is of more interest. There was a classic example of this in Luton when an old fella called Albert rang up.

We were discussing paedophilia and the debate was getting pretty aggressive when I opened the fader and said, 'Albert good morning.'

'Hi Gaunty, it's Albert here.'

'Yeah I know that, what do you want to say?'

'Well, Jon, I'm 74.'

'Who put this old fart up?'

I was shouting through to Lee and Lorraine in the production studio using the pre-fade button on my desk so that I could talk to them without the caller hearing. I was furious. I was desperately trying to drag down the average age of the caller and they had put up this silly old duffer.

I was effing and blinding and glaring at Rat Boy when suddenly Albert said, 'Well, Jon, you know like you're talking about abuse, well when I was five three blokes took me into a field and raped me . . .'

I stopped swearing. I let go of the button slowly and listened to Albert. He proceeded, over the next twenty minutes, to tell a horrific tale about how he was raped by these three men. He didn't go into graphic detail. He didn't have to. The tone of his voice and his hesitant delivery spoke volumes. He told me and of course my thousands of listeners that he had never told anybody about this rape for the best part of seventy years. He hadn't even told his wife who had died twenty years ago.

He told me that the secret had ruined his relationship not only with his wife but also with his son. He said that he never felt comfortable being alone and bathing his boy and he had not managed to tell his son about the rape before he too had died. It was an incredibly moving story and perfectly described the horror and life sentence that is handed down to victims, or survivors, as I prefer to call them, of childhood abuse. This is why I firmly believe the bastards should swing.

At times like this you can almost hear the audience putting down their teacups, or staying in their car, not able to get out and go to work in case they missed anything that Albert was to say. It was true radio magic, tragic and uplifting in equal measure. It was a moment that radio was made for, the intimacy of one voice speaking to another, and the anonymity of a caller sharing a terrible secret with everyone.

The difficulty with a call like this is, however, what to say when the caller has finished the tale because whatever you come out with always sounds likes a platitude.

'Albert, I mean, thanks for sharing that with us—'

'That's all right Jon, as I said I've never told anyone before like.'

'Well, mate, I can tell you I'm honoured that you shared that with me. Thanks.'

I was just about to pull the fader down on this man and go to a newsbreak when the most amazing thing happened. After telling me and about a hundred thousand listeners a tale that he hadn't even told his wife and family, he suddenly said, 'That's all right Jon but before I go, could I have a go at your competition?'

There was a pause. Then Lorraine and Lee laughed on the other side of the glass and I had to suppress a giggle myself but it was a truly incredible moment. This man had shared his most intimate secret with me on the radio because he trusted me and knew me because he had listened to me every day; he trusted me so much that he saw no contradiction in then wanting to have a go at the competition as well. It was the moment when I really realised that I had made it as a talk jock. I had made that one-to-one connection that Andy Wright had always talked about. It remains one of the defining moments in my career.

It also made me finally realise that I had to make my peace with my own dad. I didn't want any deathbed reconciliation scene where as he dies he tells me he's sorry. I didn't even need him to say sorry, I just wanted us to be mates. It was in the past, I wanted to forgive him and move on. By forgiving him I realised that I could release myself from my past. I was a survivor just like Albert.

Albert was one individual call that made a difference both in my broadcasting and personal life and the day the hospice was attacked and vandalised was the other. We were in the middle of another show and I was just about to interview another boring councillor when a woman phoned in and said did I know that the local children's hospice had been vandalised.

The people of Luton had been raising the best part of three million pounds to build a hospice on the outskirts of town and now some yobbos had smashed all the windows that had just been installed. I shouted for Lee to get the hospice manager on the phone and he detailed the damage to us, saying that the cost or replacements would be at least ten grand. I decided there and then to get our listeners to start a fund to raise the cash to replace them. Of course, according to BBC guidelines I should have asked permission to do this but bollocks to that, this was important and needed immediate action.

Then some stupid woman rang in and said it was the hospice's own fault because they should have had a nightwatchman. I lost it completely with this caller. I shouted her down, calling her stupid, thick and insensitive and told her, 'Of course it's not their bloody fault it's the kids' fault, you stupid woman.' There was a right ding-dong on the phones and a load of listeners called for me to get the sack but luckily many more got behind me and within days we had raised the ten grand to repair the windows.

This led to a relationship between the hospice and myself and eventually to that dreadful moment when they asked me to come up and visit the place. I hated the idea, mainly because I was scared of death. Being the father of two young girls, the last thing I wanted to see was dying kids and I dreaded having to confront every parent's worst nightmare.

However, Lee, Lorraine and I eventually did go up the centre and it was one of those life-changing moments because the hospice director made the point that a hospice is not a place of dying but a place of living. It is a place where families can get respite care and where children can find others in a similar circumstance and can enjoy their life. It was the beginning of a long relationship and although we went on to raise loads more money it still breaks my heart that the hospice movement in this country is chronically underfunded by central government and if it weren't for the generosity of people like my listeners many of them would face financial collapse.

My involvement with the Children's Hospice led me to meet another older man who was going to have a massive influence on my personal life and who probably doesn't realise how much help he gave me. His name was John Richardson and he was the Bishop of Bedford. I got to know him both from the charity work and from having him on the show as a guest. He also became a regular listener and right from the first moment I met him we just seemed to hit it off. I'm not religious, despite being brought up as a Christian, but this man had a spirituality that even I could recognise and a calmness about him that I envied.

I had got involved in a spat with a local newspaper that seemed to enjoy trying to take me down a peg or two in their downmarket rag. If I'm honest I quite enjoyed being the local celeb and this paper – which was desperately trying to be Bedford's answer to the *Sun*, without the resources, skill, intellect, wit or charm – loved taking potshots at me. They had got hold of a story that I had been given a brand new Vauxhall Frontera car and they reckoned that this contravened BBC guidelines on impartiality. They were basically suggesting that I was on the take. They doorstepped me outside the radio station as I got into the car and one of their hacks shouted out, 'Isn't earning eighty grand enough without getting a freebie, Gaunty?'

'Are you jealous, you no mark?' I snarled as I tried to run him over as I left the car park.

Later they arrived at my house and a big fat sweaty slob of a snapper took a flash photo of me as I opened the door. They splashed this all over their feature the following week to suggest that I was hiding from them when actually I had shouted, 'Get off my property, you fat bastard!'

The thing is, these parochial prats had only got half of the tale and if they had done their homework better they would have had an even bigger story.

They were right: I did have a free Vauxhall but it was hardly a secret as half of Beds, Herts and Bucks knew about it and so did the BBC. Just before we had moved down to Milton Keynes I had been involved in a bad crash on the M1. A transit van went into the back of me. I had phoned Dad from the service station where I was towed to. What with the combination of the traffic noise and his failing hearing I had to shout and repeat what had happened to me before he could give me some advice about what to do. But he was seriously concerned that I was okay and even offered to get in his car and come straight down to meet me. I told him there was no need as the car was still drivable for the moment. He then gave me all the coppers' advice about what details I had to get off the other driver. He really wanted to help and it felt great that he was so concerned.

Meanwhile, on air, Pilgrim had been holding the fort, and there was also genuine concern from my listeners when The Old Man Not a Boy had told them I had been involved in a car crash. When I eventually arrived we discussed the crash on air and this led into a discussion about insurance, road safety and motorway expansion. Again I was using the personal story to get into news and current events. It isn't rocket science but you would be amazed how many so-called talk jocks don't understand this basic technique. The discussion also led onto whether I should move down to the area permanently and so the on-air and off-air saga, or soap opera, of finding a house began. It was location, location, location live on the radio.

Out of the blue the Vauxhall press office rang up and offered to loan me a car while mine was off the road. All of this was done on air and I accepted their offer. I knew the boys at Vauxhall because we had been involved in the same charity projects and also they were the town's main employer and they knew, of course, that most of their workforce listened to me. In fact the chairman of Vauxhall, Nick Reilly, told me that if he ever wanted to get a message over to his workers he would rather appear on my show than the *Today* programme as they or their families were all Gaunty fans. This link was to prove costly to Nick years later when General Motors tried to close Vauxhall down because of course those very same workers were going to air their grievances with me.

Anyway, back to the story. By the end of the show Vauxhall had delivered a brand new Frontera. Lisa and I loved it. Environmental green jerks should skip the next bit and go and get a tofuburger. The four by four was brilliant and Lisa adored it; she loved the fact that the driving position was so high up and that she could just open the back door and throw everything in from the pushchairs, kids' toys, bikes and all the shopping. She also felt safe in it and, although the only time it went off road was in Tesco's car park, she saw no reason why she shouldn't drive it around town. It was a fashion statement, but so what? In a democracy surely you can earn your money and spend it on whatever you want, can't you? That's why she's now the proud owner of a Volvo DX90.

After a couple of weeks Vauxhall told me to keep the motor for six months, so I did, with the full knowledge of the BBC. However, it was two years later when the paper got hold of the story and by this time I must have had about five or six brand new cars. I used to joke that Vauxhall changed them when the ashtrays got full even though I didn't smoke. It was a nice perk and everybody was happy. It didn't compromise me in any way and anybody who thought it did would have had any doubts dispelled when I covered the closure of Vauxhall and won all my radio awards a few months later.

The paper suggested that the car was a clear contravention of BBC producer guidelines and in true BBC style the management had the backbone of a blancmange and instead of supporting me and telling the little paper to bugger off they made me return the car, even though I was a freelance and even though they knew about it. As a consequence they gave me a pay rise to make up for the shortfall.

It was pure hypocrisy that allowed the BBC to maintain the moral high ground while making me look like a grubby freebie grabber. It was not the first time and it certainly wouldn't be the last time that the Corporation would save its own skin at my expense.

I opened a letter about a week after the car had gone back. It was a card from the Bishop of Bedford in which he had written in Latin the words, '*Noli nothis permittere te terere*' which translates as, 'Don't let the bastards grind you down.' He had also enclosed a book that was going to change my life, *The Railwayman* by Eric Lomax.

You must buy this book, as it will change your life too. It's a story of how Eric was captured by the Japanese and forced to work on the railways during World War II. He was brutally tortured and fifty years later he decided to find one of those involved in his torture and kill him. However, at the last moment instead of murdering the brute he forgives him. The reason he forgives him is that he discovers that the torturer's life has been ruined and dominated by the actions he witnessed during the war. He has tried to make amends by working with survivors' groups and has attempted to promote reconciliation but he has been haunted by the brutal torture that others inflicted on British troops and he witnessed.

The Bishop had sent me this book because there were enormous lessons to be learned and applied to my life. The abuse and fractured childhood I experienced as a result of Dad's selfish actions was of course nothing compared to the suffering of Eric Lomax. However, I felt many of the emotions and had many of the attitudes that Eric had held onto for years.

Make no mistake, what Dad did to me was wrong and there is no way I would ever abandon my children in the way he did. However, I'm a modern man and I'm living in a different age and different society. He had no help, no guidance or support. And I suddenly realised that he had had to live with the consequence of his actions as much as I had. He carried the same guilt, the same memories and no amount of apologies or crying could ever alter the fact that by his selfish actions he put me through hell. The result was that I was damaged. I had the most incredibly short temper and until a couple of years after the birth of my two daughters I was still that little boy who couldn't trust anyone but himself. I was cold and distant and suspicious of anyone and everyone who professed their love to me.

Now I realised that this was a result of me allowing Dad and his actions to dominate and ruin my life. I always thought that I didn't deserve my success and happiness and that at any time, just like Mum dying or being put into care, something or someone would again pull the rug from under me and I would be on my own again. It was ridiculous, almost a form of self-hatred. This irrational fear, although based on bitter experience, was holding me back professionally but much more importantly mentally and personally. It was even affecting my relationships with those I was meant to love most, my wife and two daughters. I don't know how Lisa put up with me because I wasn't a particularly nice bloke even if I was successful.

For years Lisa had been urging me to have it out with him, to make him realise what a selfish bastard he had been and what enormous damage he had done to me. But this book, this one little book, made me realise there was no point in staging a big emotional scene. What good would come of me shouting and bawling at him telling him in explicit detail what happened to me in the children's home? I might have got some satisfaction out of it – what's the trendy word, closure – but it would have just crushed him, a 65-year-old bloke. Because that's the point, he couldn't make up for what he had done. It was too late, in fact it was too late the moment he pushed us out to Jock and Olwyn's.

I was also determined that I wasn't going to have some kind of Oprah Winfrey moment where he breaks down and says he's sorry and I let him off the hook by pretending to accept his apology and say everything is okay. Because it wasn't bloody okay, but I was willing to forgive him. He had made a mistake, he had fucked up, but what was the point of continuing the pain? If I released him from the necessity of saying sorry I could release myself. For fuck's sake I was a 38-year-old father of two kids. I was no longer the little boy lost outside Wilko's office. I was not a victim, I was a survivor. I was a success and I decided to love Dad and release him and at the same time release myself, and as a by-product make us both better men.

I now look at other families who carry a grudge for a lifetime. What's the point? Who wins in that situation? Absolutely no one. Like a cancer the hatred, the anger, eats away at your soul and it doesn't matter who caused the problem, who delivered the first blow, you have to let it go. If a simple man like Eric Lomax could forgive a man who was complicit in torturing him, then I could surely forgive Dad.

The forgiveness, however, was going to be unspoken and it was going to be completely in my head and in my actions. I wasn't going to prostitute myself on an altar of emotion and bullshit. I wasn't even going to tell him that I had forgiven him because that would lead to tears and the apologies and I needed neither. I was just going to love him and hope that he could love me and do you know what? He could and he did.

31

Curry on Gaunty

'Gaunty, will you please stop farting!'

Lee 'Rat Boy' Agnew was getting fed up in the back of the van. We both had stinking hangovers and the curry from the night before was making its presence known. We were parked outside the Vauxhall car plant in Luton. It was six in the morning.

The day before I had been rehearsing for the pantomime in St Albans when I had received an urgent call from Rat Boy to come back to the studio as Vauxhall had announced that they were going to close down their plant in the town.

I had been rehearsing with Vicki Michele from *'Allo 'Allo* and it was my first full-scale panto. I had been engaged as the local celebrity and I loved it. It was another validation of my growing status in the area and I had been enjoying the experience immensely.

The call to hotfoot it back to the station was also a clear sign of my importance and standing not only in the radio station but

239

in the town as well. All normal programmes had been suspended and Mark Norman, the manager, had called me in to host a special one-off drivetime phone-in show so that the town and workers could talk about the closure. I went on air at six that evening and the phonelines were in meltdown. Don't forget Vauxhall was the town's main employer and everybody either worked there or knew someone who did.

People were crying on the phones and others were simply angry but one thing was for sure: the town of Luton was not going to take it lying down. The decision had been taken by the parent company in the States and there was little the local management could do about it.

Straight after the show Rat Boy, Mark and myself decided that the next day we should do a special breakfast show live from outside the gates at Vauxhall and we should start at an earlier time of six in the morning.

That night I stayed in Luton in a hotel and had been out for a few bevvies with Lee, Lorraine and the production team to plan the guests that we would need for the next morning, hence the smell in the radio van as we went on air at six. The first hour or so went quite smoothly and we had the usual suspects on air: trade union leaders, councillors and car industry experts and then the most amazing thing began to happen. We started taking calls from inside the plant where lads were telling us that they were pushing car bodies off the track.

It was now obvious that there was going to be trouble. Lee dispatched one of our more experienced reporters down to the Vauxhall administration centre, Griffin House, with a satellite phone to try and get a word with the management. Meanwhile I told one of our youngest lads, Toby Friedner, to get down among the workers and just use his mobile to pick up anything he could.

The van suddenly rocked as a few lads banged on the roof and shouted 'Gaunty! Gaunty! Gaunty!' I was talking to a worker inside the factory who told me that they were all going to walk out and march on Griffin House and with that we suddenly saw thousands of the lads walk down the road and past us. I switched to Steve Swann who described the mob as they approached and Toby got among them and started asking them to talk directly to me on the mobile.

Meanwhile Lorraine was desperately trying to reach the management who by this time were trapped inside their own building. The whole team played a blinder and it was just one of those days that you dream about where nobody dropped the ball. I eventually got a management person to air and as I was interviewing him you could hear the mob outside. I crossed to Steve Swann who was outside the glass atrium of the admin building just as the mob surged forward and Steve was pushed into the building.

He then did the most difficult thing on radio: *he kept his mouth shut* and let the noise of the crowd paint the picture.

The lads were shouting, 'We want Reilly, we want Reilly.' Nick Reilly was the chief executive who was trapped in his office. The listeners at home knew that Steve and the mob were now in the building because the acoustic had changed. Then Toby got a worker to speak to me as he too was pushed by the surge of the crowd into the building. He then instinctively did the right thing and shut up but held his phone in the air to capture the atmosphere.

Back at base Lorraine was playing a blinder, mixing in the various sound sources and then she bellowed in my ear on talkback that we had Reilly on the line. I spoke to him live on the radio as the crowd fell silent and listened. He agreed to come out and talk to them if they went outside of the building and after a few minutes they did.

I was sweating; it had been the most exciting and dangerous piece of live broadcasting I had ever been involved in.

Rat Boy looked at me and said, 'Gaunty, not again.'

'Shut up, Lee, we've just won a Sony.'

32

Three gold stars

The phone rang, Lisa put on the light and lent over to pick it up, it was about half ten at night.

'Lisa, either someone's died or I've been nominated for a Sony.'

She raised her eyebrows and handed the phone over. It was the Station Manager, Mark Norman, I was wrong. We hadn't been nominated for one Sony at all. We had been nominated for three.

It was the most amazing turnaround because only a year earlier I thought that I was going to get the sack after beating up a former colleague at the same event.

The Sony Awards are often described as the Oscars of the radio world and are dished out every May in a lavish ceremony at the Grosvenor House Hotel. The previous year I had been nominated and on the night everyone in the room fully expected us to walk away with the Gold Award but it was not to be and I was actually beaten by Nicky Campbell and my old colleague from Coventry, Victoria Derbyshire, who were now presenting the breakfast show on BBC Five Live.

I was bitterly disappointed and very pissed. The event dragged on forever and despite reassuring Lisa I would take it steady, the nerves got the better of me and I had consumed a skinful.

Earlier on in the evening an ex-colleague from Three Counties radio when I first arrived years earlier had come over to our table and wished us all the best. I even had my photo taken with him. He was a bit full of himself because he thought he had made it as he was now producing on Five Dead.

He wandered off and I didn't think any more about him until after the awards when he came back and said, 'Bad luck, Gaunty, but don't worry eh. You're just a working class twat who's going nowhere.'

He then staggered off.

I paused. Then I took off my dinner jacket and slowly walked across the floor of the great room. I tapped him on the shoulder, he turned round and I smacked him in the face. According to the little local rag that had tried to stitch me up about the Vauxhall car I then staggered back and 'fell into the lap of pregnant TV star Ulrika Johnson' which would have been an amazing story if it was true and a fucking miracle because I had seen her leave an hour earlier.

The actual truth was a lot messier as he fell from the first punch. I jumped on him and put my knees on his chest and gave him three more digs.

The radio station had booked a limousine to take us to the event and all the way back Lisa gave me the cold shoulder. It was like a broken TV, we had pictures but no sound. The next morning I woke up and fully expected to get the sack or at least a severe reprimand. However it would appear that many people in the BBC disliked this bloke more than me and although Mark had to go through the motions of telling me off, many people thought that he had asked for it by insulting me.

Dad laughed like a drain when I told him about it and said, 'I did the same thing to an inspector years ago when the pompous prick insulted your mum. I followed him into the bogs and gave him a couple of slaps. Sometimes it's the only thing they understand, son.'

This year I promised Lisa there would be no fisticuffs as I wouldn't drink at all and as I sat down at the table the regional boss, Reggie Holdsworth, poured me a large mineral water.

We had just come back from a superb holiday and I had a great tan and all through the break I had been fantasising about winning a Sony and perhaps getting that break out of Luton. I had been there for the best part of five years and although I was still enjoying it, I wanted to move to a bigger station and play with a larger audience. I had been doing a Friday night show right across the region which I had enjoyed but that had been pulled because of costs so I felt with the audience at 20 per cent it was time to move on.

Before the Sony nominations were even announced, Keith Beech, the boss of BBC WM, had approached me and asked if I would like to do a Saturday morning show in Birmingham. Keith was a fan and really understood and admired what I did on the radio and I jumped at the chance. It was a return to my old patch and also WM was a massive station, I also clearly understood that if it went well there was plenty of opportunities for a daily gig. I hoped Mr Doolan was sweating.

Before the awards were announced I told Lisa I was just going off for a wee, which I did do, but via a mate's table so that I could grab a quick stiffener. On the way back from the toilets, Bill Ridley approached me from Talksport. Bill was their programme controller and he congratulated me on my three nominations and wished me all the best for the actual awards and then asked if we could have lunch, as they were interested in me working for them.

I said of course and walked back to the table and whispered the good news to Lisa, I went to pour myself a glass of red and she diverted me to the water. The awards started and the first time my name was read out as the winner was just unbelievable. I kissed Lisa, took a massive swig of wine out of someone else's glass and almost ran up to the stage to take my award.

They played some audio from the show and it was quite humbling to hear the voices of the now redundant Vauxhall workers again after five or six months. I thanked my team and then of course thanked the most important person, a man who couldn't be there that night, and the man who first believed in me, Andy Wright.

I remembered what he had said to me that day after I gave him that Coombe Abbey tape. 'Jon, when you get to London you'll be made.'

I tried to phone Dad but couldn't get a signal and before I knew it I was back on the stage with Lorraine and Lee picking up another Gold Award. When they called me up for the third time I made some crack about whether I should I just stay there, and then wandered back to my table to get drunk with my mates.

The Gold Awards I actually won that night were: News Coverage Award, Breakfast News & Talk Award and News Broadcaster Award. I beat the *Today* programme for Best Breakfast Show and John Humphrys for News Broadcaster and in the news coverage award the Vauxhall closure beat Five Live's coverage of the Paris Concorde crash – but I don't like to brag!

Later that evening I had my photo taken with George Martin, the Beatles producer, who had also been awarded with a Sony that evening and I couldn't resist taking the mick. I had just done a one-man tour of the three counties, with John Pilgrim supporting me, and I had gone down a storm. One of the theatres we played was Cleo Laine's place, The Stables, in Milton Keynes. I had sold it out but the previous week George had done a lecture there and only sold 75 per cent of the tickets.

'George, they call you the fifth Beatle, is that right?'

'Yeah.'

'And John Lennon said they were bigger than Jesus, yeah?'

He smiled. He knew where this was going.

'Well I sold out and you didn't so that means . . .'

The cameras flashed.

George shook my hand.

I had made it.

Two days later when the hangover had almost subsided I had a meeting with the boss of all local BBC radio, Andy Griffee, in Luton. He gave me an immediate £10,000 bonus and congratulated me and said he was looking forward to hearing me on WM on Saturdays.

I thanked him for the money and the praise but said that obviously I now wanted to move on. I was completely straight with him and told him that Talksport had approached me but that I would be interested in listening to an offer from him. He understood where I was coming from. Later that day Keith Beech phoned and asked if I would still be coming to WM on Saturdays to which I replied, 'Of course, I'm a man of my word.'

The Sonys hadn't changed anything. He replied that he would like me to come full time and take over his breakfast show. I was flattered, I liked him and I would have liked that challenge. However, a couple of top BBC bosses had other ideas.

Robey had moved to BBC London a year or two ago and was struggling to turn around the station's fortunes and increase its pathetically small audience. Pat Loughery, who was the Director of the Nations & Regions for the BBC, thought I would be the ideal person to kick the audience into life. Robey wasn't so keen and, as I understand, he had to be told by his bosses that he was having me on his station whether he liked it or not.

They came up with a package that meant I could work in London in the week and Birmingham on Saturdays. This suited me fine as it meant I always had the security of the Midlands if the London gig didn't work out. To be honest I wasn't sure if my act would work there because I didn't think I could fully rely on the support of Robey and because the rest of the output was pretty dire.

I had a meeting with him where instead of offering me the mid-morning slot he put me on at twelve. This didn't really worry me because after seven years of getting up early I was looking forward to the lie-in and the massive pay rise. Plus I knew that if it worked he would have to bow to the usual pressure and move me up the schedule and pay me even more.

33

The day the world changed

'Jon put Sky on and don't say this on air but a plane's just gone into the Twin Towers.'

It was my producer Kath Malandri shouting in my head-phones. I didn't know what she was talking about, but as the TV flickered into life I saw another aeroplane emerge out of the clear blue sky, turn and fly straight into a massive skyscraper. I had never been to New York and didn't even know what the Twin Towers were but it was obvious from these first few seconds of footage that this was New York and that America was under attack.

It was September 11, 2001 and I was on the air in London doing my new phone-in show. I had been in London for only a few months and was only just beginning to get to grips with both my team and my audience.

Robey had been doubtful that my act would work in London and was also concerned that I didn't understand the ethnic and racial diversity of London. I thought he was talking crap; I mean

I came from Coventry, had worked in Luton and I knew about diversity or so I thought. But to his credit he was right; London is a different place to the rest of the UK and just like New York, which I was to visit six months later, it was almost a different country to the rest of Great Britain as the Big Apple is to the rest of the States.

When I first got to London I had a week shadowing the guy whose job I was to take and after just one day I felt embarrassed for him and slightly awkward. He was trying to do phone-in but didn't have a clue how to do it and nobody was helping him. This bloke wouldn't get a caller if he was manning a sex line. The show was painfully dry and boring. If the callers even reached double figures they almost cracked open a bottle of champagne, it was embarrassing to listen to and even more painful to sit and watch him die on air for three hours each day. I was relieved when Robey suggested that my new producer, Kath, who was also producing this pile of car accident radio should take me on a taxi trip round London so that I could get a feel for how the whole place tied together.

After half an hour of this pointless exercise and of being stuck in traffic I was overjoyed when Kath said, 'Shall we forget this and have a drink?' I had been suspicious of Kath when I first met her and perhaps even a little intimidated. She was a big personality and an even bigger woman. She was intelligent, forthright and very strong on her politics. She wore low-slung jeans that barely covered her ample arse on which she had a tattoo of the sun rising which you couldn't fail to miss.

I thought, *Oh right love, you really do think the sun shines! I'll have to watch you.* She was also the producer of the present show and that always makes it difficult for the incoming presenter because you don't know whether or how she will transfer her allegiances. But to give her credit, she was right behind me from the beginning and worked with me rather than against me from day one.

The show was going well and mutual suspicions were beginning to fade when 9/11 happened and to be honest, just like the air crash in Coventry all those years ago, this major tragic event was going to be the test of my new team and me and also the making of the programme.

We stayed on air for an extra two hours and turned into a rolling news service for Londoners as the events unfolded. We were helped because Kath knew the city so well as her brother lived there and we managed to get some eyewitnesses to air quite quickly. The fact that her brother was in New York gave the show a real immediacy but also as the show progressed I realised just how many links there were between these two great cities. The show was a massive turning point for the programme and my acceptance by the audience; it showed them that I could really do hard news and indeed cover an unfolding event without turning to mawkish sympathy or wild speculation. I still get into taxis in London to this day and cabbies tell me how they were listening on 9/11 and how they can remember exactly where they were as we started to report on the events.

I normally expect it to take at least six months for a new audience to get used to my style but this one single event pushed that acceptance and approval day forward. That's not to say there weren't listeners who hated my guts. However the audience went up massively and the inevitable Sony and local radio award nominations came along. At the same time I developed a team around me with a great set of characters. I was repeating and only slightly modifying the formula.

Six months later I was sitting in Club Class on a flight to New York to commemorate the six-month anniversary of 9/11. I had been upgraded along with my fellow presenter Robert Elms and we were both knocking back the champagne.

Robey had come up with the idea of us both doing a couple of shows from New York on the six-month anniversary of 9/11 because of the strong links between the two cities. However, just before we had flown away he had asked me to come into his office and told me that he wanted to move me up the schedule and take over Elms's slot in the morning. Just as I had predicted he had bowed to the audience pressure and now wanted me at primetime. Of course I had accepted and taken the big wage rise. However at the same time Robey had asked me to keep quiet about this change until Elms and I both got back from New York. I agreed.

Now, sitting next to Robert, I felt a bit of a heel but unfortunately there is only one certainty in a broadcaster's life and that is that one day you will either get the sack or be moved down the schedule, so you just have to swallow it and play the game. That said, my deception or deceit wasn't helped by the fact that Robert and I got on so well on this trip. He's a working-class guy just like me but because he lived and grew up in London during the punk and New Romantic era he knew all the faces and was part of that trendy scene.

I used to take the piss out of him on air about when he used to read poetry as the support act for his mates, Spandau Ballet. I had him marked down as a bit of a middle-class poser, when in fact he was a working-class lad who had made it to the LSE and was passionate about his home city of London. He was also passionate about bullfighting and, as we flew across the Atlantic, he talked to me about his obsession with the art and culture of Spain. I liked him and despite taking his job, which on the surface he took well, we grew to like and admire each other's programmes. I particularly liked and still do his features on the architecture and history of the capital.

Seeing the devastation at the World Centre and interviewing the eye-witness accounts of those who were affected by 9/11 convinced me that the war on terror and the invasion of Afghanistan was justified. The debates over this issue again helped to build the audience at BBC London and cement my relationship with them. I also got the chance to do quite a few small films for the local TV, including some reports from New York, so there were doors opening all over the place.

It was, I'm afraid, another classic example of bad news being the best news for journalists and the events of this day had a dramatic effect on my career – but of course they also had a massive impact on the world. From now on nothing would be the same ever again. This story and its aftermath would also dominate the news agenda for years to come and unfortunately 9/11 was only the beginning of the horror that we would all face and still have to defeat to this day.

34

Once in a lifetime

Despite the success I didn't and never would move to London, as I don't believe it's the place to bring up kids, so every day I would drive to the station at Milton Keynes and commute by train. I love London, the buzz, the excitement, but by the time I had got a job there I didn't need to live there. When I first signed the deal to go to London, Michael Cohen, my agent, remarked that at least with my being older, getting a major gig in London wouldn't turn my head and he was right. It would have been different if I had got the break years earlier but now I had a family and had settled in Milton Keynes and we loved the place.

We had great friends in Milton Keynes and just like in Livingston I loved and fully signed up to the pioneering spirit of the place and the people. We had been helped to settle in by meeting up again with Lee Scriven, an old friend and performer from the Tic Toc Club days. He had been the lead singer in The Blues Collective who had regularly performed at the Tic Toc

Club and whom we had promoted at the fringe. They were an eighteen-piece blues band that literally blew the audience away or at least played them into submission. I even booked them to play at the Forum at the Kwik Fit Christmas ball.

Lee and the band were from MK and when I started on the radio in Luton he had got in touch and we remain close friends. Lee knows everybody and everything about the new city and introduced Lisa and me to all the right people, including one complete nutter who reckoned he was going to build a football stadium in the town and bring top flight football to the city. His name was Pete Winkelman; he had made his money in rock music and I first met him when Lee invited us both to go and see the amateur Milton Keynes City football team play in a cup final in some godforsaken rain and windswept city down south.

We had travelled down in Pete's Jag and he outlined his vision, which he had absolute confidence in. It was almost a carbon copy of Kevin Costner in that movie, *Field of Dreams*, although a slightly speedier version. He just knew that if he built the stadium, it would work. I thought at first he was a bit of a space cadet but over the months his enthusiasm was infectious and not just to me as he began to convince the council and other major players that his dream would become a reality.

Seven years later it has. Not only has he built a magnificent stadium but he also got a massive Asda store there and the biggest Ikea branch in Europe. The guy is truly inspirational and he again pushed me on, he loved the show and was familiar with the radio style as he had been to the States so often. His story of bringing top-class football to MK and moving Wimbledon out of London helped to build my audience in the Three Counties and then, when I was on in the capital, the London audience had a lot to say too about Pete's controversial plans to 'steal their club'. However Pete and his energy reconfirmed to me that to succeed you don't need luck, you need to work and work and work.

That's exactly what I was doing too. As well as performing in London five days a week I was now also doing regular TV films on local history and politics for BBC London TV News and a programme called *Inside Out* and working every Saturday in Birmingham on BBC WM. My Saturday show was quite different to the London show and although we still tackled serious subjects and had heated discussions I also messed around a lot more.

Keith Beech, the manager, gave me a free reign and understood the concept of 'light and shade' much more than Robey who was more of a serious newsman. The audience was older, as it is at most local stations, than in London and I loved the Midlanders' honesty and frankness. To be fair they were more used to putting their two-pennyworth in as they had been brought up on the culture of phone-in and had been developed by some brilliant local presenters such as Tony Butler, Malcolm Boyden and of course Ed Doolan.

Saturdays on WM also acted as a refuge in the early days of BBC London, almost like a security blanket that I could retreat to and regroup as I fought the battle in London to build my listening base. Of course it also provided another great source of income to the Gaunt household and allowed us eventually to trade up and buy the footballer's mansion in the country with the 'stone cladding in three different colours'.

It's true to say that although we were very happy in Milton Keynes, the house itself always felt like it was just a temporary arrangement. Lisa says that it always felt like we were just camping there and in a way we were. When we came to move, a lot of our belongings were still in the original tea chests that we had transported them in from Coventry four years previously.

I wanted to move because after the collapse of Tic Toc I no longer had a pension and I took the view that we should buy the biggest house we could manage and sit on it until the kids went to college. We would then retire and move to the seaside. It took over a year to find the house of our dreams. People often ask has it got stone cladding? And the truth of course is yes! No I'm only joking. The jokes about the cladding and the fountain of the boy pissing made out of plastic and the illegal Albanian gamekeeper are all fantasies but are also kind of taking the micky out of myself. You know, how this kid from the raggy-arsed end of Radford in Coventry can end up living this lifestyle, I'm taking the piss out of myself and unfortunately some of my listeners don't get the joke.

I'll never forget Dad's face when he first turned up at the new place. He just stood in the drive and took in the view and said, 'Bloody hell, bloody hell.'

The view from the front of the house is magnificent. It goes on as far as the eye can see. Dad walked into the house and was more excited than us and he always used to say, 'I don't want to go home, son. Who would want to leave your beautiful house?'

I know he was partly impressed by the sheer cost of the place and proud that his son could afford it but it ran deeper than that. He understood what it meant to me to have this after everything I had gone through. It was also important to me to know that he knew that I had made it. The move to the house had another unexpected twist in cementing Dad's relationship and mine. I had to have a medical at the new doctors and they discovered that I too had Type 2 diabetes.

My old man was a fantastic source of advice and support in the early days of my diagnosis as he was living with the same condition and now, instead of always remarking on my weight or size his first or last question in any phone conversation would be, 'How's your sugar?' I would then have to tell him my latest blood sugar reading and he would then dole out the advice. He was also dishing out the care that he had neglected to do when I was a child and I don't know if he was conscious of this but it meant so much to me that he cared about me and similarly I began to really care for him.

We were now more, much more than mates. We were father and son and it felt fucking brilliant.

My house is beautiful and I am immensely proud of it and the fact that it's mine. It is a symbol of how far Lisa and I have come together and indeed it is remarkable that in just a few short years we are now back and living a nice lifestyle and I don't see any reason why I should apologise for it. I've worked and continued to work extremely hard to have what I've got and I'm not going to pretend or be falsely modest about my achievements or possessions, although I'm not adverse to taking the piss out of myself.

There's a joke in local radio that when a presenter has a holiday they pretend they are staying at home to do some decorating when in fact they are sunning themselves on an exotic beach. I have never subscribed to this bullshit and always remember Andy Wright's maxim that you should never lie. That's why I tell people where I'm going on holiday to and why. The only people who get upset are the jealous ones, the real fans just think, 'Good on yer Gaunty if you can afford it, go for it.'

When I first went to Luton the BBC sent me on a course to discuss how to do a breakfast show. Each presenter had to send in a tape of their show for the others to listen to and dissect at the seminar. It was so funny as one of the tutors said, 'Yes, Jon I like it, it's got great energy but I don't think you should talk about your kids so much.'

What a jerk, I talk about my kids as a central point of my act. It's a way of getting into the issues and the listeners love that daily true soap opera of your life and what they can't stand are the lies or the falsehoods.

It's ironic that this trainer could be so wide of the mark because now that I was the star of BBC local radio the Beeb started asking me to hold training days for other BBC presenters the length and breadth of the country. They wanted me to teach others the Gaunty, or rather should I say the Wright and Conroy, techniques to get people phoning in.

It was great money and I really enjoyed passing on the tips and having the chance to talk about radio, my kind of radio, and show youngsters that local radio doesn't have to be about vet phone-ins or questions and queries about your corns, which was often the staple diet of most local radio. However, you can only bring on talent, you cannot create it. I can normally tell, within two minutes of meeting a presenter if they've got what it takes or not. If they have I can help them to improve but unfortunately too many of them haven't got it and all the seminars and tapes in the world will never get them just to be natural in front of the microphone.

I was at the top of my game with record audience figures in the two biggest radio markets in the UK, London and Birmingham. My phone-in style was being imitated and adapted across the country and there was a general acceptance that I was pioneering a new style of interactive radio for the UK. What could possibly go wrong?

The BBC could realise their mistake and re-open BBC Coventry, that's what!

35

Here comes the Sun

2005

I was pissed, again, and I was at the Sony's again. I had been nominated for an award for my Saturday morning phone-in show on WM and I was having a good drink with Lisa, Keith Beech and my brilliant young producer Jo Tidman. We didn't win but I was still immensely proud of the tape we had put in and I was loving working at WM. The show may not have won this year but it was clear that within a year or so it would be recognised as a great freewheeling, taboo-breaking phone-in.

The previous year I had also been nominated for another Sony with my London show and so the annual awards bash was becoming a regular diary entry for Lisa and I. However, this year was special because it was for WM, the place where I felt the most comfortable and where I thought I would end up full time in a few years. I was getting bored with London, not the great team I was working with or the audience but the continual sniping and jealousy from the management. I was looking for an escape route and if Beech had offered me Doolan's or the breakfast show on WM I would have jumped at it and I knew it was only a matter of time before that offer would come.

I never felt valued at London and I might be wrong but I feel that the management saw me as a necessary evil and, similar to some football managers, couldn't cope with the concept of my earning more money than them. I was now the highest paid presenter in BBC local radio.

Speech radio – and in particular phone-in – is a relatively new form in Britain and, as well as being the most interesting to listen to, it's also the most difficult to do well and certainly the most complex to manage. Most of the real great talk broadcasters are mad, with egos the size of houses, myself included. It's necessary because there are no records to hide behind, no breathing space to gather your thoughts or reconsider your position. The red light goes on, you enter the ring of fire and it's you on your own against the fruit loops, liberals and bigots. And that's what makes it so damn exciting and impossible for anyone to really manage or format. It's even more difficult for the politically correct buffoons at the BBC who are tied up by their own hypocritical producer guidelines and lefty liberal bias.

During the afternoon Keith Beech had asked me if I was going to come back to Coventry and present on the new BBC Coventry and Warwickshire. I said no but that I was negotiating to do a Friday night football phone-in for them and still do his show on a Saturday and London in the week.

The reason he was asking about Coventry was because ten years to the day almost after closing down Coventry the BBC had decided to re-open it. On the day that Greg Dyke made this announcement I was asked for a quote and I said that I was delighted and that the decision was wrong in the first place and it was fantastic that the BBC was big enough to accept its mistake and give the City of Coventry its radio station back. And I meant it but I had no intention of leaving London to work there even if I was fed up with London or more specifically the management.

The BBC had spent over three million pounds developing the station with new state of the art studios but unfortunately had forgotten the most important aspect of any radio station – the on-air talent. They had approached me a few months earlier and I had agreed to do a Friday evening show and I was really looking forward to this as it would mean more cash, but also I would be the star back in my hometown. I also liked the idea of being back in something at the beginning and I would be working with some old mates who were still on the merged station.

The months passed until here I was at the Sony's in May 2005, drinking and talking with Beech. Later that night Andy Griffee, the head of Local Radio, approached me. He was slightly pissed.

'Okay, Jon, cut the shit. What would it take to get you to Coventry?'

'I'm going, Andy. I've agreed to do Fridays.'

'Yeah, I know, but what about Brekkie?'

'Behave, why would I want to leave London?'

'It's your home town.'

'Yeah I know that, but why would I want to leave the capital?'

'What would it take? How much do you want?'

'You mean—'

'Yeah, look Jon, you know we've spent the best part of three million on it but we need a big name and you are the biggest local name, I want you to go there.'

I decided to chance my arm.

'A three-year contract, same money as London and the chance to go to WM as soon as I've got you the audience you need in Coventry.'

He held out his hand.

'Done, when's your contract up in London?'

'April next year.'

'Fine.'

'But Andy, I haven't said yes yet and we've both had a drink. Let me sleep on it.'

I did sleep on it, for a few weeks. I went up to Coventry to see the studios and they were fantastic. They were right next to the cathedral and they were all plate glass and steel. Coventry had changed too and the city's symbol of the phoenix rising was apt as again the city was regenerating itself. The footballer's mansion was only thirty minutes away by Jaguar and after having a long chat with Dad about the pros and cons I was beginning to seriously consider it.

Then the Sun quite literally shone on me. I had another one of those life-changing moments that have characterised my career. One of those occasions where my mates would again say, 'You lucky bastard if you fell into a shit heap you'd come out smelling of roses.'

The *Sun* rang and asked me if I would like to write a column for them.

'Come and have a look at this e-mail, Gaunty.'

'Not today, Abi, I don't want any grief off that idiot.' I was just walking into the BBC London newsroom as my producer, Abi Lewis, spotted me.

I was still thinking the worst and expected it to be another petty bollocking from the boss.

'No Jon, you will want to read this one.'

It was spring 2005 and the previous night Liverpool had won the European Cup on penalties and I had consumed a skinful of red wine after phoning the Beeb in Coventry and telling them that I would take their job.

I meandered over to her computer and read the mail that was addressed to her.

'Hi Abigail, I wonder if you could tell me how to get in touch with Jon Gaunt as we would like to ask him if he would be interested in writing for the *Sun*?'

Is the Pope a Catholic? Does a fish swim? Does a duck have lips? (With thanks to Flann O'Brien.) This was a dream come true.

Abi, myself and my previous producer and great friend Lorraine, who I had brought with me from Luton, had often fantasised about such an offer. We often looked at stories in the tabloids and believed, whether true or not, that they must have nicked the feature or ideas from our phone-in the previous day. Now it was going to be a reality.

From the moment in Coventry years previously when I had decided that I was born to be a talk jock, my only ambition and my total drive was directed at being on the biggest radio station with the largest audience I could find. I'm a populist. I want to talk to as many people as possible and I always remember a punk band saying that you had two choices of record deal. You could keep it real and deliver your message to a small, dedicated, fan base by signing to an indie like Stiff records or Rough Trade or you could dilute your message slightly, sign to EMI or CBS and sing to millions.

The chance of working for the *Sun* was for me the equivalent of the Pistols signing to Branson outside Buckingham Palace. I had hit pay dirt.

After the show, Robey's boss, a Scot called McFarlane, called me into his office. In between shaking and trembling he said that I should take the job in Coventry because when my contract came up for renewal in April he didn't see me fitting in with their vision of what the station should sound like. I let him sweat and then I answered, 'I'm so glad that you've now got a vision for this radio station because before I came you didn't even have an audience.'

He trembled even more, I even began to feel sorry for him but then I put the boot in. 'Haven't your bosses told you I've already decided to go to Cov so don't make out you're the hard man sacking me,' and with that I walked out.

What was so funny about this meeting was that he was concerned about my reaction to his perceived rejection of me but he clearly didn't understand that everything in my life to this point had well prepared me for rejection, plus of course I had the life-changing e-mail from the *Sun* in my pocket.

A few days later I met the *Sun* and never felt so much at home at work since I first got into radio all those years back in Coventry. It turned out that the Assistant Editor, Fleet Street legend Chris Stevens, was a big fan of the radio show and couldn't believe how much I got away with on the BBC. To be fair neither could I and if I'm truthful the only reason I did was because of the awards and the audience figures, I knew full well that the moment the figures dropped those lefty liberals would have had me out of the door quicker than they could order their next skinny latte.

Chris knew all the catchphrases and Dominic Mohan, Deputy Editor, joked that he was a Gaunty stalker. That may be, but he has turned out to be the best editor a rookie columnist could ever have and his gentle advice and tips have improved me immensely. The Editor of the *Sun*, Rebekah Wade, was at the meeting too and all three were so encouraging and spoke my kind of language, I felt at home immediately.

When you walk into the *Sun* offices there's a sign that says, 'Walk tall, you are entering Sun Country'. The corridors are filled with massive reproductions of their famous front pages; everything from the sinking of the *Belgrano*'s front page, 'Gotcha' to 'Freddie Star ate my Hamster'. It's frightening, intimidating and encouraging and on the same level as the sign in the Liverpool Football Tunnel that says 'This is Anfield'.

A few weeks before I actually started writing the column, one of the hacks on a drunken night out said, 'Gaunty you were playing in defence for MK Dons but you've just joined Chelsea.'

You drunken arrogant twat, I thought.

One column in, I realised he was right.

36

Let it Beeb

I was to leave BBC London on 18 July 2005, go on holiday for a few weeks and start in Coventry in mid-August with the station going live in early September.

I had been working my balls off for the best part of twelve years on the radio and I fancied an easier life. Because I knew Coventry so well the job would be easy and almost a semi-retirement gig with the added bonus of being a columnist on the biggest newspaper. The fantasy would be that I would get up early, drive to Cov, do the breakfast show and have all the time in the world to concentrate on the *Sun* column.

I was planning to tell the London audience a couple of weeks before the 18th that I was away when 7/7 happened. We got a newsflash that there had been a power surge on the tube but I knew almost immediately that this was more than an accident. We were the first station to get a survivor to air, which just happened to be a colleague who was on the Tube on his way to work when the first bomb went off. Just like in the Vauxhall crisis, because I had developed a relationship with my audience, the first person they thought of ringing when they emerged from the Tube was me at BBC London. We went to a rolling news service mode and avoided all sentimentality and speculation and just reported the facts.

The previous day I had been sitting in the East End in a radio car as the announcement was made that London had won the 2012 Olympics and the fact that today's programme should have been a celebration added a real poignancy to the broadcast. As well as carrying the unfolding news we had regular updates from our reporters in Singapore and interviewed Ken Livingstone from the other side of the world. A testament to just how good the programme was and how well the whole team did was the fact that a decision was made to simulcast the live show over all of the 38 BBC local stations.

My team obviously knew that I was leaving and I think all of us now began to question whether the BBC and I had made the right decision. It was brilliant radio but again it was a double-edged sword as this broadcast was based on the most tragic of events.

A few days later I announced my departure and a lot of my listeners were angry that I hadn't given enough notice and many felt that the BBC was pushing me out of the door. They were partially right and a large part of me wanted to turn the clock back, but at the same time I still had the *Sun* job up my sleeve. I couldn't tell the audience I was leaving any earlier as it wouldn't have felt right to talk about my career when people were just coming to terms with their and the capital's loss. So I kind of just disappeared from the airwaves of London on 18 July.

We went away to Tobago while my agents negotiated my contract with the *Sun*. A few days later I took a call in the pool and it was confirmed that I would start on the *Sun* on 18 October, Lisa's birthday. It was a dream come true. I phoned Dad and told him how much I was going to be paid.

'What a month? Fucking hell!'

'No a week.'

'You what? A week! Fucking hell, Sylvia come here, listen to this, you'll never believe what's happened to Jon. Bloody hell son, well done, well done.'

Forget the fucking money, this was priceless. He was proud of me.

I got back home and started working in Coventry doing the pre-publicity for the station opening. It was great to be reunited with my old mates. Geoff Foster was going to be my sports presenter and a very old mate and talented producer, Kev Lee, was going to leave WM and mastermind the show for me. I had a quiet word in both Geoff and Kev's ear and told them about the *Sun* and said I didn't know how the BBC would react but they still wanted to take the chance and join me in this new show. Geoff said, 'Surely they won't object to you writing for the biggest paper in the world?'

I wasn't so sure! Several months earlier I had been offered a column on the Sunday *Star* and I had asked the BBC if they were okay with me doing it. They had refused saying that it would be a conflict of interest, despite the fact that Vanessa Feltz who was also working on BBC London at the time was already writing a column for the *Express* newspaper group.

The money wasn't enough to allow me to challenge the BBC so I had to let it go but from that moment on I had been determined to get out of the Bloated Broadcasting Corporation. I was a freelance paying my own tax, stamp and pension. How dare these Oxbridge educated idiots dictate to me? The *Sun* was my passport out of this, so I spent the next few weeks firming up the offer and then eventually signed the contract. Meanwhile the preparations for the opening of the new Coventry station were proceeding.

Once the ink was dry on the contract with the *Sun* I told the boss of Coventry that I had got this amazing job on the paper but that I would still be able and willing to fulfil my commitment to him. I fully expected them to say okay, not least because the *Sun* was willing to have an advert on the bottom of my column saying, 'Listen to Gaunty on BBC Coventry.' I could think of no other better publicity push than this for a new station.

However, the BBC saw things differently. The boss of Coventry, to give him his due, was cool with it but his immediate bosses in local radio had to push the decision up the food chain. They asked me to keep quiet about the *Sun* job until they made their decision. I agreed to do so and for seven weeks I kept quiet and pretended that I was happy just being a local DJ.

It went all the way up to Mark Byford, second in charge of the whole corporation. Ironically he is the BBC lifer who was largely responsible for closing down the same station ten years earlier.

Eventually the BBC decided that it would be a conflict of interest and said that I had to choose between the corporation and the *Sun*. The hypocrisy was stunning, Jeremy Clarkson was working for both organisations and Fatty Feltz was now earning enough money to spend every day in the all you can eat buffet because she had been promoted to my job at BBC London. Any commercial outfit would have given their right arm to have a *Sun* columnist working for them but the BBC can afford to pretend they have standards of impartiality, when in reality they are stuffed full of liberals who relentlessly push their politically correct agenda onto the masses while simultaneously ripping off the population by levying an unfair poll tax in the form of the licence fee.

I told them to stick their job and their radio station up their arse and walked out.

I spent the next eight months writing and learning my craft on the *Sun*, bitching and swearing down the phone to Dad, moaning to my agents that I couldn't get a job on the radio and driving Lisa up the wall. As you know I love my family but if I'm honest I've also got to admit that I love closing the door behind me and leaving them to go to work.

For the best part of fifteen years I had been on the radio, having the craic with both my colleagues and the listeners. My mates all thought I was mad. I was easily earning enough from the *Sun* and the occasional guest appearances on TV or ironically BBC Five Dead not to have to get another full-time job but I was missing the radio and the regular interaction with the listeners.

Because I had burnt my bridges in such spectacular style there weren't many avenues available. The only other talk stations were LBC in London or national Talksport.

LBC sounded too soft for me and it appeared the management wanted to recreate *Hello* magazine on the radio so I wasn't exactly suited to their style. Meanwhile Talksport seemed to be against me because I had turned down their offers of work on three previous occasions when ex-*Sun* editor Kelvin McKenzie was running the station.

However, just a few weeks before Dad collapsed, my agent had persuaded Bill Ridley, the boss of Talksport, just to have a coffee with me and meet the man behind the gob. Amazingly he agreed. He didn't produce any coffee but he did offer me a couple of stand-in shifts. Dad knew all this and on the Monday before he flew to Thailand whilst he was eating his favourite meal of fillet steak and chips in my house he said, 'This is going to be your year son, I know it, I just know it.'

I think he was more convinced about the gigs than I was and he truly believed that it would lead to a full-time job back on national radio. And he was right.

37

Redemption Song

2006

I was alone. It was day two or three. It was irrelevant. The days, long days, had all merged into one and we were taking it in turns to sit in pairs at his bedside in Woolwich and talk and talk and talk. We had even brought in a Sony Walkman and put the headphones on his ears and played his beloved Bob Marley records to him, including his very favourite one, 'Redemption Song'.

I suppose there was an irony in that, because we all knew there was no redemption for Dad physically: he was going to die and there was nothing we could do about it. But for me personally, there had been a kind of redemption for both of us, for me and for Dad, and that song somehow got to the heart of it. Of course we were also playing the records to him in the vain hope that he might wake up or at least show a sign of recognition – a flicker of understanding. But so far nothing had changed.

I was hot, sweaty and knackered. It was a four or five hour round trip to visit him and the strain was beginning to show. I paced the hospital corridor and turned the mobile on without thinking. Then it rang. It was the boss of Talksport, Bill Ridley.

'Hi Jon, we would like to offer you the ten till one slot, five days a week.'

'What at night?'

'No mid-morning you fool.'

'Right.'

'You don't sound too excited.'

'No, no, I mean yes, well Bill, it's like this, I mean thanks and all that, it's just that Dad's lying in a coma . . .'

'Jesus!'

'No, no, don't worry, when do you want me to start?'

'May 29th.'

'Fine Bill, fine, thanks, thanks a lot.'

I washed my hands and rushed back into the old man with the news.

Not a flicker.

But at least now I had something to tell him, something new to share with him.

He still looked brilliant, even with all the machines and tubes hooked up to him. I asked the intensive care nurse, Emily, to brush his hair. She had already shaved him and I remarked that he would have liked that because he was a vain man. None of the nurses could actually believe that he was really 72. I laughed and told them about when we were in Miami on holiday and some listeners recognised me, which of course was flattering, but then pricked my own self-importance by asking if Dad was my brother. The silly old sod never tired of retelling this joke and to be honest even now he looked better than the rest of us.

Later, during the drive home, Sylvia told me that he had spent the whole holiday wondering how the stand-in gigs on Talksport had gone and he was convinced that by now they would have offered me a job. I regretted not upgrading his phone so that we could have spoken while he was away.

The travelling was taking its toll on all of us. Sylvia and my brothers had all set up camp in my house in Northamptonshire, to be slightly nearer to the M1 and Dad. However, it was still a three or four hour trip every day to see him. We took it turns to talk to him and get no response.

On the fourth day the doctor called us into the family room, as he had on previous occasions, to tell us that there was no hope. Dad wasn't going to come back.

'But what about the way he's flexing his hands?'

He told us that was just a sign of basic brain function and that because he had been starved of oxygen for so long the majority of brain function had been lost, he had been lost. We were no longer waiting for him to wake up but for him to die.

I asked the doctor if Dad could be moved nearer to home. The doctor refused, saying he wasn't well enough to undertake the journey and that he was worried he might sustain further damage.

'But you've just told us that he's already brain damaged,' I replied. Simon shot me a look. When the doctor left us alone to discuss things, I was alone in pushing the case to have him transferred. Sylvia didn't like the idea because she was afraid of him dying in the ambulance. I couldn't see the problem as we had already been told he was effectively brain dead. But my brothers agreed with her. They were wrong. I knew Dad better than Jason and Simon, I was his best mate, I was the one whom he told, 'If I can't wipe my arse put a plastic bag over my head', and I know he would have wanted to take the chance to get home.

Back at the pub in the village that night I was pissed and argued with Simon and Jase and I was out of order but I wasn't willing to let Simon take the lead just because he was the eldest brother. In a normal family that may and probably should be the way, but we were no normal family. I hadn't really lived with either of them for a sustained period of time since Mum died and our life experiences and attitudes were completely different. We might have been brothers, but we were strangers too.

I kept trying to make the point that they would have to go home soon and that I would be left with the burden of travelling every day with Sylvia to see Dad and that it was already killing me. I couldn't face the prospect of that drive every day, neither could I countenance the idea of leaving him there so far from home with none of his family visiting him. To me that was a statement of fact, to them it must have seemed like an implied criticism.

I wish we hadn't argued that night but then I wish Mum hadn't died and Dad hadn't been such a bastard to all three of us but I also knew that I had made my peace with Dad years ago and in their ways I'm not sure they had. Months earlier I had told them to come and see him, that he wasn't well and that I was worried, I think they probably thought I was being the drama queen again but I wasn't, I was genuinely concerned. His eyesight was failing and he was bricking himself that he was going to go blind. He had had his eyes lasered a few weeks ago but just before the final holiday he had been to the specialist and it was clear from Sylvia's nods and winks behind his back that there wasn't much hope. I think this may have been his motivation for booking that holiday.

He had also had several bad bouts of vomiting in recent weeks and the good-looking bastard had begun, at last, to look his age. He would stand in my conservatory huffing and puffing like all dads do as they stand up and talk to their sons about their fears. He would talk to me like he had never talked in the first thirty odd years of my life. He told me about his dad dying when he was fourteen and implied that his mother, my Nana, was seeing Harold, my step-grandad, before his dad was dead.

The resentment that I used to pick up as a kid from my aunties and Dad towards Harold began to make sense. He had talked about his mum's death, how she was riddled with cancer, and he tried to talk about his regret for what he did to me.

But I always stopped him as the tears began to fall, I didn't need him to say sorry or even feel sorry for himself. I had already forgiven him and I loved him.

38

Do not go gently

There were three of us in the room but it felt as if I were completely alone. I looked at Jeff; he nodded and I stared at Sylvia who looked like she had physically shrunk these last few days.

'Sylvia, you stay here for a bit, we'll come and get you in a minute.'

'Yeah Mum, it'll be best.'

Without waiting for her reply, Jeff and I left that stifling little room and headed for Dad's bed.

He still looked magnificent, tanned, clean-shaven, hair immaculate. Emily, his nurse, had done him proud but she was now off duty. This was going to be the worst twenty minutes of Jeff's life and of mine.

After the drunken row, things were tense at home and necessity did mean that Simon and Jason had to leave and return to their families and work so that's why it was down to Jeff and me to watch as the nurses took out the tubes that were keeping Dad alive.

The doctor had explained that they believed that, with only limited brain capability, if they removed the tube that was keeping the airway open, Dad's brain wouldn't be able to keep it open itself and that in all likelihood he would pass away within twenty minutes or so. I rang Simon and Jason and we all agreed that this would be what Dad would have wanted. So Jeff and I stood side by side by the bed as the nurse gently pulled out the tube. Dad writhed, gasped for breath, seemed to clench and unclench his fists, it was agony for us but the medics assured us he could feel nothing.

We were both crying, I held Dad's arm and told him I loved him, not to worry it will soon be better, Jeff was mumbling the same platitudes, we were both crying. The nurse left us alone with our dad. And he was *our* dad because although there had been the inevitable tensions between an eighteen-year-old lad and Dad when he and Sylvia first got married they had grown to understand each other. Dad had helped get Jeff out of a dead-end job as a trainee butcher and into the police. I remember being jealous of how proud he was in later years when Jeff was awarded the accolade of Britain's bravest cop after ending an armed siege where a man had doused himself, and also the hostage he had taken, in petrol.

In many ways Jeff was more like Dad than us three and his tribute at the funeral was as moving as that of any of us biological sons and after what we went through that night, it's hardly surprising.

Twenty minutes passed, Dad had calmed down but he wasn't dying and he certainly wasn't dead. The nurse returned, then the doctor, and then hope returned.

Perhaps they were wrong. Maybe he did have more brain activity? Sylvia came in after about an hour and we sat with Dad, waiting for him to die for hour after hour.

But the stubborn, strong, pig-headed bastard wasn't going to go that easy, quietly or quickly. Eventually after midnight they told us to go home and said they would ring us if anything happened. The next day he was still alive and then there were a couple more days when we hoped he might pull through.

But then one day when we arrived, they had moved him to another ward where he wouldn't get the one-on-one treatment; it felt that he had been moved to the dying room. That's not an implied criticism of the medical team, just a statement of fact. But at least now they appeared more willing to move him back to Nuneaton. Simon and Jason had come back down to see Dad and now agreed that we should take the chance and move him.

And so, two and a half weeks after collapsing they moved him. He survived the journey but within fifteen minutes of reaching the ward he was dead.

Epilogue

At times like these you tend to get lost in your own thoughts, memories and needs. It's hard to focus on the bigger picture and see how this tragic situation is affecting those around you and perhaps one of the biggest learning curves for me was realising the effect the death of Dad had on my own kids.

Bethany was ten, almost the same age as I was when Mum died. I thought that the death of Mum had hardened me to tragedy but in all honesty the death of my father hit me harder. Dad's death and my reaction to it hit the kids too and Bethany wrote about it in her RE lesson as only a ten year old could.

My Special Experience

The special experience I'm going to write about doesn't stick in my head because it was a happy memory. It sticks in my head because I admire how people coped with the situation, especially Dad.

It started on a school afternoon; my sister had made a pizza shaped like Italy at school. We were just reheating it to eat for dinner, when the phone rang. My dad answered it in his study. He shut the door of the study so that Rosie and I would not hear. The phone was put down. Dad called through Mum, they talked in hushed voices. Then the study opened, Dad ran to get his coat, Mum rushed through to explain to us that Grandad had had a heart attack at the airport and he was in hospital in intensive care. My sister and I began to cry, I had a lump in my throat. I couldn't breathe.

My nana and pop were coming down to look after us while Dad and Mum went to the hospital. The day after, Nana Sylvia (Grandad's wife) came to stay at our house and our uncles too. In our house there was a gloomy atmosphere, no one was comfortable. Everyone was very positive at first but as the weeks went on and Grandad was still in intensive care things didn't look good.

At this point I prayed every night for Grandad and I really did believe in God for once in my life. It made me feel better if I believed there was someone looking out for me. Although I prayed and believed there was something we hadn't been told.

I asked my mum if Grandad would live and she explained that his brain had been without air for ten minutes so only a small amount of his brain was working (he could only breathe, hear . . .). She said that Grandad would never wake up from his coma and we were just waiting for him to die. I had never cried so much in my life; it sends a shiver down my spine now when I think about it.

Even though there was no hope of Grandad waking, Dad wanted to move Grandad to a nearer hospital. On Wednesday 24th May 2006 Grandad was going to be transferred to a nearer hospital. When Grandad got to the hospital he had a massive heart attack but he was gone before the doctors could react. Even though I miss him, I know he is in a better place because he could have stayed in the coma for months and never got better.

I think Dad coped with his father's death well. I know he probably did cry but he never showed he was afraid. It must be scary when you have no real parents here with you and you just have to rely on yourself.

I have learnt from this experience that everything has a time and you have to make the most of what you have before it's lost . . . forever.

Everything she says is true, apart from the fact that after his death I wasn't alone, I had the love and support of my wife and two girls. It was a world away from the real loneliness I felt throughout the majority of my own childhood.

I had been having a drink with a couple of my oldest mates when the call came that Dad had died in Nuneaton. I picked up Lisa and we drove rather than raced to the George Elliot Hospital in Nuneaton. It was a different journey than the one a few weeks ago because at least now we had a certainty to face when we got there. I was glad that he was dead, not just for him as a release from his pain but for Sylvia and more importantly for myself.

I was glad when Sylvia decided to have a closed laying in wait for Dad but I was also glad and grateful to Charlie the nurse in Nuneaton who delayed taking Dad off the ward until Lisa and I arrived.

When I got to the ward I also knew why the old bugger had decided enough was enough. The first person we met was an elderly fellow with his Y fronts pulled up to his ears, another woman came up and said thanks for coming to visit her, the place was full of the mad, sad and the lonely. It really was heaven's waiting room and it was crammed full and stank of piss. My old man must have taken one look at this and realised that he was surrounded by the fishing party in *One Flew Over the Cuckoo's Nest* and thought, bugger this for a game of bananas, I'm off.

Dad hated the thought of being old, unfit, incapable; he was a proud man, a strong man and he would have hated to end up like these sad bastards.

I thought of him telling me to put the plastic bag over his head. Fortunately I didn't have to.

Charlie, the staff nurse, was chubby with pink hair and was what Dad, if he had been conscious, would have described as a right screamer or 'seems like a nice boy'. Charlie was everything that Dad worried that I would turn into if I went to university to study Drama. But this bloke was lovely and couldn't have been more caring. He told me how they had got Dad in the bed but that fifteen minutes later he had arrested and despite all their efforts they couldn't resuscitate him. I asked if I could see the body. Dad had already gone; it was just a body. Charlie said yes and pointed us in the direction of the only bed with the curtains drawn round it.

It was the second dead body I had seen. Years ago Dad took Simon and me to see Mum in Pargetters, the funeral directors in Coventry. I remember the chapel of rest was really cold and there were loads of coffins in there. Mum's was open and I peered in and felt her cold hand; she looked peaceful but I couldn't stand it and left.

He was cold, his mouth was gaping open and he smelt. He smelt of death. Lisa held my hand; I pulled away and then stopped myself. I wasn't alone, and I didn't have to cope with this on my own.

'Jon you prick, accept the love, the support. You're not outside Wilko's office now, you're a man, a father, a husband and more importantly a son.'

Eventually I did let go of Lisa's hand and lifted up Dad's cold hand, I bent over, kissed him on the forehead and said, 'Thanks Dad, thanks for everything.'